Lives Matter

A Handbook for Christian Organizing

Kimberley Bobo

Sheed & Ward

Sheed & Ward™ is a service of National Catholic Reporter Publishing, Inc.

Library of Congress Catalog Card Number: 86-61557

ISBN: 0-934134-87-1

Published by: Sheed & Ward
115 E. Armour Blvd. P.O. Box 414292
Kansas City, MO 64141-0281

To order, call: (800) 821-7926

All royalties from this book go to Bread for the World

Contents

Preface

This book is drawn from eleven years of experience in organizing on hunger. I have worked eight of those years for Bread for the World (BFW), a Christian citizens' movement on hunger. BFW focuses on national public policy issues. Consequently, most of my organizing has concerned national and international issues. For several years, I have directed the BFW organizing staff. This experience has highlighted to me the acute need for training materials on hunger organizing. I designed this book for Christians who want to work to end hunger. I have tried to make it useful for those who have worked previously on hunger issues, as well as those who are relative newcomers. A few of the hunger movement's leaders have full-time jobs in hunger, but most are volunteers. They are Christians who generously give their time to work against hunger. This book is meant to assist the many committed volunteers organizing across the country. Although directed to Christians organizing on hunger, this book also should be useful to Christians organizing on other social justice concerns. Many of the techniques and approaches for starting and maintaining a group, public speaking, lobbying elected leaders, and using the media hold true no matter what issue is addressed. The book should also be helpful for organizers who do not come from a faith perspective, but work extensively within Christian communities. It is almost impossible to organize in local communities and not work with churches. The sections on working with churches will help organizers understand how to approach churches and church related groups.

* * *

A few words on words. You will soon realize that this book contains some unpronounceable words. I have used "hmr" to mean

iv

"him or her," "hsr" for "his or her," and "s/he" for "she or he." You may find this somewhat disconcerting at first, but it is less cumbersome than always using two pronouns.

Christians use many different terms for the various aspects of religious life. I have tried to be inclusive of various denominational heritages, but I tend to use some terms more than others. Please know that I mean priests and pastors when I say ministers, and parishes when I say churches.

It is also difficult to know what to call the large group of countries with low per capita income. An extensive debate rages over the correct term. "Underdeveloped" is not proper. Some believe that "developing" is not accurate. The "Third World" has now been supplemented by the "Fourth World." Whatever term I choose this year will be perceived as wrong the next! Thus, while understanding its deficiencies, I have selected the designation "Third World."

Finally, I have referred to groups and people as hunger groups and hunger leaders. In reality, we are all antihunger groups and antihunger leaders. Rest assured that I do not want hunger to increase!

* * *

All organizers learn skills from other organizers. This has certainly been true for me. Marie Runyon, a long-time community organizer on the Upper West Side of Manhattan, gave me very valuable training. Her lifelong commitment to organizing and her deep faith have been, and continue to be, an inspiration to my work.

To the organizers with whom I have worked over the years I offer my thanks, particularly those at Bread for the World. I have learned organizing skills from coworkers and BFW volunteers around the country. Special thanks are due to all those who took the time to read the entire manuscript and offer comments: Will Alexander, Kathy Guy, Bonnie Jorgenson, Marlene Kiingati, Bob Schminkey, and Arthur Simon. A number of other colleagues offered invaluable assistance on specific chapters including Jon Buuck, Sarodel Childs, Kimble Forrister, Lloyd Goodman, Cureton Johnson, Tom Murphy, Kathy O'Pella, James Steele, and Joel Underwood.

Stephen Coats, my husband, gave support and encouragement throughout the book's planning, writing, and typing. He not only offered suggestions for the manuscript, and typed many chapters, but he listened to my ideas with interest and shared in my excitement.

Martha B. Lawrence, my sister, deserves much credit for the readability of the manuscript. She first read the manuscript with the eye of one not actively involved in hunger organizing. She then worked hours editing each chapter, making numerous improvements in grammar and style. Martha's talents as an editor and her friendship during the project have contributed enormously to the the book's development.

Finally, I thank Bread for the World for giving me time away from my regular duties to write and reflect. The entire BFW organizing staff assumed extra responsibilities. Sarodel Childs and Bob Schminkey carried the bulk of my administrative responsibilities in addition to their ongoing work. Thank you to the organizing staff.

Although many people have contributed to the manuscript, the responsibility for errors and omissions rests with me.

It is indeed my hope and prayer that this book will be of service to the hunger movement, and ultimately to those who are hungry.

1. CAN'T DO IT ALONE

Organizing can't be done alone. It needs people. Organizing needs you and those around you.

What do I mean by organizing? Organizing is empowerment. It is enabling people to act effectively to cause change. Most Christians feel powerless to confront the problem of hunger. Organizing recognizes and develops the power within people so they can work to end hunger.

I first recognized the need for this book a number of years ago when I was training a group of novice hunger organizers. They asked for materials on *how* to organize, but I found few resources to recommend. Organizers have tended to organize and not write about organizing. Of the material available on organizing, there is little written from a faith perspective. Religious principles of organizing are not contrary to secular ones. However, there are additional motivations and traditions upon which we can call in our organizing work. The worship perspective and community orientation of this rich Biblical heritage offer enormous resources, both inward and outward, to organizers.

Literally hundreds of books have been written on the problems of hunger. A few of these books devote a chapter or two to *what* people can do to work against hunger. Not one book concentrates on *how* to do it. I hope this book will strengthen the organizing skills among Christians working on hunger issues. The hunger movement needs strong Christian organizers to address today's complex issues. The political and economic changes required to end hunger in our world can only occur through intensive organizing at the community, state, and national levels.

Our history books often represent individual leaders as causing society-wide changes. Perhaps focusing on specific personalities makes the history easier to read and remember. It does not make it more accurate. Social changes occur due to widespread political and economic change. These changes are fueled by organized groups of people. They may produce a few articulate spokespersons to convey their message. Such spokespersons are needed. However, the organized groups, not the spokespersons, cause the change.

A few obvious examples come to mind. Dr. Martin Luther King, Jr. is certainly identified as the leader of the Civil Rights Movement. His leadership played a critical role, but the Civil Rights Movement made lasting changes in U.S. society largely because of the numbers of people who were organized and ready to act, and the ability of that many people to take significant political and economic actions. Civil rights organizing empowered people to believe that they could make a difference, and orchestrated specific actions to meet their goals.

Dr. Martin Luther King, Jr. is frequently compared to Gandhi. Gandhi was another great leader, but he did not single-handedly bring about changes in India. Gandhi organized people, and recruited others to organize people. The large numbers of people who boycotted products and challenged the political and economic balance of power caused the change. Gandhi's organizing empowered people to make these changes.

A final example is Mao Tse Tung and the Chinese revolution. None can deny that Mao was a brilliant general and leader, but he did not bring about the Chinese revolution. Thirty years of grassroots organizing in small villages throughout China created the revolution. People came to believe that they had a role to play in changing the government. They then took concrete steps to alter the economic and political order. Regardless of what your personal views on the change may be, you cannot deny that organizing caused major social change that affected one-fourth of the world's population.

People organizing themselves to take effective political and economic action caused the changes just discussed. This required many committed people organizing at the local level. One key person is identified with each situation, but the key person did not work in isolation. Hundreds of volunteer organizers worked patiently to build the movements. Thus, in working to end hunger, we must work together. We cannot think that we will solve the problem by being a lone, brilliant speaker or by persuading one "influential" person.

However, while all these movements involved many people, the people actually constituted a relatively small percentage of the overall population. The message for us as hunger organizers is that we need to keep increasing the number of people involved, but we can accomplish change far beyond what we might expect from our existing numbers. Indeed, this has already been the case in the work of the hunger movement in this country.

You should be aware that organizing can, and often does, cause conflict — even when it is to achieve a generally accepted goal such as ending hunger. This is partly because change makes people anxious and uncomfortable, so they resist change. It also occurs because people have different values. For example, hunger organizers lobby congress to include generous funding for domestic feeding programs and famine relief in the federal budget. At the same time other groups are lobbying for everything from tobacco price supports to military aid. Since government dollars are limited (at least to some degree), not every group can get everything they want, and conflicts arise.

Neither the concept of empowerment nor the likelihood of conflict are foreign to Christians. Christian faith empowers us to confront sin, even when it brings us into conflict with others. By sharing our faith with others, we build a community (or organization) of believers who are able to support one another in life's conflicts. We gain the power to overcome conflicts.

For Christians, seeking justice is fundamental to faith. While knowing that we cannot bring forth the Kingdom of God, we use that kingdom's standards as those toward which we strive. If seeking justice requires social change, we must organize to achieve social change. If that causes conflict, we must find courage to face the problem.

Christ is our best organizing model. He chose twelve people and asked them to join him. He did not simply post a notice and hope people would show up. He asked people individually. He worked with them and they learned by doing. He gave them responsibilities. He empowered them. Then he sent them out to tell even more people and to organize them into groups. Sometimes they came into conflict with other people because they changed things and had different values, but they faced these conflicts with courage and ultimately prevailed.

Christ organized the disciples because it was effective. It was the way he chose to spread his message to the people. Although he traveled about, talking with people, staying in their homes, and giving speeches, Christ did not try to work alone. Christ organized a group to help him. We can't organize alone. On a personal and practical level we need to work with others, organizing so we are empowered to confront the problem of hunger and make changes. These may be small changes in the beginning, opening a food pantry, helping people get food stamps, or sending food aid overseas, but they offer hope. That hope empowers us to do more.

Christians working together can claim the power to help end hunger at home and abroad by organizing. Hungry people need you to organize.

2. CHARACTERISTICS OF AN ORGANIZER

Have you ever found yourself saying, "It's just easier to do it all myself?" If you have, you are not alone. Many people find that performing a specific task is easier than motivating and coordinating others to do it — at least in the short run. Nevertheless, in the longer run, no single person can do all the work of a hunger group without being overburdened. More importantly, organizing means involving others, even if it sometimes seems easier to do the work yourself.

Organizing is a particular kind of leadership. Not all the hunger movement's leaders are organizers, but if the movement is to grow and develop, more of its leaders need to become organizers. A leader assumes responsibility for achieving tasks. An organizer involves others in achieving tasks. A group's spokesperson is usually a leader, but s/he may or may not be an organizer. Organizers often play "back seat" roles and encourage others to be seen in public roles. An organizer is a leader who empowers people.

One common difference between a leader and an organizer/leader is the way in which they view themselves in the community. The leader who is not an organizer often becomes isolated from the rest of the community because of hsr positions. S/he sees hsr role as challenging and shocking people with the truth. This is often described as a "prophetic" role.

Prophetic leadership on hunger issues is provided by people such as Tony Compolo, Bishop Gumbleton, and James Cone. They confront us and move us to new commitment. Too frequently, however, the term "prophetic" is used to describe actions and leadership which are simply ineffective. I have seen strongly committed people berate others, alienating themselves from all around them, including those concerned about hunger. Many of those who behave in this fashion are leaders, because they assume leadership tasks. Nevertheless, they are not organizers.

An organizer works *with* people, trying to involve them in hunger work, even if initially it is at a very basic level. The organizer continues studying hunger issues, but does not try to "shock" people with new information. S/he believes people will develop an understanding of hunger better by being involved than by being told by the organizer.

I believe that underlying the approach of many local hunger leaders who do not seek organizing skills are two faulty beliefs. The first is that the truth in one's message will "trickle down" to those who are concerned about hunger. I have found that *speaking* "the truth" to people and helping people *discover* truth for themselves are quite different. My experience in hunger work leads me to believe that most people grow in their understanding of hunger by being involved rather than by hearing a message.

The second faulty belief is that if we articulate our message clearly enough, the moral imperative of our position will convince those in power to make the changes necessary to end hunger. Major changes rarely occur that way. As indicated in the previous chapter, significant social changes occur when groups of people challenge the existing way things are done.

The question of the kind of leadership stressed by the hunger movement is fundamental. Until recently, too little emphasis has been placed on developing leaders with organizing skills. One reflection of this is the energy devoted to making statements, passing denominational resolutions, and criticizing groups for being insufficiently prophetic. Although this is changing, more energy must be focused on developing leaders who are organizers.

Let's look at some of the characteristics of an organizer.

First and foremost, an organizer empowers people. S/he involves others in planning and acting. S/he identifies people concerned about hunger, and helps them find ways to use their talents. S/he asks them to assume appropriate responsibilities. S/he enables people to develop leadership skills, and helps them discover their abilities.

An organizer is persistent. Hsr interest in hunger is not fleeting. S/he is committed to working over the long term, and will keep working even if only a few attend a meeting or a project falls flat. S/he is strongly motivated and is not deterred by strong opposition. S/he learns from failures as well as successes.

An organizer is a good listener. S/he is interested in what people are saying, and sometimes in what they are not saying. S/he learns to ask questions and listens carefully to the answers. S/he listens not just with ears, but with eyes, body, and expressions.

An organizer helps others listen. S/he tries to make people comfortable in new situations, and avoids rhetoric. S/he develops a non-threatening style and avoids mannerisms or styles of dressing which will distract people from listening.

An organizer speaks clearly and simply. S/he does not speak simplistically, but rather tries to explain things as simply as possible. Although an organizer must do hsr homework on issues, s/he does not seek to impress people with hsr knowledge or vocabulary. An organizer tells stories and gives examples to make issues clear and concrete more often than s/he recites facts and statistics.

An organizer is joyful. S/he is a bit like Tom Sawyer — s/he makes involvement in hunger look like so much fun that others want to be involved.

An organizer respects others. S/he tries to understand their positions even if s/he may not agree with them. S/he treats people courteously and with respect. S/he does not expect everyone to agree with hmr. S/he realizes that change does not occur overnight. S/he respects people's need for time to think and pray.

An organizer is honest and can be trusted. Sound like a Boy Scout? It's important. If an organizer says s/he will do something, s/he makes every attempt to fulfill that promise. S/he will answer truthfully if s/he cannot do something, and will not commit to anything if s/he cannot deliver.

An organizer is a good administrator. S/he keeps track of records, details, and requests. Only by being a good administrator will s/he be able to gain people's trust for delivering on a promise. Organizers have to develop good file systems and ways for recording meetings and information, because they juggle lots of projects, names, and details. Some good organizers I've known keep card files on those they meet, listing spouse's and children's names, skills, areas of interest, and best times to call.

An organizer is a continual student. S/he is always learning new skills and developing hsr understanding. S/he challenges hmrself to read and stay abreast of the issues s/he is working on. S/he never claims to have "the truth" but continually seeks the truth. S/he is always willing to say "I don't know."

An organizer has vision and enthusiasm. S/he looks toward the long-term vision of a hunger-free society, but concentrates on the short-term steps needed to alleviate hunger and empower people. S/he peaceably reconciles the difficulty of working for small changes in the midst of overwhelming problems.

An organizer is realistic. S/he sets sensible goals and objectives, in line with the human and financial resources available. S/he makes realistic evaluations that allow people to learn from their successes and failures. By being a realist, an organizer becomes a good strategist. S/he gains experience in designing campaigns which meet objectives and empower people.

An organizer is self-assured. S/he does not think of hmrself as perfect, but basically likes hmrself. S/he tries to do the best job possible at any given time, knowing that s/he will be able to do it better in the future with more experience. Because s/he has confidence in hmrself, s/he is able to encourage others to be leaders. S/he helps others receive credit and praise. S/he does not need continual recognition. S/he is able to accept criticism because s/he wants to do the best job possible. S/he also knows when to quit and allows hmrself to take needed breaks and recreation.

It takes a good deal of self-assurance to continue inviting people to become involved, because the invitation is frequently rejected. The organizer cannot take that rejection personally. Occasionally hunger organizers canvass door-to-door, inviting people to be involved in their group. Doors are slammed in their faces and people can be rude. They also find the people who are thrilled that they stopped by and want to get involved. The organizer has to have confidence to keep knocking until s/he finds those people who want to get involved.

An organizer is creative. S/he is creative because s/he is open-minded about new approaches, flexible in changing how things have been done in the past, and confident in hsr abilities. S/he does not feel threatened by new ideas. S/he is confident enough in hrmself to offer new ideas even if they might be criticized.

Finally, an organizer is hard working. Organizing is difficult. The issues are hard to explain simply, the strategies are complicated, and people can be unpleasant.

Does my organizer sound like a super person? Obviously, no organizer, either volunteer or professional, has all these qualities; however, they are the qualities which make a good organizer, and thus are the qualities we must strive to develop.

Christian scripture and history offer some excellent models of organizers, including Christ himself. Observe the model he offers of gathering people together, providing a vision of a better way, empowering friends and neighbors, and encouraging people to take leadership roles. Our faith can help develop many of the characteristics of a good organizer.

The book of James is full of practical advice for organizers. Every organizer should read it on a regular basis. Here is a brief summary of some of the excellent instruction offered in the book:

Chapter and verse	Guide for organizing
1:2	Be happy.
1:3	Exercise patience.
1:4	Don't try to squirm out of problems.
1:5	Pray for wisdom.
1:19	Listen much.
1:19	Speak little.
1:19	Don't become angry quickly.
1:22	Don't just talk, but act.
1:26	Control your tongue.
2:1	Respect people regardless of income.
2:8	Love your neighbor as yourself.
2:13	Be merciful.
3:1	Don't be too eager to teach people or to tell folks their faults.
3:5	Don't boast.
3:13	Perform deeds with humbleness and wisdom.
4:7	Submit yourself to God.
4:11	Do not criticize or judge one another.
5:8	Keep your hopes high.
5:12	Don't swear.

5:13	Pray for yourself.
5:14	Pray for others.
5:16	Admit faults and sins to one another and then pray for one another.

While I have not highlighted all the important points that James makes in the book, I have tried to illustrate what a powerful and helpful guide the Bible is in doing the work of justice. It can help us gain many of the qualities necessary to be good organizers.

In the same way that we all fall short of the glory of God, we will also fall short of the perfect organizer. Nevertheless, through prayer and practice we will become better organizers, and through the grace of God our work will help hungry people.

3. EMBRACING DIVERSITY

People of all different ages and backgrounds are concerned about hunger and eager to contribute to its solution. Everyone must be encouraged to work together if the problem of hunger is to be solved. Hungry people need *everyone's* contributions. This means that in our organizing we must extend welcomes to all people, actively soliciting their ideas and encouraging their participation.

Involving many different people in hunger work is vital for two practical reasons. First, the more people, and the more diverse people that we can involve in hunger work, the more resources we can direct toward solving the problem. Second, diversity in membership gives the hunger movement a resiliency that it could not have with a homogeneous makeup. When many types of people are represented the movement can appeal to more people, and people of diverse backgrounds and experience can bring a broader range of analysis, insight, and ideas to bear on the problem at both a local and national level. In addition, as Christian groups we seek to be the body of Christ. By encouraging diversity we make ourselves more reflective of the body of Christ. The diversity of the Christian community is a strength for the hunger movement. We must be sure to nurture that strength.

As we go about organizing work, we will find barriers dividing Christians within our communities, and sometimes within our churches. These barriers are deeply embedded in our society, and unfortunately, within us as well. Although we may feel naturally drawn to work with people who are most like ourselves, we must recognize that calling for help upon only those like ourselves excludes all others. The very fact, moreover, that we are uncomfortable with people who are unlike ourselves indicates that we each have some degree of prejudice which we must acknowledge and overcome, if we are to be effective organizers.

The barriers that divide people working against hunger are based most often on differences of politics, religion, age, gender, race, or income. This chapter is not intended to analyze the origins of these barriers. Rather, it is intended to help the reader recognize and eliminate behaviors that erect barriers, and suggests ways to embrace, rather than fear, diversity.

Embracing Political Diversity

Hunger is a nonpartisan issue. People from all political parties are concerned about the problem. Ideas for ending hunger will and do come from a broad range of political perspectives. We must understand, that while each of us may choose a particular political party with which we wish to align, we should not suggest that everyone concerned with hunger must agree with our choice. In your local hunger group, it is important that people from different political perspectives be represented. On the public policy level it is essential. Few policies will be changed at the state or national level without strong bipartisan support.

I have most often seen "political prejudice" manifested in pronouncements that the Democrats are always more concerned than Republicans about hunger. Republicans are made to feel excluded and their comments unwelcomed. You should always presume that the people in your audience or local group are concerned, and everyone should feel welcomed and encouraged to speak. Recognize also, that the Democrats are *not* always more concerned or effective on hunger issues. If fact, some of the strongest Congressional leadership on hunger has come from Republicans such as Silvio Conte, Benjamin Gilman, Mark Hatfield, and Chris Smith.

Avoiding generic statements is the easiest way to overcome

this barrier. Refrain from making sweeping generalizations about either party, the president, or other highly recognized partisan politicians. Stick to the specifics of each issue, e.g., "We don't agree with so and so on this particular issue for this reason." This approach will help keep peace between people representing the two major parties, and will enable us to seek ideas and solutions from all sources. We must make hunger a concern for all parties if we are to make the changes needed to end it.

Embracing Religious Diversity

Christians from many religious backgrounds are concerned about hunger. Not every religious denomination has a hunger program per se, but a program is not needed to involve church members in hunger activities. As Christians we can and should work with people from many different denominations to end hunger.

The predominance of one or two denominations within a group is often an indication of religious barriers. If you have chosen to organize a hunger group within your congregation, it will by definition be of one denomination. The same will likely be true if you have chosen to organize on campus and your college campus is strongly affiliated with one denomination. In these circumstances, you should not be concerned that your group is of one denomination unless you are unable to cooperate with other denominations. If, however, your group intends to be interdenominational, and you find yourselves appealing to only a small sector of the Christian community, you should be concerned, and seek to eliminate the barriers that have limited participation.

The predominance of one or two denominations does not necessarily indicate barriers. In most counties in the United States at least 25 percent of the church-going population belongs to one denominational group. In a surprising number of counties, at least 50 percent of the church-going population is from one denominational group. Thus, it will not be uncommon to find strong participation in your group from particular denominations.

The simplest way to get a sense of the denominational character of your community is to look at the phone book. Make a list of how many churches of each denomination are in your community. Use this information to assess how representative your group is of the church community. Having perfect numerical representation from each denomination is not the goal. If you find a large discrepancy between your group and your community, however, you should seek ways to encourage participation from the underrepresented denominations.

Another manifestation of religious barriers is the way Christians talk about Christians from different denominations. I have heard "mainline" Protestants suggest that evangelicals and fundamentalists are unconcerned about hunger and social justice. I have also heard statements implying that Roman Catholics don't "belong" in the South. These kinds of statements not only indicate the lack of understanding between religious groups, but they are also divisive — barriers in and of themselves. They will isolate us from our sisters and brothers in Christ and will be destructive and harmful to building a movement of Christians concerned about hunger.

One time I was leading a seminar in Arkansas. Participants represented an excellent cross section of the Christian community. For many of those present, it was the first time they had shared with Christians from other denominations. I heard two statements that really struck me. One was from a Southern Baptist woman who said, "I didn't know there were Catholics who loved my Lord." Another was from a Roman Catholic woman who said, "I didn't know Baptists cared about feeding people." At the seminar, people had a chance to discover common concerns and not to dwell on our differences.

We each choose to worship with a particular denomination because we grew up in that denomination, or we enjoy its worship style, or we agree most closely with its theology. It's understandable that if we choose to be involved with one denomination, we think it's the "best." We may not understand certain practices and positions of others, but we must be careful not to judge those involved.

Opening our hearts and developing a nonjudgmental spirit is the first thing we all must do. Doing so will help us accept other people and allow us to learn from one another. Having the right attitude, although necessary, is not sufficient. We also must become informed about different denominations, so we can find ways to cross denominational divisions. We must become sensitive and knowledgeable about different denominations.

Learning about different denominations is a rewarding experience. A good way to begin is to learn from those in your group. Ask people to share about their denominations. Ask different people to lead worship in a style that is traditional for their denomination. Consider attending one another's church services to experience the forms of worship.

Intentionally reach out to churches and Christians from a wide range of denominations. Do not assume that certain churches will not be concerned. If you are sending out speakers' bureau flyers, send them to all churches and denominational publications in the community. If you are calling all the churches in town, don't skip over certain ones because you think they will not get involved.

There may be separate ministerial associations in your town — one for "mainline" Protestants and Roman Catholics and another for evangelical and fundamentalist churches. Many towns also have separate white and black ministerial associations. Seek ways to speak with ministers from all denominations and races. If you plan commmunity action/education programs, include church leaders from across denominational lines. Ask a priest to lead the opening worship and a gospel preacher to lead the closing worship. Ask leaders from both black and white churches to participate. Endeavor to make the leadership represent the diversity among the Christian community.

The last section of this book contains a chapter on understanding denominations. The chapter discusses differences between denominations. It will help you understand how important it is to learn about different denominations and will highlight areas of particular sensitivity. Knowledge and sensitivity are necessary to work across denominational lines effectively.

Including All Ages

Most groups on hunger, perhaps with the exception of small undergraduate campus groups, should involve people of all ages.Young, middle-aged, and older people all have contributions to make toward ending hunger.

Some hunger groups do not include young people. Those still in school or just out of school are passed over for leadership tasks or dismissed when they offer their ideas. The greatest problem most groups have is not tapping the energy and experience of older people. We live in a youth-oriented culture, where people are encouraged to hide graying hairs, cover up wrinkles, and rejoice when people think they are younger than they are. Older people are often put on a shelf and underutilized, if not ignored.

Retired people are a great untapped resource for the hunger movement. They often have time they can offer the organizing work. They have experience from working with people, raising families, and developing careers. They are often sensitive to the problems of people on low and fixed incomes, and open to looking at the world from different perspectives.

Look at the composition of your group. Are there people of different ages? If not, make special invitations to people of different ages. Speak with groups which are normally associated with certain age groups. For example, if there are no young people involved, speak with a campus ministry group. If there are few older people involved, speak with the American Association of Retired Persons, the Gray Panthers, or other groups of older people. You may also want to consider contacting retirement and senior citizen centers.

Draw on all aged people as leaders, volunteers and consultants. If there are physical limitations associated with age, such as mobility, find ways to overcome them. Arrange for people to be picked up for meetings, and schedule meetings at conducive times and places. Above all, welcome and respect contributions of time, leadership, and ideas from all ages.

Including Both Sexes

People in the United States have become increasingly aware of sexism in our society, and yet it is something with which we must all struggle. The hunger movement in general can be quite proud of its inclusiveness of both men and women in leadership roles. Nonetheless, we must all be careful that our language and actions are not exclusive toward women, and that we do not allow gender to color our judgment about people's suitability for leadership and other tasks.

The most common manifestation of sexism in the hunger movement is the dominance of men in meetings. This is usually a somewhat subtle thing, but it is a pattern that I have observed visiting many groups. Men ask more questions, interrupt people, and speak more often. Obviously, this is not true for all men or for all groups. Nevertheless, in most groups, both men and women need to be more careful that the traditional patterns of speaking and behaving in meetings do not dominate, preventing some from participating.

Sexist language is another common manifestation of sexism in our society and churches. Some words are easy to change.

Others are difficult and awkward. I recommend to all hunger organizers that they practice eliminating sexist words and phrases. It takes time and effort, but it is worth it to express ourselves in phrases which make everyone feel included.

If you are speaking to a group, you may have someone correct your noninclusive language. This can be disruptive and frustrating. I have found it best to acknowledge the correction, thank the person for the assistance, noting that changing speech patterns is sometimes difficult, and then continue. Since public reproof is discomfiting to a speaker, I suggest you talk with someone individually about speaking patterns or attitudes which are bothersome, rather than correcting someone in the middle of a presentation or sentence.

One difficult issue that requires extra prayer and sensitivity is reading from the Bible. Some argue that the sexist language in the Bible should be changed to more closely reflect the true will of God. Some Christians are extremely offended to hear words changed. I do know that many Christians would be quite upset to hear changes made in the Bible, and might well focus on the word changes rather than the concepts expressed. Thus, I personally choose to alter the words of songs, prayers, and readings to nonsexist language, but to read the Bible as the particular translation is written; however, this is just one person's decision on a controversial matter.

Sexism is a problem against which all men and women must work. Both men and women exhibit sexism, and both must struggle to include all people in as many ways as possible.

Welcoming Racial Diversity

People of all races are concerned about hunger, and are working to relieve it. Unfortunately, racial divisions separate our churches and our social groups in the United States, and if we do not make a special effort to eliminate them, they might separate our hunger groups as well. Black church groups, for example, historically have worked against hunger and poverty in the local community. Newly formed non-black groups are often unaware of what the black churches have accomplished. Why? Black and white churches have not worked together consistently. Hispanic congregations are separated by language as well.

Your hunger group should be open and welcoming to people of all races, but this may not occur without some effort. People generally ask their close friends to participate with them in hunger projects. Thus if the group is predominantly one race, it will tend to grow the same way, unless some conscious steps are made to invite and include people of other races. A similar result may occur in working with church groups. Dr. Martin Luther King, Jr. said that the most segregated time of the week is Sunday morning. Given the small number of integrated churches in this country, hunger groups based on church affiliation will probably not be racially mixed unless a special effort is made to work with the churches of different racial groups.

In addition to the hurdles created by nonintegrated churches and social groups, individual racism discourages people of different races from working together. This individual racism can express itself in many fashions. There is the overt racism of those who won't speak to people of other races or will make racial jokes. Most racism among hunger groups is much more subtle, and though unintentional, no less a problem.

Black colleagues at Bread for the World have recounted comments made when they were speaking among white groups that I, as a white person, have never experienced. Examples include:

- Making special reference to "all their black friends."

- Talking repeatedly about their involvement in civil rights activities twenty years ago.

- Assuming a black person will know another black person in a very large town.

- Expressing surprise that s/he has a college education.

These kinds of comments, however well intentioned, make the object of them feel differentiated from others in the group and excluded.

If you live in an integrated community and your hunger group is not somewhat reflective of the community, perhaps you should consider why not. Hunger groups and organizations have many excuses for why they are not more integrated, but most of them relate to personal and institutional racism.

I've frequently heard comments such as those below used by white groups to explain why people of other races are not involved in their group:

- They are just not interested in world hunger.

- They are not educated and find the economics and politics of the issue confusing. Some of them don't even read well.

- They like to work through their own churches.

- I'm afraid I will come off patronizing or racist if I talk with them.

- I've tried a few times but they just weren't interested.

- They respond only to crisis situations.

These comments sound terrible and foolish when written

down, but I've heard them, and somewhat more sophisticated versions of them, frequently.

As Christians concerned about social justice, we not only need to confront the racism in us and in our institutions, but we also need to become racially sensitive. We need to become aware of the pervasive nature of racism and how to deal with it in others, in our society, and in ourselves. Organizers need to be sensitive to how a group can become and remain integrated and truly reflective of the Body of Christ.

Below are a few suggestions for achieving a more racially inclusive hunger group. It is by no means an exhaustive list. If your group discusses ways to broaden itself, you can probably generate many more ideas.

- Speak with church groups that reflect other races.

- Many towns have segregated ministerial associations. Be sure to meet with all of them.

- If your goal is to attract more black members, consider contacting black sororities and fraternities. Black sororities and fraternities are strong on many college campuses and the clubs remain active after graduation. Black sororities and fraternities tend to have a stronger service focus than white ones. Also, contact other organizations such as the NAACP and the Urban League.

- If your goal is to attract more Hispanics, see if language is a barrier to participation. If so, consider offering translations at meetings and bilingual materials. Members of your group may choose to make a long-term commitment by learning to speak Spanish.

- Hold your meetings in different churches. The image that is projected if all meetings are held in chuches of one race is exclusive and will discourage participation by other races.

- Invite speakers of different races for meetings and educational programs. Be conscious of the racial mix of leaders who represent your group.

- Seek coverage in newspapers and on radio stations with audiences underrepresented in your group. If your group is predominantly black, be sure to advertise meetings in white, Hispanic, Native American, and / or Asian news mediums. Personally meet with media contacts from races least represented in your group.

Racism is one of the most difficult barriers to break down. Sometimes even those of us with good intent perpetuate racism unknowingly. Forgiveness and a reconciliatory spirit are necessary on everyone's part. We need forgiveness for the hurt we cause one another, and a reconciliatory spirit to bring together Christians of different races.

Welcoming All Income Groups

Rich and poor people alike are concerned about hunger. Everyone who wants to help has something to offer to the hunger movement and to your hunger group.

The United States is the least "class" conscious society among industrialized countries. Many of us would like to pretend that income classes and barriers do not exist. Nonetheless there are very real barriers between people of different incomes: where we live, where we work, where we socialize, and often where we worship. There are actually contemporary theories on church growth which stress that homogeneity — particularly of race and income — results in the most "successful" church. Such homogeneity may increase attendance, but I question whether it is healthy. I am sure such homogeneity is not best for your hunger group.

Reach out to low-income people. Low-income people are most likely to have experienced hunger directly or to know people who are hungry. Their experience will keep a hunger group from romanticizing hunger and poverty.There are a number of ways your group can facilitate the participation of low-income people. Most basic is to hold your meetings where low-income people can attend. If people do not have cars, hold meetings in places accessible to public transportation, or arrange for people to be picked up. Meetings held during the day will be difficult for working people. You may also want to consider child care so that low-income parents do not have to find babysitters.

I have frequently heard upper-middle class Christians express the belief that low-income people are not concerned about hungry people overseas because they are so concerned about day-to-day survival. I personally have found some low-income churches to be the most responsive to the needs of hungry people, in both this country and overseas. Don't assume low-income people will be uninterested or unconcerned.

The key to organizing with low-income people is to suggest responses beyond simply giving money. Although low-income people cannot be "successful" at giving lots of money, there are plenty of things low-income people can do well. Low-income people, for example, can help your group articulate the effects of cuts in federal food programs or what it means to be poor in the United States.

Reach out to high-income people. Invite them to participate in your group. Do not just ask them for financial contributions. You need their experience and ideas as well. People from high-income groups often have contacts in influential positions which would be useful to your group. Find the best way to use these contacts.

Remember to involve the entire group in projects that capitalize on the contacts of a few members. For example, if a high-income person happens to know an elected leader, s/he should not be the only one to meet with the elected leader. Perhaps s/he could help arrange the meeting, and a cross section of the group could participate.

Few rich people know any poor people. Similarly, few poor people know any rich people. It will take conscious efforts to reach across income lines to build an inclusive hunger group. The group will need to be conscious of tendencies to judge rich people and patronize poor people. Both will alienate.

Christ is our model for reaching across income levels. Christ invited all to join him, rich and poor. He circulated among people from all income levels, sometimes to the distress of the disciples. We are called to do no less in our work against hunger.

Of all the barriers discussed in this chapter, income and racial lines are probably the hardest to cross. Yet, we all must struggle together to do so — white, black, Hispanic, native American, and Asian, rich and poor. We need to morally, because it is right. We need to strategically, because we will be a stronger movement if we have a broad base of Christians seeking solutions together. Only by working together can we find creative solutions and can we influence the direction of our society. Diversity makes good political sense.

Breaking down divisions is hard. It is hard for us as groups and harder for us as individuals. Acknowledging the barriers within ourselves — a necessary first step — is painful. But through God's help we can change and be forgiven. We can be reconciled to one another. Through prayer and struggle, we can celebrate our diversity, and build a hunger movement which is truly reflective of the whole body of Christ.

4. ORGANIZING A GROUP

Convinced that you can't, and shouldn't do it alone, you've decided to organize a group. So where do you begin?

Form a Planning Committee

Talk with a few friends about your interest in forming a group to work on hunger issues. Personally ask these friends to meet with you about the possibility of forming a group. Two or three interested people are all you need to form a planning committee. This committee should draft answers to the who, what, why, where, and when questions for your hunger group, so that it can seek institutional support and organize the first meeting.

The planning committee should first attempt to decide who is to be a part of the group. Do you want to be the First United Methodist Hunger Committee whose members are from that congregation? Alternately, do you want it to be a citywide Methodist endeavor, or an interdenominational community effort? The answer to the "who" question defines the target audience for your group.

What is the group's purpose? The answer to this question will relate to the target audience you have selected. If the group will be within a church, integrating hunger issues into the life of the church may be its goal. If the group is denominational, the purpose may be to increase concern and response on hunger in many churches within the denomination. If the group is interdenominational and community-wide, it may try to increase food availability within the country, or heighten awareness and response to world hunger, or both.

Why should people become a part of the group? A well-thought-out answer to this question is important because you will have to answer it when you invite people to the first meeting. Review the following questions that people commonly ask before joining a group: Is the group effective? Will individuals' time and talents be used? Will ideas be welcomed? Will the group be fun? Will people meet others? Take time to think through answers to these questions. Urge members of the planning committee to anticipate questions people will ask and develop thoughtful responses.

Finally, you should determine when and where the group will meet. You don't have to decide precisely how often to meet, but the planning group should develop a general idea about meeting frequency (weekly, monthly, or bimonthly). Similarly, you need to prepare some guidelines on where to meet. Should the group meet in church or a home? Should it rotate among churches? Like the frequency question, you don't need to finalize a policy on this issue — except for the first meeting site — but it is helpful to prepare some initial thoughts before soliciting support and planning the first meeting.

Once your planning committee has worked through these questions, you will be able to seek institutional support and then plan the first meeting. Be prepared for your answers to these questions to change as others become involved. Your initial decisions are necessary to get the group started and provide focus as you solicit support and plan the first meeting. They are not immutable policy choices.

Seek Institutional Leadership Support

What institutional support should you seek for your hunger group?

If you are working within your church, you will want the support of your pastor and other church leaders. Your pastor's support is more likely to be gained if you anticipate hsr likely concerns. Make clear that (1) You do not intend to add to the pastor's workload, and the program will not end up in hsr hands within a short period of time. (2) Your hunger group will support existing church work. For example, you will increase funding for established hunger relief programs. (3) Your work will be nonpartisan and open to all members of the congregation. You will also probably want the support of other church leaders, like the parish council, the missions committee, or the elders. Think through your church leadership and talk with those you think would like to know about your group's formation.

The main reason to talk with established church leaders is to spark their interest and solicit their help in starting your group. Use your meeting with them to ask for specific assistance. For example, ask the pastor to announce the meeting at the church services. Ask the missions committee to allow a section of the bulletin board to be used by your group. Ask the parish council to endorse the group and encourage members to participate. Unfortunately, given human nature, you must also consult with key leaders so you avert conflict and avoid even the appearance of competition. Key leaders may be offended if their advice and support is not sought. Others may feel that by starting another group you are ignoring or belittling their past efforts. Most of these problems can be forestalled by talking with church leaders, and drawing on their experience and seeking their support.

In doing this, do not set yourself up for failure if institutional support is not forthcoming. The organizing of your group does not depend on leadership support. Therefore, when you discuss the organizing of your group, do not imply that its formation is in question. For example, don't ask "Should we start a hunger taskforce?" Rather, say "Several of us are excited about the idea of forming a hunger taskforce. Do you have suggestions on ways we might get started?" Be sure to convey the certainty of the group's establishment as well as your sincere desire for the person's support and advice.

Seeking key leadership support in a community or city-wide effort is more difficult, but equally important. Since planning committee members have limited time and energy, you will need to set priorities for seeking leadership support. Among the key leaders to consider contacting are church leaders (e.g., ministerial alliances, key pastors, bishops, presbytery executives), political leaders (e.g., mayor, city council, republican and democratic party leaders), and community leaders, particularly those already involved in hunger-related activities (e.g., Salvation Army, Urban League, League of Women Voters, Church Women United). The range of support being asked from each person or group needs to be thought through ahead of time. Church, political, and community leaders can often provide excellent help in publicizing your group's formation and continued work. Their endorsements also carry weight. Ask if you can use someone's name in talking with other key leaders. In all your discussions keep the aims of seeking support and avoiding conflict and competition firmly in mind.

Remember: Your efforts to organize a group do not depend on support from institutional leadership. However, your work will be much easier if you laid the proper groundwork with institutional leaders when starting your group.

Choose a Meeting Site and Date

No day, time, or meeting spot you choose will suit everyone. Do the best you can to accommodate peoples' concerns, but once you have weighed the concerns, go ahead and decide. If later you find a better time or place, you can change. The following questions may help select the day and time:

1. Do you want working people to attend? If so, you've probably eliminated the hours between nine and five o'clock, Monday through Friday.

2. Do most potential members attend meetings or programs at certain times? For example, Sunday morning is unsuitable for most church groups.

3. Are there other times which can be eliminated? Most groups find they can quickly eliminate Friday and Saturday nights.

4. Can you time your meeting to piggyback on other meetings or events? For example, if you are a church group, you might consider a Sunday morning breakfast meeting before services. (It's better to have your meeting *before* rather than *after* something.)

5. Is a breakfast meeting a possibility? Breakfast meetings at a local restaurant are very popular. Consider the times from 7:00 to 8:30 A.M., realizing that you'll lose thirty minutes on ordering and eating. A bit later on Saturday mornings is also a good time.

6. How early could an evening meeting start? You don't want to start much later than 7:30 P.M. because people will be tired (the only exception to this is student groups whose days tend to start and end later).

7. Are there major events, such as the Super Bowl, already scheduled? The sports enthusiast on your planning committee can keep you informed of such matters.

Consider these questions in choosing a meeting site:

1. Is it convenient for most people? Your site should

be centrally located and easy to find. It should be especially convenient for your "target" membership.

2. Is it accessible by public transportation? This is an important question if your group will include people without cars.

3. Is it accessible for physically handicapped people?

4. What reputation does the site have? This question is more important than you may realize. As a group concerned about justice, you must consider a site's reputation. For example, if a church is chosen, it should be one that both blacks and whites feel comfortable entering. Similarly, a lavish restaurant is unsuitable for a hunger group meeting.

5. Is it safe? This is especially important if you choose a night meeting.

6. Is it quiet? A busy restaurant without a private dining room is too distracting to hold a meal meeting.

7. Is it comfortable? It's far more important for a meeting site to be comfortable than fancy. In most cases a smaller room is more comfortable than a huge room.

8. Is it cheap? Avoid spending money on a meeting site. Meeting in someone's home is certainly cheap and can be done if it meets the other criteria.

Plan the Agenda

Once the date, time, and site of the first meeting have been determined, you need to work on the meeting agenda. You will certainly want to begin your meeting with a worship service. It should be uplifting, but not too long. Ten minutes is probably about right. One or two familiar songs help by involving people at the very beginning. Worship is an important beginning because it allows people to share something in common, places our work against hunger in the context of our faith, and sets a good tone for the meeting. Following worship, you will want people to introduce themselves and share something about themselves. Useful topics include why they came to the meeting, how they got involved in hunger issues, or what they hope the meeting will accomplish. Expect to spend ten minutes or so on people getting to know one another. If there are lots of people, you may want to break up into small groups for people to meet one another.

One or more people from your planning committee should then present your thoughts on the need for the group and what its goals should be. The tone of the presentation should be one of sharing initial thoughts, not conclusions set in concrete. The thoughts are presented to stimulate other ideas, and to establish some common ground for the meeting. The presentations should serve as an orientation for new people. You will then want the group to discuss its goals. Spend some time working through what kind of group the people want. You might ask each person to list some goals for the group. Then ask each person to name hsr top three goals. This will enable you to discern which goals are the most important for the majority of people. (See the chapter on using creativity for other ideas.) Don't allow the group to get bogged down in the wording of goals. Get the general idea and then assign a few people to work on the final wording for the next meeting. Most groups have a few members who are very detail oriented. They are good people to serve in finalizing the wording.

If time permits, the group should select one or two concrete projects. These projects should be small to assure success and to demonstrate from the very beginning that yours is an action group. It is helpful if the planning group can have a few suggestions prepared. However, better ideas may emerge at the meeting.

Make assignments for the next meeting. It is important that everyone who is willing take on a task, no matter how small. There should be some projects undertaken beyond just planning for the next meeting. The tasks needing further work will flow out of the discussion at the meeting. Once tasks are assigned, formally close the meeting with a song or a prayer.

Be sure to plan some sort of refreshments after the meeting to encourage people to stay and talk. The social time is very important in developing a sense of community. People will be more likely to get involved and make commitments if they feel part of the group. Building relationships among people is an important part of organizing a group.

Thus your meeting agenda will probably look something like this:

Opening Worship	10 minutes
Introductions and Welcome	10 minutes
Presentations of Possible Goals	5 minutes
Discussion of Goals	30 minutes
Discussion of First Project	15 minutes
Assignments for Next Meeting	10 minutes
Closing	2 minutes
Refreshments and Social Time	

This agenda uses approximately an hour-and-a-half. That is about as long as a meeting should go, since people get restless in longer sessions.

You will want to pass around a sign-up sheet for names, addresses, and phone numbers. You may also want to ask people to indicate what meeting times are best for them. Do not have a group discussion about meeting times. Such discussions are a poor use of your group's time.

One good way to get information about people is to ask everyone to fill out a profile sheet. It can record basic data such as address and phone numbers, as well as gather information about the talents people would be willing to contribute. Your form might look like this:

SAMPLE PROFILE SHEET

Name: _____   Home phone: _____

Address: _____   Work phone: _____

_____   Church and other hunger
involvements:

_____   _____

The following times would be okay for meetings:

	early morning	lunchtime	late afternoon	evening
Monday				
Tuesday				
Wednesday				
Thursday				
Friday				
Saturday				
Sunday				

I can offer skills in the following areas:

___ typing	___ media/public relations
___ drawing	___ preaching
___ layout	___ singing
___ writing	___ musical instruments
___ speaking	

I am willing to help in the following areas:

___ making phone calls	___ assisting with childcare
___ stuffing envelopes	___ leading worship
___ preparing refreshments	___ planning agendas
___ arranging publicity	___ conducting research

In addition, I have skills in the following other areas and/or would be willing to help in another way: (please describe) _____

_____

Once you've drawn up your preliminary outline for the meeting, you should again review the questions raised earlier in this chapter. Be sure that your agenda and plan address most of the questions a person will be asking.

1. Is the group effective? This question is one reason you want to have an action plan from the very beginning. People want to join a group that is doing something — not just meeting. People should leave the first meeting seeing how the group's work will help hungry people.

2. Will individuals' time and talents be used? This is part of the reason for making assignments immediately. It is also why you want to survey the skills in the group.

3. Will ideas be welcomed? Demonstrate from the very beginning that the group will be listening to ideas. The tone of the person facilitating the meeting is critical. Openness and flexibility are key to the success of any group.

4. Will the group be fun? Again, the best answer to this is demonstrated in your meeting. The worship should be a joyful time. The leadership in the meeting should be positive. The refreshment and social time should be fun.

5. Will people meet others? Make sure this happens at the beginning of the meeting and then again during the social time.

These questions are basic for recruiting and keeping people involved. Every meeting should answer these questions positively. Especially at the beginning, you might want to review these questions on a regular basis.

Once the meeting agenda is outlined, you need to decide who will do what. One person should be asked to facilitate the overall meeting. This person should be comfortable leading meetings and should be able to set the warm tone desired by the planning committee. Other members of the planning committee can take responsibility for specific aspects of the agenda, such as planning and leading worship, presenting the initial thoughts, or leading a closing prayer. You may want to ask key institutional leaders to handle one part, such as lead the worship. Some members must handle the logistics and details. Here are a few to review: refreshments, sign-up sheets, nametags, an agenda for people to look at, worship aids or song books, audiovisual equipment, signs to find the room, chalkboards, and newsprint. Whichever items are desired, be sure that someone is assigned to bring or check on each item.

Publicizing the First Meeting

The most effective means of getting people to a meeting is through personal invitation. Each person on the planning committee should agree to personally invite ten people from their family, circle of friends, or church. You should probably call those who express interest the night before the meeting and remind them of the time and place. That kind of personal attention tells people you really want and need their participation.

A personal invitation is most effective when it tells a little bit about the planning committee's dreams and why the person is needed. For example, "A few of us in the church have been talking about forming a hunger group in our congregation. We think there is a lot that could be done to raise awareness, increase our contributions to world hunger, and maybe even to start a pantry. We would like you to join us because we know you are concerned, but also because you are such a good teacher. We need people who are skilled at planning adult education programs."

If your group is to come mainly from your church/parish, you will want to focus attention primarily at the church level. You might want to use posters on the bulletin board and around the church building, announcements in the church bulletin and/or newsletter, and spoken invitations during announcement of "minute for missions" times. Many churches have committees and various groups that meet on a regular basis. Type up a brief announcement about the meeting and ask that it be presented at the various meetings held in the church. Separate copies to each group or committee leader will increase the chances of its being read.

If you are forming a group among churches in your denomination, you will want to publicize the meeting to all the churches. If you have time, place an announcement in a denomination publication. In addition, individual announcements should be sent to each congregation. I suggest sending several different items: (1) a flyer which can be posted; (2) a letter to the pastor/priest asking hmr to announce the meeting; (3) an announcement which can be placed in the bulletin (sent with the letter to the pastor/priest); plus (4) a letter to the social concerns committee, missions committee, church and society committee, or whatever grouping in your denomination's church structure that you think would be most interested in the formation of a hunger group in your area.

If your group is hoping to appeal to churches across the community, you will want to do even wider publicity. Below are a few suggestions:

1. INVITATION LETTERS — Mail invitation letters, including a flyer if possible to all the churches in the area. The listing of churches in the Yellow Pages is probably as good as any. There is also a listing in the Yellow Pages under "religious organizations." Some cities have interdenominational organizations, such as a Council of Churches, which publish a listing of all churches in the area.

2. MINISTERIAL ASSOCIATIONS — Most communities have some sort of ministerial alliance. Try to find a minister who will announce your meeting, or ask if someone from your group can attend and make the announcement. You might also want to distribute flyers and ask the ministers to post them. It is good for the ministers to hear about the meeting through both their association and the invitation letters. Don't worry about them getting duplicate information.

3. NEWSPAPER ANNOUNCEMENTS — Most newspapers

have a community bulletin board section. It's quite easy to get your meeting announced in this section. You might also want to send news releases to local papers. For suggestions on this, see the media chapter.

4. RADIO/TV ANNOUNCEMENTS — Much like the newspaper, many of the radio and TV stations have a community bulletin section. Make sure your meeting is announced here. You may even be able to arrange an interview to discuss the formation of the group on one of the Christian radio stations.

5. PERSONAL INVITATIONS — Despite the wide reach of all the above forms of publicity, personal invitation will still be your most effective means for attracting new members. Don't spend so much time mailing publicity materials that you forget to invite your friends and neighbors. If you ask at your meeting how people heard about the meeting, you will probably find that the majority came through a personal invitation.

Set up for the Meeting

There are always a number of things that need to be done right before the meeting. It's a good idea to have the planning committee meet an hour or so before the meeting is scheduled to begin. The planning committee should begin by praying for the meeting and praying that their leadership will be as effective as possible. This prayer time together reminds the planning committee that they are about the Lord's work.

Signs need to be put up to guide people to the appropriate room; this is particularly true in most church buildings. Chairs should be arranged in a circle if at all possible. Don't assemble too many chairs. It's better to widen the circle than have empty chairs. Put the agenda where people can see it. You may want to hang a poster on the wall, write on a chalkboard, or use an overhead projector. It's good to let people know what will be happening in the meeting.

Make sure your sign-up sheets or forms are ready and available. Have nametags available if people won't know one another. Arrange the refreshments ahead of time so no one has to miss the last part of the meeting preparing food. Coffee or tea available during the meeting is helpful if the meeting is during the evening.

Distribute worship aids, such as music or reading materials. It's easy to place these on people's chairs. Extras should be readily available in case chairs need to be added. If you will be using any audiovisual equipment, get everything set up ahead of time. Murphy's Law that anything that can go wrong will go wrong definitely applies to audiovisual equipment. Check where the room's light switches are, whether the bulbs work, and if you need an extension cord or screen. Someone should bring a spare bulb, just in case.

All of the arrangements should be completed ten to fifteen minutes before the meeting begins. The planning committee should be available to meet and welcome people. Take this time to make new people feel welcome.

Run a Good Meeting

The impression people get about the first meeting will play a large part in their decision about whether or not they want to become part of the group. Thus, it is important that the meeting be run as well as possible.

If members of the planning committee have been welcoming people as they enter, a good tone will have been established before the meeting begins. Opening the meeting within a few minutes of the planned time will indicate that the group is serious in its task. The worship time will help set the right tone, as well as give stragglers a few more minutes to arrive.

During the introduction time, the meeting facilitator should listen intently to each person, looking them in the eye. This will emphasize the message that the group's planning committee is interested in each person. The facilitator should ask people follow-up questions if s/he feels they would be of interest to the group.

The meeting facilitator should watch the time carefully throughout the meeting. There will be a tendency for the presenter(s) from the planning committee to talk for a long time because they are excited about the potential of a new group. Do not allow this to happen or the new people will feel left out of the group's planning and formation. They will feel they are being handed a finished product. As quickly as possible move the group to discussion.

During the discussion time, the planning committee will be tempted to dominate the discussion. The facilitator should intentionally ask others what they are thinking. Draw everyone into the discussion. General discussion can go on for quite a while, so the facilitator will need to move the meeting along. If the facilitator is good at summarizing, s/he should summarize how the group wants to proceed and what it wants to do. If the facilitator is not good at this, s/he should ask someone else in the group to do so. Group members need to feel that the discussion moved the group forward and that there is a cohesive ending to the discussion.

Decide on one small project to work on at the first meeting. This decision will set the group's tone as an action group. Let me emphasize that the project should be a small, manageable one. It will be critical for the group to have an early success, which is best assured by choosing an achievable target.

The assignment time of the meeting is crucial. It is the point at which people will decide whether or not to be part of the group. Do not pressure people to assume responsibilities, but ask people individually. General questions like "Will someone do this?" will not receive as good of a response as "Belinda and Angela, would you two work together on this project?" People are free to say no, but they will be more likely to say yes if asked directly. The facilitator can ask people, or other members of the group can do so. You should have a good idea of who might do what, based on people's background and the items they expressed interest in during the meeting.

Once assignments are made for the next meeting, bring the meeting to a close. The meeting should end at the time agreed upon. Invite people to stay around and talk more over refreshments, but allow those who need to leave to do so. People will start leaving or be irritated if the meeting runs beyond its scheduled time. There is nothing more disruptive to group dynamics than people leaving before the meeting ends.

Close with a song or prayer or something affirming. Some groups stand and join hands for the closing. Others have a time of shared prayer where anyone who wants to pray can do so. Thank everyone for coming and repeat the invitation for people to stay for refreshments.

Immediately after the meeting, the planning committee should talk with as many people as possible, especially those who seemed somewhat quiet. Ask someone who seems interested and is able to stay for a few minutes to help in cleaning the room. From the very beginning, establish the practice of asking others to help with tasks or assume responsibility.

Do Follow-up Immediately

First, someone should send a formal note thanking the appropriate person for the use of the meeting site. Ask someone who likes writing to send the note. Next you should follow up on those tasks that people agreed to do in the meeting. Call people and find out how things are going. Ask if they need help. Depending on the size of the group, you may want to call everyone and thank them for coming. Follow-up letters can be sent, but calls are more personal.

Just after the first meeting is one of the best times to get media coverage. Take advantage of it. Send a press release announcing your group's formation. Call the local religion reporter and ask if s/he would like to talk with you about your group's upcoming plans. Do the same with radio talk-show hosts. The formation of a new antihunger group in the community is news. Thus, even though you may not feel ready to jump into the world of media, there's no better time to begin developing your press list. See the chapter on media for "how-to's" on working with the media.

Finally, find a way to celebrate the formation of your group. Send thank you cards to other members of the planning committee. Go out for a celebration meal. Do something special. Organizing a group is hard work. You've passed the first stage. Celebrate!

Take It from There

There are several tasks that your newly-formed group must accomplish within the first two to three months after it is formed. You must set and accomplish some achievable goals, you must assess your leadership and member composition, and you must develop an acceptable level of organizational structure.

All newly organized groups need achievable goals. They should be targets which can be achieved quickly, within the next month or two. These kinds of achievable goals help solidify the group. People within the group feel good about being part of a group that does something. People outside the group see it as a group that is active. Both are important for the group to grow and develop.

Later chapters deal extensively with the kinds of goals and

tasks that are appropriate for young groups, but let me stress that your early meetings should focus on more than just getting more people to the next meeting. There is nothing more depressing than waiting until more people show up before you really decide to do something. Work with whomever shows up and take concrete actions with the folks you have. Remember, Christ only chose twelve, and at least one of them wasn't so great.

In door-to-door canvassing, if I talked with forty people, about half would express interest in hunger issues. About half of those (ten) would make some financial commitment. Two or three people would join Bread for the World. Similar figures can be expected in organizing a group. If you personally invite forty people, half may express an interest. Two or three will actually come to a meeting. Six or eight others will be supportive enough to help out with specific tasks, if asked, or to attend a special event.

The point of these numbers and figures is to encourage your hunger group to have realistic expectations about its size, and to realize that a lot can be accomplished with a committed core of people. The fact is that most hunger groups are small, with a nucleus of eight to ten people. Some sociologists say that from five to ten is the perfect group size, so if your group is small, think of it as "the perfect size."

If your group is small, identifying key leadership roles such as a president or coordinator, can be done informally. If the group is larger, you may need to hold elections. The main thing is to assure that the leadership quickly expands beyond the planning group.

You should also assess the overall composition of those who come to the first meeting. For example, if your target audience is your congregation and you notice that there are no young people involved, then you should actively seek some young people to be part of your group. If your target is all the Catholic churches in town and you seem to have only representation from one side of town, then consider holding your next meeting on the other side of town, or finding out how to involve others. If your group is supposed to be interdenominational, and you only have white "mainline" Protestant churches represented, then you need to actively seek Roman Catholic, Evangelical, and black church participation. It is important to be representative of your target group from the very beginning stages. This will offer you the greatest diversity of ideas and potential for broad outreach. A young person is likely to have the best ideas for involving young people; and so with the others.

One pitfall that many groups fall into is spending many hours and meetings struggling over bylaws and finances. Unless you really need bylaws, don't bother with them. At the least, wait until you have accomplished some goals and have had a chance to see if you really need them, before establishing bylaws. Work with as informal a structure as your group can. Funds needed in the first few months are best raised by passing the hat and asking for contributions. Asking each member to pitch in what they can will usually cover expenses and will allow people to express commitment to the group. If more funds are needed later, you can find ways to raise them that do not take much time. Fundraising, like bylaws, should be a low priority on a newly organized group's agenda.

Organizing a group may sound like hard work, and it can be, but it is also rewarding. Once you have your first meeting, and people have agreed to meet again, your group is off and running — and you are not working alone. There are others not only to share the tasks, but to share the pain and joy of working on hunger issues. Give thanks to God for those who came, even if only a few, and ask for guidance as your group moves forward.

5. MAINTAINING A GROUP

Maintaining your hunger group will require at least as much energy as organizing it, and will be far more important in the long run. Long term maturity and development is necessary if your group is going to make a difference in your church or community. It is also a major ingredient in developing social justice leaders.

Task/Maintenance Functions

Every group performs both task and maintenance functions. For a group to mature and develop it needs both task and maintenance leadership. What do we mean by these terms?

Group members perform task functions when they exhibit behaviors that facilitate meeting the group's objectives. Examples of task functions in a meeting include:

- providing an agenda
- recommending objectives
- determining key questions
- suggesting ways to accomplish specific objectives
- clarifying information
- moving the group to action or decision-making
- recording information and decisions
- opening and closing meetings.

Maintenance functions relate to *how* a group goes about doing its tasks and how people in a group relate to one another. Other terms for maintenance functions and leadership are emotional functions and emotional leadership. Ideally, the group maintenance occurs in such a fashion that members of the group feel supported and included. Maintenance functions in a meeting include the following:

- welcoming and introducing people
- actively listening to people's ideas
- including everyone in discussions
- encouraging shy and quiet people to speak
- thanking people for contributions and for coming to the meeting
- giving positive feedback to speakers.

All members of a group offer both task and maintenance behaviors, but most people tend more toward one function or the other. You might want to look over the lists above and think about which activities you are most likely to perform in a meeting to determine if you are more task- or more maintenance-oriented.

Maintaining a local group requires solid leadership in both task and maintenance functions. Tasks must be set forth and accomplished, but members of the group must feel included and positive about the way the group established and accomplished its goals. The complaints and meeting descriptions listed below are typical of ones I've heard when a group was weak in either task or maintenance leadership. Review the lists and try to determine which leadership functions your group needs to strengthen:

- The meetings seem so businesslike.
- The same people always seem to dominate discussions.

- No one pays attention to my ideas.
- I feel excluded from the group because I don't know as much.
- I feel like I might get jumped on by someone if I don't say the right thing.
- New people never feel welcome.
- The women never seem to talk.
- People interrupt one another constantly.

THE GROUP
NEEDS STRONGER
MAINTENANCE
LEADERSHIP

- We really enjoy one another, but we never seem to accomplish anything.
- Our meetings never have agendas or objectives.
- I'm never clear what we have decided.
- We seem to be meeting just to be meeting.
- I don't feel like I'm learning anything.
- No one knows what happened the last meeting.

THE GROUP
NEEDS STRONGER
TASK LEADERSHIP

Task and maintenance leadership are needed in all aspects of a group's life, both during and between meetings; but, attention must be devoted particularly to the functioning of your group's meetings. Meetings are the times when the entire group interacts. Meetings must be productive and enjoyable to sustain the work that occurs between meetings.

To assure that your meetings have solid task and maintenance leadership, you might want to leave five minutes at the end of each meeting to evaluate the meeting. Ask people what they liked about the meeting. Then ask what they would like to see changed or improved for future meetings. This approach will usually bring forth suggestions for improving task leadership. However, it does not always allow maintenance leadership questions to surface. Therefore, in addition to formal evaluation times, leaders need to talk with people on a regular basis. Ask if they felt included and listened to. Ask if they have any observations on how the group interacts. New people can often provide useful insights into the interactions of a group. Accompany a new person out to hsr car or bus stop and ask for hsr reflections.

Based on the group evaluations, and the feedback you hear about the group and its functioning, take deliberate steps to strengthen leadership in the weak areas. If your task leadership is weak, spend time preparing an agenda. Ask others to look at the agenda ahead of time and make suggestions for improvement. Think about realistic objectives for the meeting. Write them down for the group to approve. See that key questions for discussion are determined before the meeting so the group can use its time efficiently.

If your group has trouble keeping its meetings focused, moving to decisions, recording decisions, or opening and closing meetings on time, then the person or people facilitating the meetings need to take stronger task leadership. If the group has agreed to the agenda and the key questions, then the group will want the facilitator to keep the group on track. The facilitator must gain the confidence to suggest that the discussion is a bit tangential and suggest that the group go back to the initial question at hand. This kind of focusing is only possible if the facilitator is serving in a facilitating role. S/he can not be actively involved in the discussion and expect to facilitate as well. By helping the group focus its attention, the group is in a better position to actually conclude a discussion and make a decision. The facilitator must then see that the decisions are written down.

In addition to a group facilitator, one person should be appointed at each meeting to serve as the timekeeper. S/he can let the group know when the time allotted for a particular agenda item is nearly up. If necessary, the facilitator can be the timekeeper as well, but it is better to have separate people. Although a meeting facilitator should provide leadership in task areas, task leadership should be exercised by all members of the group. Everyone should help the group maintain its focus, keep its goals, and stay within the time frames.

If the group evaluations and the feedback heard indicate you need stronger maintenance leadership, think about the behaviors within the group that discouraged participation. Were opinions sought from those who normally do not speak? Were new people welcomed and urged to participate in discussions? Did people listen well to one another? Involving everyone in meetings and helping people listen to one another are two of the most important maintenance tasks required in meetings.

The meeting facilitator, as well as every other member of the group, should seek to equalize participation in meetings. This does not mean that each person has an allocated amount of time. It does mean that those who speak frequently should be encouraged to draw others out more, and those who seldom speak should be asked their opinions on matters. The facilitator should assure that each person's ideas are treated with respect.

Helping people in groups listen to one another is not as easy as it might sound. Many of us are more concerned about what we are going to say next than with what another person is saying. As a result, we do not listen well. Listening well means watching the person speaking, asking clarifying questions, and giving verbal and nonverbal signals that you have heard and understood. Nonverbal listening signs are such things as nodding your head or leaning forward in your seat. Good listening skills should be strived for by the group as a whole.

Stages of Group Development

Sociologists and our own personal experience tell us that groups go through various stages of development. The term "stage" is a term to help us understand the changes a group is undergoing based on the experiences of other groups. Your group may be somewhat or entirely unique. However, if your group is like the vast majority of groups, there will be certain patterns in its development. As a group organizer, it is helpful to understand what is likely to happen — what stages the group will experience. There seem to be five fairly distinct stages.

STAGE ONE IS THE INTRODUCTION OR EXPLORATORY STAGE. This is when the group members are "checking out" one another. People ask questions like, "What are the goals of this group? Are there people here I'd like to get to know? Do we share similar values? Will the group want my talents?" Each new person who joins a group goes through this type of questioning. It is reasonable then if a group is new that the entire group would go through this stage.

Stage one is the first stage at which people choose whether or not they want to be part of the group. Their decisions will rest on what they perceive the group's goals to be, whether they want to work with the group, and whether they think the group wants their contributions. People join a group wanting to give and receive.

The group's organizers at this stage need to provide structure and guidance so people can have their questions answered.

Beyond this task leadership, the emphasis needs to be on maintenance leadership. Everyone should be welcomed warmly when they arrive, even if late. Time should be spent letting people get to know one another. People should be encouraged to ask questions and share their goals and dreams for the group. This stage is a time to explore one another and the group.

STAGE TWO IS THE EVALUATION OR TRANSITION STAGE. This is the stage where having gotten to know one another better, some fears and hesitations emerge. It's similar to what happens with two people in love. At first they are overjoyed with one another. Then they begin to realize that the other person isn't perfect and they themselves feel somewhat vulnerable. It is a time of questioning and evaluation.

Stage two is a difficult stage for groups and individuals. It is the time when the group begins to determine what kind of leadership it wants and discusses concrete actions in relationship to the group's initial goals. There's a lot of talking in this stage — evaluative talking.

Some people refer to stage two as the "adolescent" stage. That in itself says a lot to us. Adolescence is the time when people question leadership and its decisions, and can be hypercritical. It can be a creative time, but also a difficult one. Many parents wish their children could bypass adolescence. You may wish your group could too. However, neither a child nor a group can skip this stage. However, the ease of transition is greatly affected by the tone and direction of the meetings. Developing a team spirit is important in this stage. More time should be spent on people getting to know one another, sharing goals and concerns, and listening to various ideas. The organizer/s should be open, respectful and nondefensive, especially to people who seem to be asking questions in a confrontational manner.

The group should begin working on a project or task, both as a way of clarifying its direction and as a means of developing the team spirit. The project should be a modest one to assure success on the group's first project. Take adequate time to work through the details of the project with the entire group. Distribute tasks and responsibilities in such a way that everyone assumes some kind of responsibility. This will begin to confirm people's commitment to the group.

Stage two requires patience and love. It also requires direction to move into some beginning projects. This stage requires both strong task and maintenance leadership. This period is the one where members either decide to leave or commit themselves to the group. You should expect to lose some people at this point, but the way in which this stage is handled can minimize departures. Open and clear communication is important.

Most groups enter this rocky period by the second or third meeting. Sometimes this period goes quickly, and other times it takes longer. It is not a "bad" stage, just a difficult one. But as with many difficult times, it is a time filled with much potential.

Each new member of a pre-existing group experiences this kind of transition. It's like a new staff person in an office setting. The first week or two is the honeymoon period where everything is great. Then, the person questions everything and it appears that the person thinks the organization has been sitting on its hands until that person arrived. The same is true to a lesser extent with any new person in a group. At the first meeting, they are likely to be thrilled to have found such a group. After a few meetings, they will question the group's goals, leadership, and activities. This can irritate other members of the group. However, the group members must realize that each one of them went through a similar process.

STAGE THREE IS THE CONFLICT STAGE. After people have gone through a period of questioning and evaluating, usually some conflicts arise. These conflicts result from differences of opinion or philosophy. It is perfectly "natural" for people to have differences of opinion or philosophy, and thus conflicts should be expected.

Occasionally there are conflicts that can not or should not be resolved. However, most of the time conflicts can and should be resolved. Resolving conflict in a healthy fashion is creative and strengthening for your group.

Resolving conflict in a healthy fashion requires the group to analyze the conflict. Sometimes there is less conflict than originally thought because people express themselves differently and misunderstand each other. Take time to question and listen carefully to the various positions. Once the actual conflicts have been identified, you should assess how these conflicts relate to your goals. Are the conflicts actual conflicts in goals? More likely they are differences about how to reach the goals. Many conflicts, although stated as a conflict in goals or priorities, actually are conflicts in strategy. Conflicts in strategies are easier to resolve because different strategies can often be undertaken to reach the same goal.

With the conflicts analyzed and assessed, you are better able to resolve the conflict. Actually resolving conflict requires strong maintenance leadership.

People need to be listened to, respected, and treated fairly. People will be willing to alter their positions or change their strategies if they feel respected and accepted. If people do not feel treated fairly, conflicts cannot be resolved.

Sometimes the conflict stage involves large segments of the group. Other times the conflict is concentrated between a few people. Either way, the conflict should be resolved. However, how the conflict is resolved may vary. For example, if the conflict is between two people who trust one another, they should be encouraged to resolve the problem and bring some solutions which are acceptable to them both back to the group. If there are two people whose conflicts are disruptive within the group, either the group needs to accept responsibility ("we, the group, have a difference") or a facilitator should offer to meet with the two people.

In the third stage, it is not uncommon for the group to split into two or three subgroups. This usually reflects unresolved conflict. If one or more of the subgroups feel their ideas are not being integrated, they may leave the group unless this conflict, whether perceived or real, is addressed.

Unfortunately, Christian groups in general, and Christian hunger groups in particular, prefer to skip this stage. Addressing the conflict is seen as un-Christian. However, by skipping this stage, growth is curtailed. Creative solutions are not discovered, goals are not clarified, and group members are not challenged by one another. The group may well lose members because conflict was not addressed.

Too often in groups where conflicts are not addressed directly people complain and discuss the conflicts in small groups. The temptation to murmur and gossip is great. By not addressing the conflict in a Christian manner, we are tempted to sin. In the short run it may seem easier to avoid the conflict but in the long run, it is not the most healthy way to proceed. We need to realize that addressing conflict is neither Christian nor un-Christian. *How* we address conflict (i.e., how we treat people) is an expression of our Christian faith.

STAGE FOUR IS THE ACTION STAGE. Stage four is the most productive and the most enjoyable stage of a group's life. It is the stage in which the group best makes decisions and undertakes tasks. It is a period when group members take on new responsibilities and develop leadership skills. At this stage, task leadership is very important. It is a time to enjoy accomplishing tasks.

During stage four, the group learns to set realistic goals. It learns to develop measurable steps, timelines, and responsibilities for achieving those goals. Group members begin to celebrate the accomplishments and enjoy spending time with one another. At the same time the group and each individual continues to expand knowledge and skills.

The group can and should be reaching out during stage four. It is a time to involve new people, incorporate different perspectives and ideas, and undertake difficult projects. The group is strong enough to push and challenge itself. The group as a whole is in a good position to welcome new people (who are in the exploratory stage), respond to questioning people (who are in the transition stage), and grow from challenging people (who are in the conflict stage).

THE FIFTH AND FINAL STAGE IS THE CONCLUDING OR TERMINATION STAGE. The group ends during this stage. It can occur by default or by agreement. If a group of people are "hanging on" out of guilt, rather than because they want to be part of the group, the group should conclude so people could use their energies and talents elsewhere. If possible, the group should end with some formal closure and celebration.

Often, however, groups that should end and individuals who should leave, are plagued by guilt. These guilt feelings cause the individuals or groups to find fault with one another to justify leaving or terminating the group. This is not healthy for anyone. Formally ending a relationship with a group is better than resentfully participating in it. The person who needs to leave a group, but continues to participate, is usually a burden to the rest of the group with hsr negative attitude. Similarly, groups that are ready to end, but do not, are a burden to all group members.

Therefore, it is important that the group be affirming and joyful in this last stage. Review and celebrate the group's accomplishments. Make recommendations for other organizations. Set aside time for people to share with one another one last time. Give thanks to God for the time the group has been together. A positive final closure is important for the group and the individual.

At this point, you may be wondering "should my group just die?" Perhaps it should if no one wants to participate in it. However, if you are wondering this because people are questioning the group's purposes, there are conflicts within the group, or there aren't as many people actively involved as you would like, then the group should not end. These are normal problems that groups experience. The organizers in the group should help the group work through the various stages and persevere with the people they have.

In addition to occurring at the full group level, these patterns occur to some degree with individuals joining a group. Any new person will evaluate the group. If s/he feels welcome and interested, s/he will continue with the group. Fairly soon, the new person is likely to disagree with how something in the group is accomplished. There will be some conflict. If the conflict is resolved in a positive manner, the person will probably become an active member of the group. After several years of active participation, the person may need to stop working with the group.

One can also observe these five stages in each group meeting. The first part of a meeting is introductory. Group members greet one another and welcome new people. Maintenance leadership is exercised at the beginning of any meeting. The next part of a meeting is evaluative, looking at what has been accomplished and what needs to be done. This requires a combination of maintenance and task leadership. The third part addresses conflicts that have arisen during the evaluations and discussion. Maintenance leadership is needed during this part so conflicts surface and are resolved in a healthy fashion. During the next part of the meeting, the action part, people make plans and agree on responsibilities. The group requires strong task leadership during this part. Finally, the meeting is closed. Maintenance leadership is exercised to thank people for coming, review the meeting's accomplishments, and celebrate.

These stages are not rigid. They are merely useful categories for understanding the development of a group. You *do not* need to be a social scientist to understand and apply these stages or to work well with a group. The stages apply to groups as a whole, to each of us as individuals, and to each meeting. Understanding each phase can help you and your group be more patient, anticipate problems, and recognize what type of leadership (task or maintenance) is needed at a particular time.

Worship/Study/Action

Worship, study, and action are the major activities of both community- and church-based Christian hunger groups. The balance of activities varies depending on each group's interest and stage of development. New groups (in the exploratory, transition, or conflict stage) tend to have stronger worship and study components and weaker action components. Groups in the action stage have stronger action components and groups in the termination stage focus primarily on worship and study. A balance of these three components should be maintained during every stage.

Worship helps individuals and groups keep their perspective in focus. It reminds us that we alone will not be able to end world hunger. Worship can also facilitate group maintenance by helping members share with one another, listen to others' true feelings, and include new people. In an interdenominational group, worship enables people to share different worship traditions with one another.

In addition, beyond supporting faith on a personal level, worshipping together sets a tone for group interaction that is difficult to reproduce in a nonreligious group. As an organizer, you want to think of worship not only as something spiritually beneficial and necessary for us as individuals, but also as a dynamic component of group maintenance.

Study focuses our thoughts and plans. Young groups may undertake structured study programs to develop shared understandings of the problem of world hunger, for without study, action may be misdirected. Understanding the causes of hunger is fundamental to action. As the group grows, most of its study will be linked with action. People will learn through doing and by reflecting on their actions. However, if at any point the group feels it is not learning enough, it should set concrete study goals. Hunger groups and concerned individuals should never cease studying.

Study requires both task and maintenance leadership. Those offering task leadership set out questions, determine the major points to be covered, summarize the group's findings, and make sure the proper materials are given to each person. Maintenance leaders make sure everyone is heard, encourage people to ask questions and disagree, keep people from interrupting one another, suggest breaks when needed, and involve people in education.

Worship and study lead to action. Hunger groups want to end hunger. Members do not want just to pray and learn more about hunger. They want to make a difference. Action plans should be achievable and measurable. They should also be projects which the group will enjoy and will involve many members. Action projects should challenge the group to learn new information and new skills. Action projects should be evaluated and reflected upon to learn as much as possible from each one.

Action also requires task and maintenance leadership. Each project must have goals, steps outlining how to achieve the objectives, timelines, and specific responsibilities. But along the way, the project should be satisfying. People should work together and enjoy one another's company. New people should be included and given jobs which draw on their talents. And at the end of an action project, people should be thanked and the group should celebrate. This manner of working on a project, involving people and celebrating, is the maintenance part of action.

Worship, study, and action should occur over the course of a group's life. They should also happen in each meeting, to the extent possible. For example, you might open a meeting with prayer time, study and discuss a particular issue, and then write letters to your elected leaders about that issue. Thus, in one meeting, you would have integrated worship, study, and action. Simultaneously, you would have involved people in the worship in the introductory stage, evaluated the issue and addressed conflict during the study stage, taken action during the action stage, and closed the meeting in the concluding stage. Thus, the five stages described earlier occur within the context of worship, study, and action.

Shared Leadership

All groups need leadership, but group leadership need not, and should not, become the responsibility of just one or two people. Marlene Kiingati, a regional organizer for Bread for the World, once pointed out to me the number of leadership functions (both task and maintenance) mentioned in the Book of Acts. It is really quite startling. Look at just a few of them:

- Peter   preached (1:15)
- Matthias   witnessed (1:22-26)
- Stephen   distributed money (6:5)
  and Philip
- Dorcas   did good works (9:36)
- Cornelius   gave alms and prayed (10:2)
- Agabus   warned of coming
                            problems (11:28)
- Barnabas   taught and prophesied (13:1)
  and Simeon
- Judas
  and Silas   exhorted and confirmed
                            people (15:32)
- Lydia   gave hospitality (16:15)

This list demonstrates the wide variety of leadership roles filled *and* the sharing of leadership that occurred. Within groups, leadership is also best exercised when shared by many people.

We talk at church about giving of our financial means. The same principle holds true of our talents. Each person has special gifts and leadership talents to offer a hunger group. The key is identifying them and using them creatively. Sometimes overly narrow definitions of leadership keep us from recognizing leadership talent. For example, some people have a special gift of making new people feel welcome. Though not normally thought of as leadership, this is clearly important maintenance leadership. This gift should be recognized and appreciated. You might even want to assign this leadership job a title, such as "New Member Greeter."

Nearly everyone who is committed to a group and its goal will assume some responsibility and some leadership tasks if asked and encouraged. Once people are into the transition stage in a group, they should be asked to make some commitment to the group by taking on some kind of responsibility. Many organizers believe that everyone should leave a meeting with something to do. This is a good rule of thumb by which to measure that leadership roles are being shared as broadly as possible.

Naturally, this does not mean that everyone can do all jobs. Nor does it mean that new members of the group should be asked to undertake jobs which are more suited for experienced members. That would be foolish. Rather, think of all the leadership roles you need filled and ask people who seem to have matching skills. Work to develop the leadership skills of all involved.

The following are some responsibilities that new group members can be asked to assume:

- Calling a certain number of people about an upcoming meeting.
- Sending notices about a meeting and event.

- Greeting and signing in people at a meeting.
- Setting up before, or cleaning up after, a meeting.
- Preparing a display area.
- Designing posters.
- Assisting an experienced member to staff a booth on hunger.

People who are becoming more involved can be asked to assume additional responsibilities such as:

- Staffing a booth or table.
- Leading or planning worship for a meeting.
- Writing a letter-to-the-editor.
- Delivering press releases.
- Assisting with an outreach presentation.
- Making a presentation at a meeting about a proposed project.

Experienced members can handle broader responsibilities including:

- Coordinating outreach presentations.
- Arranging or giving media interviews.
- Chairing meetings.
- Directing a special action or project.
- Leading a hunger study.
- Coordinating overall activities.

There are plenty of responsibilities for all interested. The trick is to have everyone assume some responsibility without anyone assuming too much. If one person feels burdened, others should handle more responsibilities or projects should be dropped or scaled back. Realistic goal-setting, taking into account limited people power, will avoid burnout and give the group a sense of accomplishment.

It is advisable to have one or two people serve as overall coordinators for the group. Overall coordinators should integrate various projects, assist people in developing leadership skills, and assist other leaders during special events. Overall coordination is a good leadership role to rotate on an annual or biannual basis.

Once a group has identified some of the leadership roles it wants or needs performed, it might want to use the following exercise to identify gifts found among the group's members. The exercise is taken from Bread for the World's paper "Shared Leadership" by Marlene Kiingati.

Tools: A sheet of newsprint for each leadership
                role you want to fill.

                Masking tape and markers.

                A list of talents and
                skills (caring, liturgical,
                precise, good with numbers,
                patience, etc.)

                A pack of index cards.

                One pen for each person.

Activity: 1. Brainstorm talents and
                skills needed for each leadership
                role. (As ideas are called out,
                they should be recorded on the

correct sheet. All ideas should
be recorded without discussion.)

2. Post the idea sheets and
give each participant one
index card for each person
present.

3. Everyone should label one
card for each person in
the room.

4. (Five minutes) Everyone
should list two talents on
each card, skills they recognize
in the person whose name they
have written at the top of
the card.

5. Distribute cards to people whose
names have been written on them.

6. Each person now has many cards,
all with his/her name on them.
They will see their talents as
others perceive them.
People should match their talents
to the newsprint that lists the
talents closest to their own.

7. Discuss the experience.

8. Ask people to commit themselves
to the leadership role they feel
most able to do for six months.
If the group chooses to wait a month,

wait. But be sure to share the
responsibilities for next month's
meeting. Some tasks that can be assumed
immediately are agenda, telephoning,
refreshments, and worship.

This exercise is best used with a group that is fairly well acquainted so participants have a sense of one another's skills and talents. It is especially good after a group has met three or four times and is trying to determine leadership responsibilities.

Unfortunately, many groups allow one or two people to assume all the leadership functions. This is detrimental for both the individuals and the group. The one or two people who are assuming the majority of leadership tasks for the group are bound to feel overburdened and overwhelmed. These people become likely burnout victims. When they do leave, they feel guilty because the group may fall apart after their departure. Sharing leadership enables groups to continue functioning even when one or two active people leave town or become less involved. Leadership is always in transition. Groups need to expect and plan for transition.

One exercise that can be used to address this kind of situation is for the group to identify all the tasks being done by "the group." Then list who is assuming responsibility for each task. One hunger group in northern Mississippi identified ten tasks being done, and the same person doing them all. That particular person was a wonderful person, but it was obvious to him and the group that others needed to assume leadership roles.

Another hunger group in western Kentucky used the same exercise. One leader had been assuming twenty different leadership tasks. After assessing the tasks and discussing the need to share leadership, other members of the group volunteered for ten of the leadership tasks.

Another leadership problem I have observed frequently, occurs when one person has been "the" leader for quite a while, but is not really assuming the needed responsibilities. Others are willing to assume the tasks, but find it hard to step forward as long as someone else is the official leader. For example, a number of times I have observed groups in which one person had been the leader for five or six years and was no longer active. In talking with the person, s/he would express the desire to play a less active leadership role, although in reality s/he had done little for quite a while. Nonetheless, when we discussed the need for new leadership in the group meeting, the person would act as if s/he was still the leader and wanted to remain such. No one wanted to be in the position of pushing the old person out and so new leadership did not emerge.

This scenario sounds ridiculous, but it happens. A person wants out of a leadership role, or maybe out of a group altogether, and yet feels guilty about quitting. In such situations, it is important to help people out of leadership roles or to assist them in terminating their relationship with the group. One positive way to help people out of a solitary leadership position is to hold a special meeting or party celebrating the person's retirement from the leadership position and highlighting all hsr contributions over the past few years. This helps people feel honored, rather than guilty.

When they first form, most groups have one or two organizers. The goal must be to develop and share leadership skills, particularly those skills of an organizer. No group can have too many organizers. A strong cadre of committed Christians who understand the basic principles of organizing and maintaining groups can move mountains — if not literally, then at least small mountains of discouragement and cynicism.

No group starts out strong. Social justice movements grow out of small groups. Art Simon began Bread for the World with a handful of people. The group met monthly. Not everyone showed up regularly. During the first year, Art was thrilled when ten or twelve people came, because somtimes only one or two came. Out of that small group developed a national movement of Christians working to influence public policies on hunger. The movement of people against hunger in your church and your community will not spontaneously ignite. It will develop from the steady work of your small group over an extended period of time.

Perseverance is a must for the key group organizers seeking to maintain a group. Perseverance is needed when only a handful of people show up at a meeting. Perseverance is needed when the group questions its goals and works to resolve conflicts within the group. And perseverance is needed when a strong leader in the group leaves.

Never bemoan the size of your group. As long as two or three are gathered together, Jesus has promised to be with them. If those in your group want to meet and work together, go with those you have. Be patient with the group's growth, especially through the transition phase. Keep a balance of worship, study, and action. And share leadership among yourselves.

"Let us not give up meeting together, as some are in the habit of doing, but let us encourage one another, and all the more as you see the Day approaching." (Hebrews 10:25).

6. SETTING GOALS

Clear goals are important for you as an individual organizer, for each project, and for your hunger group as a whole. Each goal must be accompanied by steps for achieving the goal and reasonable timelines. Goals and steps serve as maps for the future, guideposts along the way, and means for measuring success at the end. Without goals, we're not sure where we're going, and even if we get there and have achieved great things,we're not confident we found the desired location.

Hundreds, if not thousands, of experts have written books that define goals, steps, and timelines. Without getting caught up in the debate over terms, or claiming to be an expert, let me define how I will use the terms. Goals are the measurable changes or specific accomplishments for which we strive. Steps are the actions we take to reach our goals. Timelines set out the time periods within which we accomplish certain steps, or the final deadlines by which we complete them. Our most fundamental goal is to end hunger. While this is measurable, it's not likely to be achieved anytime soon. Thus, ending hunger is a fundamental goal or *purpose*.

Some people argue that not all goals are necessarily measurable. This is certainly true in a general sense. However, for organizing I believe it is important that goals be measurable. In some cases rewording is all that is needed to turn a hope into a goal. For example, "educating people on hunger" is not a goal by my definition because it is difficult to measure whether people have been educated. However, changing the hope to "providing empowering educational programs on hunger" makes it a measurable goal. Our goals will be more useful to our work if we require them to be measurable and realistic.

Individual Goals

As an organizer, there are certain kinds of qualities, skills, and knowledge you wish to develop. To do so, you need to think about what progress you want to make in the next three to five years. Then, consider what activities could move you in that general direction within the coming year. Do not spend much time outlining specific steps for three to five years into the future — people's lives usually change too much in three to five years for specific goals to remain suitable. However, it's important to think about the future so your specific plans will have some overall direction.

When setting specific goals for the coming year, think carefully about how much time you have available. Be realistic. For most of us, time — not money — is our most limited resource. How we use it is extremely important. As organizers, we seldom value our time highly enough. Nonetheless, it is extremely valuable and should be "spent" carefully.

If assigning an arbitrary monetary value to your time helps you to treat it as a valuable resource, do so. For example, you might think of your time as being worth thirty dollars per hour. Use this measure to evaluate the "cost" of the goals you have selected and the steps that you will have to take to reach them. Revise your goals as necessary so that you set goals that will make realistic and productive use of your time.

Below are examples of individual goals and steps you might select for yourself:

Goal: Develop skills in public speaking.

Steps: Take a public speaking class in the spring.
        Prepare and deliver a minute for missions presentation on hunger in the spring.
        Volunteer for two additional presentations in the fall.

Goal: Expand my understanding of hunger issues.

Steps: Read the monthly Bread for the World news-
         letter.
         Read a book on hunger issues every three
         months.

Goal: Act on my concern for hungry people.

Steps: Write one letter per month to an elected offi-
         cial.
         Assist in forming a hunger group in my
         church.
         Volunteer for some leadership task.
         Attend meetings regularly.
         Get three friends or family members to par-
         ticipate in the CROP walk.

Goal: Nurture my faith through concern about
         hungry people.

Steps: Pray daily for hungry people and my church's
         hunger group.
         Fast once a week during Lent.
         Lead worship for my hunger group at least
         once this year.
         Study Isaiah, Micah, Acts and James this
         year.

Your goals and steps should be *specific* and *realistic*. If you are concerned that you are not studying enough, set a goal to study hunger and be specific by reading four books on hunger issues in the coming year. More would be great, but that may not be realistic. If you know two books that you want to read, list them in your steps. Decide which books you want to read in which months. The more direction you provide yourself, the better.

Examine your goals at the beginning of each month. Check the steps and the times you set to see how you are doing.

Revise your goals, steps, or times as necessary. It is fine to revise goals when situations change. We never know what unexpected situations will arrive in our lives which will necessitate changing our goals.

Members of your hunger group may want to share their individual goals with one another. If so, you may want to divide up into two-person support teams. You can share your goals with one another initially, look at them together at the beginning of each month, and pray for one another on a regular basis. This kind of sharing supports individual members and develops closer relationships within the group.

Most people need monthly calendars and weekly worksheets to translate the year's goals into actions. Use the monthly calendars to keep track of future dates, deadlines, and schedules. Use the worksheets to prevent details from falling through the cracks. Everyone has to develop hsr own system for planning and organizing work during the week. You may want to integrate your hunger activities into your current system for planning home or office work. Specify time to study, write a letter to an elected leader, or attend a hunger meeting. Even fill in phone calls you need to make. Most people find that if tasks aren't written down, they aren't all done. In addition, if tasks are written down, and marked off when completed, you have a greater sense of accomplishment. If at the beginning of the week, you plan your tasks realistically, then you can use your time wisely and complete your work without rushing madly about. Our work for hungry people must be as organized as any other part of our lives.

Here is an example of a weekly worksheet:

Mon.	Tues.	Wed.	Thrs.	Fri
Call Bob	Buy food for mtg.	Choir	Hunger	
Call Maria	Call Todd	Prepare food	meeting	
	Call Pam			

Sat	Sun
Write rep.	Church
Read one hour	Plan for
	subcommittee
	meeting

Other	Bob	Next week
Send card to Tommy	Next meeting?	Tues — subcommittee
	Car tires	meeting
	Sue and Joe	

Although there certainly are better systems, this particular one is simple. It allows you to keep track of items which need to be done on specific days, has space for the other things that should get done sometime during the week, and helps you keep track of things coming up the next week. Under each person's name, list items you wish to discuss with that person but which you might forget.

Event/Project Goals

Too often well-meaning groups undertake projects or organize events without first thinking through their goals and deciding how they could be accomplished most effectively. Without clear project goals, it is impossible to determine if your project was a success. And the odds of it being a success are much greater if you have defined your goals and how you will achieve them.

Several years ago, a peace concert was held at the Episcopal Church of St. John the Divine in New York City. This particular church is one of the largest in the country and can hold a large crowd. The goals of the concert were presumably to raise money and involve more people in the peace movement. The financial goal of the concert was probably realized, but I doubt the other was. The church building was absolutely packed, and enthusiasm was high. Speaker after speaker urged people to become more involved in peace issues. However, no one explained how to get involved. There were no sign-up tables, no listings of existing peace groups, and no literature on organizing new peace groups. People were motivated and invited to become active, but were given no opportunities to do so. If simple sign-up sheets had been available, hundreds of people would have joined peace groups. But none were available. Thousands of dollars and hundreds of hours were put into the concert, and yet one of its goals was not met. Few people got involved because the organizers had not thought through *how* they were going to meet the concert's goals of involving people.

As an outsider, one wonders how the planners could possibly have forgotten to take advantage of the large audience. Yet, many of us make similar errors when planning smaller events.

Recently I was invited to a denominational social justice conference. It was the first time that denomination had planned a conference on social justice. The conference's goals were unclear to me after I had read the agenda, so I asked one of the conference planners what they were. He was unable to answer my question. Because clear goals had not been set, the agenda did not contain time for commitment, planning, or other goal-oriented objectives.

The conference had good keynotes and workshops, but no time for people to commit themselves to action as a result of the conference. I'm confident that the conference planners wanted concrete actions to result from the conference, but they never set out what the actions should be.

Goals should not be kept a mystery. Had the conference planners articulatd a specific goal such as "to organize a hunger Sunday in every district," they could have organized the conference to accomplish that goal. At the beginning, a conference planner could have suggested the idea to people and urged them to think about it over the course of the seminar. District-wide groups could have met over meals or at regular times during the conference enabling people to become acquainted. A special time could have been set aside for people to set district goals and plan their district's hunger Sunday. The conference would have had more specific outcomes if the agenda had reflected such goals.

Since no goals were established for the conference, the agenda just offered good presentations. That is nice, but not adequate. It is inadequate because it does not use the money and time of the planners and attenders to the maximum efficiency. Hungry people need us to get the most out of any event or project we plan. We are unlikely to do that without realistic and specific goals.

Event or project goals need to be specific. General goals like "to educate people" are impossible to measure. Think about how you will measure your goals. For example, if you decide to hold a family night program on hunger in your church, what are your goals? Obviously, you have a general desire to educate or raise awareness, but that isn't a measurable goal and won't greatly affect how you organize the program. Some measurable, realistic goals might be: to get two people to take the hunger course being offered the next month, to get three people to join Bread for the World, or to get five extra volunteers to work at the soup kitchen during the summer.

Specific goals affect the design of the program. For example, if your goal were to get five extra volunteers to work at the soup kitchen, you might organize your program as follows:

10 minutes   Introduction, mentioning that a goal of

the evening is to get five new volunteers.

40 minutes	Slide show and presentation describing how the soup kitchen works.
20 minutes	Question and answer time.
5 minutes	Invitation to volunteer.

You would place literature about the program, and a sign-up sheet on a centrally located table. Designing a program to achieve specific goals seems obvious, but many groups fail to do it. Never undertake a project without specific measurable goals. General ideas and dreams are important, but they should never generate projects without goals.

Group Goals

Any hunger group, whether newly formed or older, needs goals. A new group might set six-month goals, so it can measure progress within a short period of time. Annual goals are appropriate for existing groups, although they may choose to set goals more often than once a year.

The process of setting goals is a healthy one. Group members get to know one another, gain a better understanding of different perspectives, and articulate hopes and dreams for the group. Frequently, the group discovers that some members have differing goals for the group. It is healthy for conflicts to emerge. You then have the chance to resolve the conflicts and develop goals on which all agree. The group may adopt some goals that all hold in common and some that are of particular interest to a few members. The group should not adopt goals with which some members disagree or which generate little interest.

There are several ways that the group can develop its goals.

Whichever particular method you choose, be sure to involve everyone in the process, determine if you have the resources to achieve the goal, and decide how you will measure the results. The following is one process for setting goals.

MEETING I

20 minutes   Ask members to call out goals as they think of them.

20 minutes   Group together similar goals, ideas, and projects.

20 minutes   Decide on the top five (or some other limited number) of priorities.

10 minutes   Divide responsibility for developing steps and timelines for the five priorities. Ask one or more people to develop each goal for the next meeting.

Each person or pair responsible for developing a goal should draft steps and timelines. Everyone should use a similar format. You might consider handing out sheets to be completed. Copies of each goal's sheet, with steps and timelines, should be made for those attending the meeting.

MEETING II

20 minutes   Review the proposed goals. Do the steps and timelines seem reasonable for achieving the goal? Cut or add steps as needed.

20 minutes   Consider who can accomplish each step. If your group has already divided leadership tasks, many of the steps may fall within the task areas for which members have already accepted responsibility. If your group has not divided leadership tasks, you must ask people to accept certain tasks.

20 minutes   Discuss the quantity of tasks proposed. Cut tasks until the group is confident it can accomplish them. Entire goals may need to be eliminated or altered. (There is a tendency for people to list what they would like to do as opposed to what can or needs to be done. Writing names next to steps helps people assess the group's human resources realistically. If members are not willing to undertake certain steps, they must be eliminated.)

15 minutes   List what each person has agreed to do. Evaluate whether a few people have assumed too much responsibility. If so, ask others to assume more, or cut back further on goals or steps.

One person should type up the final goals, steps, timelines, and responsibilities. Copies should be made for all members of the group.

Attached are some sample goals for a newly formed hunger group in a church. You may wish to copy the format.

Six Month Goals for Church Hunger Group (Jan-June)

	When	Who
1. To organize and develop the hunger group.		
a. Meet biweekly	ongoing	all
b. Give minute for missions, inviting people to join the group.	January	Bob
c. Rotate leading worship at meetings	ongoing	all
2. To provide educational programs/resources on hunger.		
a. Make a hunger bulletin board	February	Maria
b. Lead a Lenten study course on hunger in the U.S.A.	Feb-March	Jon and Deb
c. Place information about hunger in the bulletin once a month.	monthly	Bob
3. To influence public policies on hunger.		
a. Write letters to elected leaders once a month at group meetings.	monthly	all
b. Get five people in the congregation to join Bread for the World.		
1. Place brochures in the tract rack.	February	Maria
2. Invite members of the hunger group to join.	January	Maria
3. Place information in the church bulletin one month about Bread for the World.	March	Bob

4. To support the CROP Walk and the Denominational Hunger Appeal.
   a. Recruit ten people from the church to participate in the CROP walk.

1. Explain the walk in the bulletin.	January	Bob
2. Place information about the walk on a display table.	February	Todd
3. Give a brief presentation recruiting walkers to all Sunday school classes.	March	Todd & Kim
4. Confirm all walkers.	by April 15	Kim
5. Make a banner for the church walkers.	by May 1	Lou Ann
6. Walk.	May 10	all
7. Host a party for the walkers.	May 10	Jean

   b. To raise two thousand dollars for the denominational hunger appeal.

1. Write for information on how the money is used.	January	Deb
2. Place information in the bulletin on how the money is used.	March	Bob
3. Ask for the Fifth Sunday contribution.	January	Phil
4. Ask for special contributions.	May/June	Phil

At the end of the time period you set for accomplishing your goals, be sure to evaluate them. Did they work? Why or why not? Were the timelines realistic? Were the project's goals sound? What improvements should be made in future goals and events? Setting realistic, achievable group goals cannot be stressed too strongly. Goals that are too ambitious set up a group for failure. It is far better for a group to exceed its goals than to miss them. The group must outline all the steps carefully so that people understand the work involved, and then honestly assess the group's resources.

7. DEVELOPING AND USING CREATIVITY

"When you don't have money, you must be creative."

Have you ever heard this saying? Sometimes I think it was conceived for the hunger movement. Hunger groups are not known for their vast financial or material resources. Thus, they must use what resources they do have creatively. Unfortunately, groups often do not solicit and use creative ideas as well as they could. Some groups, in fact, discourage creativity.

Often a damper is cast on new ideas because the hunger group has too much work for the number of people. New ideas are seen, sometimes correctly, as additional work. If new ideas always add to existing heavy loads, then they will be viewed negatively. New ideas should offer alternative means for carrying out programs and projects, or offer alternative — not more — programs and projects.

Creativity must be channeled in a helpful fashion. New ideas must further the group's goals. No matter how good an idea is, if it doesn't support the group's goals, it should not be considered. If a new idea does support the group's goals, it should be compared to the other ideas for accomplishing the goal. If the new idea is preferred, change steps, dropping some of the previous ones. Do not merely add more steps. Assuming that a group has set goals which match its resources is a sensible working premise in most cases. Therefore, if more steps are added, the workload will exceed the group's capacity.

Although everyone has both creativity and the ability to critique ideas, most people are decidedly stronger in one of the two areas. Both skills are needed, but usually not at the same time. For example, if the strong critiquers begin their analysis too soon, they will squelch the idea providers. Thus, if you are trying to generate and develop new ideas, you should distinguish between the two functions.

Creativity can and should be strongly encouraged during the goal setting process. Once the group establishes its three or four basic goals, it can take more time to develop creative steps. Finally, creativity should be encouraged in solving problems. If your group does not use its creative resources to best avail, you may want to employ the method suggested below. Use creativity to serve your group's plans.

The following technique for generating and developing ideas at a meeting seems to work fairly well. (An abbreviated version of this technique can be used for solving problems. Just be sure to separate idea generation from critiquing and voting.) You will need some sort of newsprint or chalkboard, and a notetaker for keeping track of comments and ideas.

1. *Statement of Purpose.* The chairperson should summarize what the group wants to accomplish and make sure that everyone is in agreement with the purpose, e.g. to generate ideas on obtaining media coverage of an upcoming issue. The statement of purpose should normally take just a couple of minutes.

2. *Quiet Time.* Give the group five to ten minutes of quiet time to think of ideas and jot them down on paper. Most groups jump right into brainstorming (putting ideas up on newsprint) without this quiet time. I find that this quiet time increases both the number and quality of ideas.

3. *List Ideas.* Ask everyone to offer their ideas. List them on newsprint or a chalkboard so everyone

can see the ideas. Encourage people to add other ideas or modifications that are stimulated by the ideas. Urge people to be brief in explaining their ideas so as not to inhibit creative ideas from others. This should take ten to fifteen minutes.

4. *More Quiet Time.* Ask people to take another two to three minutes to generate additional ideas stimulated by the list.

5. *List Ideas.* Take a couple more minutes to list additional ideas. You will probably now have a long list.

6. *Combine Ideas.* Ask the group to see if there are ideas that are similar and ought to be combined for future development. If anyone disagrees with combining a certain idea, don't combine it. Do not spend more than five minutes on this.

7. *Vote.* Ask people to vote for their top five (or four or six) choices of ideas to be developed. Limit people's voting to a specified number. This technique helps people make choices without having to have lengthy discussions on each idea. The voting should take no more than five minutes.

8. *Identify Top Vote-getters.* It is usually pretty obvious which ideas are the top vote-getters. If there are borderline ideas that are clearly not in the top vote-getters, but have some support, I ask the group if anyone wants to argue strongly for keeping one of the ideas. If someone does, I list it, without hmr presenting hsr argument. The only exception I make to this is if someone in the group won't let go of any of hsr ideas. Then I ask the group for

a specific vote cut-off. The reason for listing an idea if someone feels strongly about it is that usually it's from the person who generated the idea and s/he may have some creative thoughts about it that people in the group don't yet understand. Identifying the popular ideas should take about five minutes. At this point, you should have five to ten ideas that the group wants to think about and develop.

9. *Break*. Thus far, you will have taken approximately 45 to 50 minutes for the more creative part of the process. Now it's important for people to shift to a more critical mode. You will probably want to take a ten-minute break before continuing.

10. *Select Objectives for Remainder of Meeting*. At this point, you need to choose your objectives for the rest of the meeting. You can either further narrow your options, or you can develop several of the ideas. In either case you will want to get more information on each idea. Be sure to schedule how much time you have for each idea and stick to the time limits. An hour for this activity should be plenty of time.

11. *Describe and Critique Ideas*. Ask the person or persons who offered each idea to describe it in somewhat greater detail, answering clarifying questions. Then ask the group to identify the pros and cons of the idea. This is where the strong critiquers should excel. Don't be concerned if people find some aspect of an idea to be both a pro and a con, and don't let one or two people get into a debate over some issue. Getting lots of feedback

out onto the table is more important than resolving specific issues. Encourage people to keep their criticisms focused strictly on the idea, not the idea giver, and to be nonpersonal in their criticism. Five to ten minutes for each idea is plenty. Watch the time carefully based on the number of ideas you want to discuss.

12. *Eliminate Ideas.* Ask for recommendations from the group on ideas which should be eliminated, based on the discussion and critiques. Often, the person who suggested an idea will suggest that it be eliminated after hearing the critiques. If no ideas are eliminated, and the group feels the list needs to be narrowed, you will need to ask people to vote for their top three or four choices. If ideas have been described adequately and understood, no idea should be left on the list if it doesn't receive enough votes.

13. *Identify Outstanding Questions.* Before a final decision can be made, some outstanding questions usually must be answered. Determine what those questions are and assign people to seek answers.

14. *Set Future Meeting Date.* Determine the earliest date upon which people can have answers to the questions, and schedule a meeting at which final decisions can be made. It is important, if at all possible, to allow people to think about ideas for a few days. Not all people need that time, but some do. I know several people who instantly oppose any new idea; however, if given a few days to think on it, they will come back and support an idea or have improved and developed it. If they

are not given the time to think on an idea and mull it over, they feel taken advantage of by the process. People function in very different ways, and procedures should accomodate them whenever possible to generate the most positive input from everyone.

15. *Continue Thinking.* Tell people to use the time before the next meeting to develop ideas, get further feedback, and to create new ideas. There is no need to cut off new ideas until you are ready to make a final decision and move on.

At your next meeting, ask people to share the findings to the questions, as well as new reflections and ideas. Ask people not to repeat comments made the previous week. It usually helps to put the sheets that you used the previous meeting back up on the board, or to hand out typed-up copies of the comments made on each idea. People need to see what had been said previously.

Occasionally a group is reluctant to suggest something obvious because strong values or feelings are attached to a particular idea. For example, one time I was working with a group discussing its overall workload. No one wanted to consider new ideas because of a large seminar that was being projected a year ahead. After listening to the group for a while, I began wondering if the group wanted to do the seminar. Finally, I asked for a straw poll on how many people thought the seminar should be dropped for the coming year. Every single person thought it should be dropped. And yet, because of the strong feelings about the seminar, no one would suggest dropping it. You may, therefore, want to use straw polls to get a reading on people's positions.

Sometimes the direction a group wants to go becomes obvious in the process of discussion. If so, great. If not, the facilitator of the group may need to encourage the group to make a decision.

The tendency in many groups is to postpone a decision. Ask the group if there will be more information which will help in making the decision if the decision is postponed. If not, go ahead and make the decision.

Helping a group move toward a consensus is the best group process, because it builds ownership in the idea from the entire group. Different members of the group should "take a stab" at stating a consensus, thus allowing the group to move forward. One caution on consensus decisions is to stress that group decisions be made on facts and analyses and not just feelings. Feelings are important, but they need to be backed up by analysis. If not, ideas can be watered down and a consensus developed which is merely the least common denominator, as opposed to a composite of the group's best thinking.

By the time you are selecting from the group's top few choices on ideas, they are all good ones. Your group may not choose the "best" idea, but it will choose a good one. At a certain point, it is important to make a decision rather than spending additional hours in analysis. The object is to take good actions and not just to develop ideas. Whichever idea is chosen should have the ownership and commitment from the group.

In closing this chapter, I would like to make a few suggestions to facilitators of groups hoping to use and develop their creative ideas and to people trying to develop their own creativity.

TO FACILITATORS:

Encourage creativity. Discourage people from ridiculing or laughing at any idea. It's very important to establish an atmosphere where people feel free to offer ideas, no matter how wild, without being made fun of or put down in some fashion. Most people have ideas, but it takes confidence to offer them. Your job is to help provide that confidence.

Encourage critical analysis of each idea. Each idea that the group wants to develop must withstand critical questioning.

This must be done *after* an idea generating session, but it must be encouraged. You will need to help idea generators understand the importance of this time and not become defensive about their ideas.

TO GROUP MEMBERS:

Creativity is strongly related to self-confidence. People lacking in self confidence are afraid to offer their ideas lest someone not appreciate them. People often will laugh or make rude comments about new ideas. To be able to generate ideas, you must learn to ignore such reactions. You must also learn to forgive people who make such comments. The best ideas have sometimes been laughed at for being "crazy." Learning to risk offering your ideas requires developing self-confidence.

Creativity also requires that you be open-minded. Some procedures are givens, but usually far fewer than imagined. Try looking beyond how things have always been done. Assume as few "givens" as actually exist. Attempt to address each problem or idea from a fresh perspective.

Finally, learn to separate yourself from your ideas. Once you have put forth an idea, let it go. The idea becomes the group's property to reject or develop. It is extremely hard to see ideas rejected or improved if you become personally attached to them.

Have confidence to put forth lots of ideas. Then let them go.

8. BEGINNING A HUNGER MINISTRY

Many Christians concerned about hunger decide that the best place for them to start working is within their own churches. This makes perfect sense. The church is an institution which can provide support for hunger work. We meet with friends who share our values at church. And working against hunger is part of the very mission of the church.

First, you will want to assess your church's existing hunger ministry. What hunger work is already a part of the church's ministry? What areas do you need to develop? At the end of this chapter you will find a sheet you can use to help you evaluate your church's hunger ministry. Be careful not to be too critical of your congregation in your assessment. Most churches require years of work by a hunger committee to place pluses in most of the categories. Evaluate your church now, set some concrete goals for the next few months, then reevaluate and set some more goals. A year from now you can reassess your church's hunger ministry using the same form and see your progress. Changing a few minuses to pluses each year is a positive and reasonable expectation.

If a hunger group does not already exist in your church, an early goal should be to organize one. You need others to work with you. Invite a few members in the church to meet with you about the possibility of starting a hunger group. Use this small core of people to seek leadership support within the congregation and to determine the best way to form your group.

As discussed in Chapter Four, Organizing a Group, it is very important to seek initial leadership support. Doing so provides legitimacy, endorsements, recognition, and support. If overlooked, church leaders may feel suspicious, jealous, or hurt. The latter is harmful and easily avoided. Identify the key people within your church. Ask for their suggestions on starting a group and ask for concrete help in such areas as publicity or education.

There are two main procedures from which you can choose when forming a group in your church. You can organize a group and set early goals that include a hunger study and an easy first project. Or, you can organize a hunger study and/or an easy first project and form a group out of these initial programs. Be sure to read the chapter on organizing a group. Basic principles outlined there will apply to work in your church.

Either way, involving people new to hunger activism is vital to the growth and development of your group. Your hunger group must attract new people if it is to expand and effectively work against hunger. Moreover, you do not want to be perceived as just the "same old group of activists". Involving new people will ward off this stigma and enable you to reach out to a broader range of people in the church. People of all ideological persuasions are concerned about hunger. It is an issue which can and does attract new people.

Hunger Study

Many church organizers choose to form a hunger group following a hunger study. This is a good, common, and easy way to start a hunger group. You should offer at least a four-week course, and preferably a six- or eight-week course. Discuss the idea with the adult education or Sunday school committee. You are likely to get higher attendance if the study is offered during a normal adult education time, such as Sunday school, Wednesday night Bible class, or a Lenten study series. The disadvantage of these previously scheduled times is that they are seldom longer than 45 or 50 minutes. A somewhat longer period — one and a quarter to one and a half hours — is more conducive to building friendships. The friendship and trust developed during the hunger study are important to creating a core hunger group. You will need to think about where and when to offer a course, weighing carefully the advantages and disadvantages.

A number of excellent hunger study courses designed for use in a church are available, several of which are listed in Appendix A. Using a specifically Christian study course is preferable because it sets the issue of hunger in the context of Christian faith. Most of the study courses recommended include worship ideas.

You and/or another person or two who are committed to the formation of a hunger group in your church should lead the course. You need not be an "expert" to do so. Most of the study courses have a leader's guide, or are easy to lead without one. None of the recommended studies require the leaders to lecture or give formal presentations. Rather, the leader's role is to be familiar with the course, encourage discussion, and facilitate the sessions.

From the beginning you should express your desire that a hunger group be formed out of the study. Do not open the issue for discussion at the beginning. Just mention it so people can mull it over during the span of the course. Do not draw on an outside expert like a college professor to lead the course unless s/he is committed to the formation of a hunger group. Instead, you may want to ask hmr to be a special presenter during a session or two. Demonstrate from the start that your group is not dependent on outside resources.

By leading the group, you can start developing the kind of community which will want to continue working together on hunger. In addition, leading the group will help you and the other leaders develop stronger group facilitation skills. Finally, those who lead a course always learn the issues as well or better than anyone else involved. However, if this is not your gift, one of your first tasks is to find a person who shares your dream of starting a hunger group and ask hmr to lead the group. Work at developing some common bonds and real friendship among those in the group. If the group decides to meet during Sunday school or another short formal time, arrange a social time for the group such as a potluck dinner or lunch so group members can get to know one another better.

Consider offering the hunger study twice. One course can be scheduled for a time and place that is conducive to building a small nucleus of people committed to the formation of a hunger group, such as 7:00 — 8:30 P.M. one night a week in someone's home. This course will not attract as many people as a course held during a regularly scheduled study time and is apt to attract those already quite concerned. This small group of people can learn together and form the core of your hunger group.

Another member of the "core group" can offer the other course during the regularly scheduled church education time. This course can be geared to reach those with some interest, who are not committed enough to attend an extra study session each week. Those who want to get more involved as a result of the course can join the newly formed hunger group. People should be invited and encouraged to join throughout the course.

Throughout the hunger study, find ways to support and encourage new people. Make sure they don't feel left out or passed over because they were not part of the original core group. Help everyone be open to new ideas, avoid rhetoric, and respect differences of opinion. Conformity is unnecessary, and requiring it may discourage new people from getting involved.

Easy First Projects

Another way to organize a group in your church is to form a task force to work on a specific hunger-related project. It should be a relatively easy first project to assure success and to build a community which would want to continue as an ongoing hunger group in the church. If you have chosen to form a hunger group first and then set your initial goals, you will also want to undertake one or two easy projects in your first few months. These projects should involve all members of your group, establish your reputation among the church as an active (different from an activist) committee, and be achievable in a short period of time. A newly formed hunger group needs an early accomplishment — a victory, so to speak.

In organizing theory a term called "organizational mileage" is used. It describes the process of undertaking projects which will help build and develop your group. Obviously, you care about the outcome of the project, but especially at the beginning you need to be concerned with choosing projects which will strengthen your group. The kinds of questions you should ask are:

1. Will the project involve everyone in the group? Can we work together and build the relationships within the group?

2. Will the project develop skills within the group?

3. Can we accomplish something fairly quickly? (Achieving goals empowers groups to take on larger and more important goals in the future. It is better to start small and have overwhelming success than to start too large and fail or become discouraged.)

4. Can we build support for our group within the church? Can we add members as a result of our project? (Generally, your first project should be noncontroversial so you establish credibility within your church.)

The following projects answer the questions affirmatively, and are fairly typical projects for newly formed church-based hunger groups.

Raising Money for Hunger Relief and Development

Raising money for hunger relief is a positive and easy first project. While most people involved in hunger work believe that raising money is not the most important function of a hunger group, funds are always needed. Set your financial goals modestly so you can be sure to achieve them, and choose a project which will build unity and about which you can do some educational work. Do not choose a project which is controversial or difficult to explain.

Raising money for your denomination's hunger fund or relief and development agency is an excellent place to start. It establishes a relationship between your group and your denomination's agency, reinforces your commitment to working within your church, and educates members of the congregation about the work of the hunger fund or relief and development agency. See Appendix C for a list of addresses for denominational hunger programs and agencies.

The staff in denominational agencies are very willing to support your fundraising efforts. Write to the fund or agency for fundraising ideas and materials, including educational materials that can be distributed to the entire congregation. Invite a denominational staff person to speak or preach. If your denomination's hunger agency has a suggested program, consider using it. Operation Ricebowl among Roman Catholic parishes, for example, is an excellent way to involve entire families in raising money for Catholic Relief Services.

Raising funds for the interdenominational soup kitchen or food pantry in your area is another suitable early project. Such fundraising can educate your hunger group on the hunger needs and responses in your community, including the contribution of area churches. It can also introduce your group to the need for more adequate national public policies on domestic hunger.

If your denomination supports Church World Service/CROP, you may consider participating in one of their fundraising efforts such as a CROP walk. CROP walks are excellent activities in which to involve your group. You will meet other concerned Christians in the community including hunger committees from other churches. Organizing a CROP walk is too large a task for a first project. Organizing your church's participation is an excellent first project. Get whole families to walk together. Carry a banner or poster for your church's hunger committee. Take pictures of yourselves at the walk and post on a bulletin board in the church. Publicize the amount of money raised by members of the congregation. Such pictures and publicity are fun and give your group recognition for being effective.

The means for raising money should be participatory and fun. Think through ways to involve families and youth. Keep colorful charts and records. One example of a fun and easy fundraising project for rural and suburban churches is to hold produce sales. People are asked to bring excess produce grown from their gardens and donate it to a produce table. Other members of the congregation purchase the produce. No one even needs to collect the money. A jar can be left on the table and people asked to donate the proper amount. This project requires little investment and involves the whole group.

You could divide the work into smaller tasks as follows:

- Presenting brief explanations of the produce table's purpose and operation to the congregation.

- Drawing posters that explain the produce table's purpose and operation for use on bulletin boards and at the table.

- Collecting paper bags to package people's purchases.

- Recruiting people to donate produce.

- Reminding those who have agreed to donate produce to bring it to church.

- Preparing the produce table before church each Sunday during the produce season.

- Setting and marking produce prices (not necessary if you use the "pay what you want" system).

- Putting away the produce table after church each Sunday.

- Collecting and recording the proceeds each week.

- Delivering the unpurchased produce to a local soup kitchen each week.

Distributing the work in this fashion provides everyone with some responsibility and does not unduly burden any one person. Sometimes one or two people will volunteer to do everything. They should be thanked warmly for their willingness but not assigned all the work. Discuss with them the importance of involving everyone in planning and completing projects and engage their assistance in finding others to undertake some of the tasks.

Other fundraising projects that I have seen undertaken successfully include benefit concerts, rummage sales, auctions, plant sales and bake sales. They all draw on locally available resources and give the group experience in working together. If the work is divided into many tasks and shared among group members in the manner described for the produce table, they are well within the resources of a newly formed hunger group.

Benefit concerts and talent shows using local, free talent are fun and require little financial investment. If children's groups perform, parents will generally attend. Rummage sales, using donated goods, can raise several hundred dollars and have the added benefit of emptying a number of basements. If you choose to hold a rummage sale you may wish to specify "no clothes" as clothes are difficult to sort, display, and sell. However, if you have plenty of volunteers, clothing donations are usually plentiful and leftovers are welcomed by shelters and other charitable organizations.

Auctions can be lots of fun and raise a fair amount of money. Potential contributions include services as well as goods. For example, someone may be willing to offer a weekend's use of a vacation cabin. Younger contributors can donate services such as babysitting or yardwork.

Plant sales are simple and enjoyable if your group contains a few "green thumbs." Ask people to make cuttings of their house plants and start the cuttings. A few months later, sell the young plants. If inexpensive pots and potting soil are purchased in quantity, the total investment is small. Such sales are particularly successful in large cities where houseplants are expensive.

Bake sales may be fun if group members enjoy baking, but they seldom raise much money, since baked goods are time-consuming and expensive to make. Some groups that raise money with bake sales meet at their church to bake together, making the work more fun.

Volunteering in Direct Feeding Projects

Your hunger group may decide to volunteer in a soup kitchen or shelter. This can be an educational experience for those with little direct exposure to hunger in the United States. Your group can volunteer on a one-time or short-term basis during the summer months or the Christmas holidays, when soup kitchens need short-term workers to fill in for regular workers on vacation. You should refrain from making a long-term commitment until your group has "gotten on its feet" and you are sure you have the sustained interest and   rces neces ry to fulfill a long-term commitment. You don't want to undertake too little, but neither do you want to commit to more than you can handle.

Planning a Hunger Sunday

A special hunger service, being easy to plan and conduct, is a good first project. The hunger service provides education on hunger to the congregation and places the issue of hunger in the context of faith. Your group will also gain widespread recognition of its concern and will develop confidence for future projects.

Each church or denomination has a different approval system for matters regarding worship. Approach the proper committee or person (with a person experienced in church policy if your group has one) and present your request to have a special worship service on hunger. It is possible that your request will be rejected. However, it more likely will be approved, particularly if you are flexible about dates and are willing to work closely with the people or person in charge of worship.

A number of excellent worship services on hunger are available for you to use or adapt. Your denomination's hunger agency or program may be able to provide some sample worship aids, as can groups such as Bread for the World. It is always helpful to look at suggested services even if you don't follow them exactly.

If your minister or priest is available, it is usually proper to ask hmr to give the sermon or homily. Discuss the themes you would like covered and the Biblical passages you consider suitable. You may want to provide sermon notes from the worship services you obtained from your denomination or Bread for the World. Some clergy, however, are offended by the suggestion of sermon notes. You will have to judge whether to offer them.

Your minister or priest may not be available. (The worship service on hunger is sometimes timed to fill in for a vacationing minister or priest.) Invite a neighboring minister or a member of your hunger group to speak. If you cannot find anyone who feels able to speak, call your area hunger relief agency or the local Bread for the World chapter. Chancel dramas, small skits, and special characterizations are also effective in worship services. Dramas using children will often involve whole families in the hunger issue.

Some members of your group should concentrate on song

selection. The music should relate to the theme of hunger, and at least one hymn should be a familiar one to the congregation. Additional songs on hunger can be taught to the congregation or sung by the choir or special musicians. If you have an artistic member, s/he should be asked to prepare a bulletin board or banners with a hunger theme.

Some groups are able to include a focus on hunger in the Sunday school classes as well as the main worship service. This is wonderful, but may require more people and time than your new group is able to supply. Offering an informative and well-conducted worship service is more important than "covering" both the classes and the worship service.

At the end of the service you must provide the congregation with opportunities to take action on the hunger issues you have presented. If your church agrees, part of the normal offering or a special offering can be sent to support your denomination's hunger agency or another designated program. You can also set up a letter-writing table for church members to write their congressional representatives about anti-hunger legislation. Finally, you should have information and sign-up sheets available so people can express their interest in becoming more involved with your hunger group.

Collecting Food

If your church does not already have a food pantry or collect food for a community-wide food pantry, consider a food collection as one of your first projects. This is a concrete project that can involve everyone in your group. It is also likely to be successful, since nearly everyone is willing to donate food.

The main job in a food collection drive is reminding people to bring their donations. Find a closet or box to designate as your "collection center." If you use a box, place it in a visible spot. If you use a closet, be sure it is clearly marked. Have artistic members of your group prepare posters promoting donations to your food drive.

Set aside specific days or weeks as donation times, and use posters, bulletins, newsletters, telephone trees, and announcements to remind people to bring their donations. Each member of your group can take responsibility for promoting the food collection in a different medium, or for reminding a certain portion of the congregation.

If the food needs to be transported to a central food center, consider asking church members who are not part of your hunger group to carry it. Someone who does not want to become part of your hunger group might be willing to drive the church's donations to the food center. By actively participating in the food drive, s/he may become interested in greater involvement in the future. Take the extra few minutes to recruit someone for the job, rather than doing it yourself.

Collecting the food is a much more manageable job than distributing it. Unless you have many volunteers, you should collect the food and allow a food center or soup kitchen to distribute it. Establishing a well-run food distribution which complements what is already being done in the community requires careful research and a long term commitment of resources. Most newly formed groups are not ready for this kind of project initially. See Appendix A for resources on starting an emergency feeding center.

* * *

Discussed above are just a few of the many projects that are suitable for newly organized hunger groups. The essential aspects are that they involve all the members of your group and that they have realistic, achievable goals that your group can meet successfully. Such early successes are critical to the group's growth and development.

ASSESSING YOUR CHURCH'S HUNGER MINISTRY

In the spaces provided to the left, enter either a plus or minus sign to indicate the level of involvement of your church. Leave blank if not applicable.

_____ 1. Does your church have a hunger committee or task force?

I. LOCAL HUNGER

_____ 2. Has your church, or a group in your church, ever tried to determine who is hungry in your community, or in a neighboring community?

_____ 3. Does your church conduct or participate in a local feeding program or pantry?

_____ 4. Does your church, or a group in your church, assist with Meals on Wheels?

_____ 5. Does your church provide financial support to any local hunger effort?

II. FINANCIAL ASSISTANCE

_____ 6. How often does your church receive an offering for hungry people? (If twice a year or more, put a plus.)

_____ 7. Does your church provide financial support to your denominational hunger program and/or relief agency?

___ 8. What percentage of your church's total income goes to assist hungry people or others in need? (If less than five percent, enter a minus.)

III. WORSHIP

___ 9. Has your church conducted a special hunger Sunday in the past year?

___ 10. Are there special services and/or regular prayers for hungry people in your church's worship calendar?

___ 11. Does your church have banners or other displays that reflect hunger concerns?

___ 12. How frequently are concerns for hungry people lifted up in sermons? (If less then four times in past year, enter a minus.)

IV. EDUCATION

___ 13. Has your church, or a group in your church, offered a special presentation on hunger (film, filmstrip, guest speaker) in the past six months?

___ 14. Has a story course in hunger been offered during the past year?

___ 15. Is hunger education included in regular church school classes?

___ 16. Has your church, or a group in your church, conducted a fast with a focus on the needs of hungry people during the past year?

___ 17. Does your church library or resource table contain books and pamphlets on hunger?

V. ADVOCACY

____ 18. Do the members of your church understand citizen advocacy as an important response to hunger? (If your estimate is less than ten percent, enter a minus.)

____ 19. How many people in your church are members of Bread for the World? (If less than five percent, enter a minus.)

____ 20. Has your church ever conducted a Bread for the World Offering of Letters?

____ 21. Has your church ever sponsored or participated in a voter registration drive or a get-out-the-vote campaign at election time?

____ 22. Has your church ever played host to a local BFW group meeting or event?

____ 23. Has membership in Bread for the World ever been encouraged in your church — either from the pulpit or by distribution of BFW brochures?

____ 24. Is your pastor a member of Bread for the World?

____ 25. Does your church, or a group in your church, participate in any other advocacy activity on behalf of hungry people on a regular basis?

- -

A glance at the column at the left should give you and your committee a reasonably good idea of the strengths and weaknesses of your church's hunger ministry. Which of the five categories has the most plusses? Which has the most minuses? Are there other ares not addressed by the assessment sheet which need considering?

A careful study of the assessment sheet should indicate the areas upon which to concentrate your planning needs. Consider what resources are available for each of the five areas to assist you in your planning (e.g., denominational hunger programs, local hunger ministries, Bread for the World, other national agencies).

While Bread for the World "majors" in the area of ADVO-CACY, we can provide resources and aids in the areas of WOR-SHIP, HUNGER EDUCATION, and LOCAL HUNGER as well. Contact your denominational hunger office or relief agency for information on special appeals for direct relief and "second-mile giving" projects.

BREAD FOR THE WORLD
802 Rhode Island Avenue, N.E.
Washington, D.C. 20018

NOTE: This assessment sheet can be used for purposes of evaluation. Toward the end of the year, run through the check-list again to see where progress has occurred and what needs to be worked on again next year.

*This survey is used with permission from Bread for the World's *Guidelines for Covenant Churches.*

9. MOVING FORWARD IN YOUR CHURCH

Once a hunger group has been started in your church and you have successfully completed a few initial projects, you will want to consider ways to integrate hunger concerns into the ongoing life of your church. You will want to establish study programs that address the underlying causes of hunger, and initiate actions that combat hunger. Building a hunger ministry in your church requires a balance between worship, study, and action. These three facets should comprise the work of your hunger group, and should be included in the plans you make for moving forward in your church.

Worship

Within your hunger group, always begin your meetings with a prayer or reflection time. Do not assume that because you are working within a church setting you càn worship together at other times. Worship unites your group and gives direction to your work. Perhaps you can rotate the leading of worship each meeting so everyone can develop skills in leading worship.

There are many ways to integrate hunger into the general worship life of your congregation. Take time to think about the parts of worship in your congregation. Consider how hunger concerns could be addressed in the sermons, music, prayers, readings, announcements, and offerings. Your group's creative ideas can assist the church leadership in planning meaningful worship services for the entire congregation.

Sermons or homilies on hunger are key places for establishing hunger ministries. The Bible addresses hunger and justice so strongly that the issue should "naturally" be discussed frequently. If your minister or priest speaks on hunger regularly, offer hmr support for doing so, and thank hmr for faithfully "covering" the issue.

If hunger is rarely mentioned from the pulpit, arrange a time to talk with the minister or priest. Politely express to hmr your desire that s/he speak on hunger more often. Ask hmr if there are ways you could support hmr in doing so. If it seems appropriate, you might offer to supply good sermon resources available from Christian hunger groups and your denomination's ministries. You will need to approach the matter of sermons cautiously to assure the minister or priest that you want to support hmr, and not undermine hmr in any way.

Ministers and priests need to take time off from their regular preaching schedules. Offer to arrange for a hunger speaker to fill in when your minister or priest is sick or out of town. Sometimes visiting speakers are able to cover issues that others cannot.

If your congregation's worship service includes a children's sermon, focus it occasionally on God's concern for hungry people. Alternatively, the children could present a drama on hunger during the service. One good dialogue on hunger for children is "All God's Children" which is listed in Appendix A.

Special adult dramas, designed for use in worship services, are powerful tools for motivating people in the context of worship. Two particularly effective ones, "Voices from the Quiet" and "Behold, I Am Making All Things New," are listed in Appendix A. A great need for more such dramas exists. If your group includes people with skills in writing and developing worship dramas, don't feel confined to those dramas suggested. Encourage your group to write new dramas and share them with the wider Christian hunger community.

If your church uses liturgical dance as part of worship, the dancers may be willing to express hunger concerns in their dances. One suggested model for a liturgical dance on hunger is described in a written piece available from Bread for the World. This model is quite moving when well executed.

Music is an important part of most worship services, and many traditional song texts express God's concern for hungry people. For example, the text from Luke 1, "He has filled the hungry with good things, and the rich he has sent away empty," has been set to music many times. Identify songs in your songbooks whose texts concern hunger and justice. Ask that those songs be sung. Talk with the choir/music director about whether the choir might sing songs related to hunger.

Ask musicians within the congregation to write or sing special music on hunger. An increasing number of Christian musicians are writing songs about hunger in our world. It does takes some effort to track them down, but there are many more songs available now than there were just a few years ago. Music helps us reflect on important issues, and also helps us feel and express our concerns. If a song gets in our minds, we will carry it around for days. Thus, music on hunger can be an important medium for raising awareness of hunger problems and solutions.

Consider how the format of your congregation's prayer times can be used to raise hunger concerns. If prayer requests are given to the minister/priest before the service, request prayers for hungry people regularly. If members of the congregation pray aloud, ask different members to remember hungry people during the prayer time. If there are special prayer requests listed in the weekly bulletin, submit requests for prayers to end hunger. Some churches use prayer cards (small cards with prayer requests on them that can be carried around in wallets or pockets). If your church uses prayer cards, consider designing and printing prayer cards about hungry people in specific countries. A map of the country and information about the number of people facing hunger could be printed on one side. Suggestions on what to pray for might be printed on the opposite side.

Many congregations use responsive readings and meditations during their services. There are many excellent ones prepared on hunger. Write to your denominational office or Bread for the World for listings of readings and meditations already prepared. Or, consider writing one yourself. Neither a responsive reading nor a meditation is too difficult to write, and by doing it yourself, you can include particular community hunger concerns and interests of the congregation.

Place bulletin inserts on hunger into the bulletin on a regular basis. This is an easy way keep hunger concerns before the congregation. Like readings and meditations, there are many excellent bulletin inserts on hunger already prepared. A number are produced for use on special holidays such as Thanksgiving, Christmas, and New Year's Day. Again, the largest collections are available from denominational offices and Bread for the World.

Does your church have a special time in the service for "minute for missions" or community concerns? If so, schedule members of your hunger group to speak on a regular basis about hunger. Even though the allotted time seems short, preparing a good "minute for missions" or brief presentation takes a fair amount of preparation time. Plan to rotate this responsibility within your group.

Offerings are a regular part of most worship services. Use the prayer time before the offering to highlight the missions work being done by the congregation or denomination to help hungry people. Many congregations have special offerings for hunger. The more that this can be built into the regular worship services of your congregation, the better it will be. Some congregations have special hunger collections once a month, or once a quarter. A few congregations have two offerings *every* Sunday, one for the regular work of the church, and the other for hunger and emergency needs. Such "institutionalizing" of hunger concerns helps to integrate them into the ongoing life of the church.

Study

Although this section discusses study ideas separately from action ideas, the two substantially overlap. The best study programs involve action, and becoming involved in action projects is usually the best form of education and study. Study alone without action can be an intellectual exercise which does not help hungry people. Action without study can be misdirected and ineffectual. Study and action must be integrally connected.

The previous chapter recommended forming a hunger study group as a means for identifying the nucleus for a hunger group in your church. Providing adult hunger study programs on a regular basis establishes a means for involving more new people in hunger action. In addition, it can deepen the understanding of those already concerned by having them rotate the leadership of the study courses.

Change the focus of your study each session. For example, offer one class on domestic hunger, and another class on land and hunger. Choose whatever forums are most appropriate, such as adult Sunday school classes, Wednesday night Bible classes, Lenten studies, or summer education programs. A number of excellent adult hunger studies are listed in Appendix A. Most are designed for six to eight sessions.

Numerous speakers on hunger are available without charge to supplement your group's teaching efforts. If you hear someone speak who impresses you, invite hmr to come speak at your church. It is simplest to ask the person to speak with your hunger group and then to invite the congregation at-large to attend. Tell the speaker you expect a small group, primarily your hunger committee, but that you have invited others. If a lot of people show up, terrific. If they do not,neither you nor the speaker will be disappointed. Plan to meet in a small comfortable room in the church, knowing you can move to the auditorium or another large room if needed.

Local university professors are a source for speakers, although they may be less action-oriented than you might like. Ask students about professors known for their concern about hunger. Be prepared to supplement a professor's talk with action strategies.

Missionaries on furlough are an excellent, underutilized resource on hunger. Generally, missionaries are asked to discuss their efforts to gain conversions, increase church membership, and build churches. Many missionaries working in Third World countries would be pleased to speak about hunger and development in their countries. My parents-in-law, who are missionaries in Thailand, have expressed their interest in speaking on hunger and development in Thailand. I know they and others would be excellent speakers.

Foreign students in your community are another underutilized resource. They can offer firsthand accounts of hunger in their countries. As with missionaries, you will want to be clear with them about what you want them to address.

Staff or elected leaders with local hunger groups, farmworker organizations, and welfare rights groups are often articulate speakers about hunger in the community. Many people working with the WIC program, or other government social service programs are good speakers, but you should know something about the person before inviting hmr to speak. Some social service workers are very concerned, others are seemingly there just for the job. Obviously, you want the concerned worker to speak with your group.

If you hear that a speaker from a national or state hunger organization is coming to your town, or nearby, and you would like to have the person speak, do not hesitate to invite hmr. Call the local contact person arranging the trip, or the person directly. People involved with hunger groups will try to make time for another meeting if it is at all possible.

Consider offering an educational program using audiovisual resources. A huge number of audiovisual resources exist on hunger and development overseas. The selection on domestic hunger is more limited. Films, filmstrips, or slide shows can be shown followed by a short presentation or discussion, or they can be a small part of a larger educational program. During 1984 and 1985 when churches were raising money and awareness about Ethiopia, a number of congregations sponsored family-night programs on Ethiopia. They offered an Ethiopian meal, a short film presentation, and a brief presentation inviting people to contribute money and write a letter to an elected official urging more generous government aid. Audiovisuals can serve as supplementary educational material, or as the centerpiece for a program. See Appendix B for distributors of audiovisual materials.

Special education programs geared to children are also important. The constant presentation of material items such as recorders, clothes, and toys as "needs" gives children a distorted view of the world. Church education programs alone can not counteract such bombardment, but they do provide opportunities to present the world from a different vantage point. Children and youth from financially secure families in the U.S. need to understand that not all children here in the U.S., let alone in the Third World, have adequate shelter and enough to eat. Most children from low-income families in the U.S. are far better off than children in Third World countries, and thus need to learn both how to help themselves and others.

The church needs to complement the teaching that occurs at home. New hunger study programs have been developed within the last few years for use with children and youth of all age groupings. There are Sunday school materials, a few vacation Bible school materials, and a couple of youth retreat programs on hunger. In addition, several organizations have designed special fundraising/awareness programs for youth. Several of these programs include all-night fasts and programs in the church building. These programs can be fun and educational. The adults working with these programs deserve special recognition and thanks! See Appendix A for a listing of study/action programs for children and youth.

Simulation games are good teaching tools for both adults and youth, because they allow people to feel and understand the study materials, rather than just hear or read them. Fewer good simulation games are available than one would like. (If you know someone with a special gift in designing simulations, please encourage hmr to share them with other hunger groups.) A few ideas for simulation study are discussed below.

The "tried and true" hunger awareness meals, also called Third World dinners, hunger banquets, or global buffets, are effective illustrations for those who have not previously experienced them. People are given different amounts of food depending on whether they are supposed to be from rich, moderate-income, or poor countries. A small number of people, from rich countries, are served lavish meals. A large number of people from Third World countries are given just rice or a plain broth. Experiencing the arbitrary nature of food distribution based on place of birth is a powerful teaching tool.

You can design your own simulation exercise on hunger in the U.S. Have people take public transportation to the nearest food stamp office and apply for food stamps. In a more modest version of the simulation, ask people to fill out a food stamp form. Either way, the magnitude of forms and questions to be answered, the strict eligibility requirements, and the low benefits are illustrated. If people are unaware of the difficulty of obtaining food stamps or question how families could run out of food stamps before the end of the month, this exercise will help them understand more about the program, and what it means to be poor in the U.S.

Another simulation for U.S. Christians who have never been poor is to be *served* at a soup kitchen. It usually is much more pleasant to serve than to be served. This simulation lets people experience being the object of charity, and helps them develop some sympathy and understanding for those who receive charity. As with any simulation exercise, it is important to help people explore their feelings following the experience.

Action

As I've travelled through the U.S., meeting with hundreds of Christians involved with hunger, I've asked many people why they became involved. Overwhelmingly, personal experience — not reading a book or hearing a lecture — sparked their interest. For many people visits to Third World countries first stirred their concern. Others cite work in a soup kitchen or personally being on food stamps or needing food. At least 90 percent of those I've asked can point to a few specific experiences which were life-changing for them. As an organizer, you will want to encourage church members to undergo experiences which will be life-changing for them.

Travel is often just such a life-changing experience. As costly as it is, if traveling changes a person's use of time and money for years to come, it is worth the investment. Therefore, if sponsoring a trip to a Third World country is within the financial resources of your group, it is likely to be beneficial. Many denominations and regional church associations sponsor educational tours to Third World countries. In addition, the following programs offer educational tours and short-term volunteer experiences in Third World nations:

Center for Global Service and Education, Augsburg College, 731-21st Avenue So., Minneapolis, MN 55454. 612/330-1159.

Children of the Americas, P.O. Drawer 21707, Santa Barbara, CA 93121. 805/963-2189.

Global Awareness Through Experience, Mt. St. Joseph, Cincinnati, OH 45051. 513/244-4623.

Los Ninos, 1330 Continental Street, San Ysidro, CA 92073. 619/691 1437/1441.

Oxfam America, 115 Broadway, Boston, MA 02116. 617/482-1211.

Puentes de Cristo, 513 Beaumont Street, McAllen, TX. 512/682-0292.

Many other "education through experience" opportunities are available closer to home. Therefore, once your hunger group is established and has completed a successful project or two, it should undertake actions that will alleviate hunger or address the causes of hunger while challenging and empowering the congregation. Although many of the actions involve public policy issues and will be discussed in the following chapter, a number of actions can be taken in your local community which will both alleviate hunger and provide learning experiences for group members.

Most hunger-related programs are in desperate need of dependable volunteers. For example, Meals on Wheels needs volunteers to deliver food to shut-ins. Soup kitchens need people to prepare and serve food. Food pantries need people to screen recipients, and collect food. As your church's hunger commitment grows, you may decide to start your own soup kitchen or food pantry. Such a decision is a big step and should be approached carefully. Be sure to see the resources recommended in Appendix A.

Your church group may seek ways to assist low-income people in purchasing food inexpensively such as organizing a farmer-to-market program. Arrange for farmers to sell their products directly to consumers, cutting out retailing costs. Although farmers may wish to sell in more affluent communities, the program is more beneficial to low-income people if it is located in poorer communities. If no site can be agreed upon in a low-income community, be sure that the site is accessible by public transportation.

Alternatively, your church could decide to organize a SHARE co-op in your town. In SHARE co-ops, each family pays a set amount — around twelve dollars a month — which purchases a package of food valued at thirty to forty dollars. The package varies each month depending on product availability and cost. In addition to the dollar commitment, each family unit must contribute two hours of community service per month. Approximately 40 percent of the service time must be used to bag and distribute the food. The other 60 percent is available to meet other community needs. Although the program has no income limitations, it has been organized primarily in low-income communities. It is an excellent program, but requires some initial financial investments and substantial time commitment from the sponsoring group. For more information, write SHARE, 5255 Lovelock Street, San Diego, CA 92110.

Only about half of those eligible for federal food programs receive benefits. A great need for outreach and application assistance exists. Your group could start an information and assistance program related to federal food programs. Following an assessment of your community's needs, your group could advertise the availability of suitable programs such as food stamps and WIC. You could provide transportation to application sites, and supply volunteers to help people wade through the forms and ensure that caseworkers treat applicants respectfully. In areas where language is a barrier, your group might provide translation.

Your group may decide that the critical need in your community is to increase awareness. You could sponsor a day-long tour of public and private agencies working on hunger issues for community leaders and the press. Visit food stamp offices, WIC clinics, food pantries, and other local centers. Talk with program administrators and program recipients. Inquire about program changes in the last few years and why these have occurred. A hunger awareness tour can spur community leaders to take action, and can gain media coverage of hunger concerns.

A more intensive survey of hunger in your community can be undertaken by using *Hunger Watch U.S.A.* This sixty-page manual, available from Bread for the World, includes questionnaires about the operation and effectiveness of U.S. food assistance programs. It will help your group document hunger in the community and use the information you have gathered to gain media coverage of the results.

Federally funded school breakfast and lunch programs are often less effective than they could be because children don't like the food served. Your group could work with the students and meal planners to get nutritious food, which is liked and thus eaten by the children, into the school menus. In addition, your group could encourage and assist parents of poor children to return forms for free and reduced-price meals.

Unemployment is a major cause of hunger in the U.S. Your hunger group may want to combat hunger by assisting people in finding, getting, and keeping jobs. Perhaps you could organize a jobs training program, where skills are taught in writing resumes, interviewing, and dealing with conflicts on the job. There may be ways the church's investments could be used to encourage businesses in low-income neighborhoods which could provide jobs.

Many single parents have trouble keeping jobs because of the high cost of childcare. Many churches have allowed their church/school facilities to be used by daycare centers. If your church has facilities which are unused during the week, consider offering the space free of charge or "at cost" to a daycare center which serves low-income families.

Product boycotts can be promoted and undertaken when the campaign is one your hunger group wants to support. A few years ago, there was a large boycott against Nestle's products because of Nestle's promotion of infant formulas in Third World countries. The promotional campaigns encouraged mothers to use infant formulas instead of breastfeeding, even though breastfeeding was generally better for the infants. The boycott was organized to pressure Nestle into changing its promotional efforts. Thousands of churches participated in the campaign by boycotting Nestle's products. For many years, boycotts have been organized to support the union drives of farmworkers. After looking into the campaigns, you may decide to join these or other boycotts. If so, provide complete information in the church newsletter, bulletins, and on bulletin boards. Collect coupons from the company and return them to the company explaining why you chose not to use the coupons.

*   *   *

Moving your hunger ministry forward in your church requires applying many of the same principles discussed in getting started in your church. Goals for your group should be realistic and achievable. Projects undertaken should strengthen and develop your hunger group, and draw on as many people as possible, as well as combat hunger. Meetings and tasks should be both fun and efficient.

Once a group has gotten started and had a few successful projects, it needs to consider two additional issues. The first is how to integrate hunger issues into the ongoing life of the church — how to "institutionalize" hunger ministries. To some extent, the goal is to work the hunger committee out of a job. If hunger concerns were considered by every committee and regularly addressed in all areas of the church's life, there would be no need for a hunger committee. Your group's job is to make hunger a part of the "regular" ministries of the church.

The second issue is to help the congregation address the causes of hunger and not just the results. Feeding people *is* an important ministry of the church. Countering the injustice that causes hunger, however, is also part of the church's ministry, and because it is harder, it is sometimes neglected. Your hunger group will serve the congregation well if it educates the congregation about the causes of hunger, in this country and abroad, and it provides a few effective responses to the causes of hunger.

Public policy is so important in responding to the causes of hunger that a separate chapter has been devoted to advocacy. Although separated here, advocacy should not be isolated in your group's planning. It is an integral part of moving forward in your church and should be integrated with worship, study, and action, into the ongoing life of your church.

10. ADVOCATING WITHIN YOUR CHURCH

If you filled out the church assessment form in Chapter 8, and if your church is like most, your rating in advocacy was the lowest. Few churches are active as political advocates for hungry people. The more one learns about hunger both here and abroad, however, the clearer the political and economic dimensions of hunger become. If our churches are to have a significant impact on hunger, we must acknowledge these dimensions. Consequently, we as individuals *and* as churches must participate in forming public policy to benefit hungry people.

When encouraging advocacy within your church, you may encounter church leaders who say, "We don't want to mix religion and politics." Don't take offense. They don't mean that Christians should shirk their duties as U.S. citizens. They are likely asserting the time honored principle of separation of church and state.

One of the best responses I've heard to the concern about mixing religion and politics is a statement made by Arthur Simon, executive director of Bread for the World. He says, "The separation of church and state should be affirmed. The separation of religion from life, however, is pure heresy. To take major areas of life — those having to do with social and economic decisions that vitally affect all of us — and put them outside the boundary of faith contradicts the confession that Jesus Christ is Lord."

There are at least three types of teaching to consider when thinking about the separation of religion and politics. Biblical examples are one type. Joseph, for example, not only influenced the most important political leader of his day, but he also advocated policies that prevented starvation. Joseph became a respected counselor of the Pharaoh. In this capacity, he urged the Pharaoh to store food from plentiful harvests to be used in the times of famine. This wise advice was heeded and lives were saved.

Similarly, God chose Moses to speak to the Pharaoh about freeing the Hebrews. When God called Moses to lead the people, Moses made many excuses about why he wasn't the right person to address the Pharaoh. Many of us sound like Moses in our fear of meeting with officials. One of Moses' excuses was, "I have never been a good speaker, and I haven't become one since you began to speak to me. I am a poor speaker, slow and hesitant" (Exodus 4:10). God agreed to let Moses' brother Aaron accompany him, but Moses was not free from his responsibility to speak.

We all know the story of the plagues God sent to Egypt to encourage the Pharaoh to free the Hebrews. Needless to say, we do not have plagues at our disposal, but we do have our voices and a number of resources which can be used to influence current-day problems.

God's prophets and prophetesses also influenced public policy. Esther used her influence with King Ahasuerus to save the Jews. First, Esther organized a three-day fast among the Jews found in Susa. Then she risked the death penalty to approach the King without being summoned. She received an audience, and after serving two banquets, she pleaded for the lives of the Jews. Esther courageously "lobbied" the King to benefit her people as well as herself.

Isaiah's prophetic words were spoken not only to the people at large, but to the officials of Israel. He warned them of the Lord's judgment if they continued "grinding of the face of the poor." He also gave guidance on military and economic matters. Isaiah addressed King Uzziah, King Ahaz, and King Hezekiah about their decisions on pressing matters of the day.

During the reign of King Josiah, people cleaning the temple

discovered a book of the law and needed help understanding it. King Josiah sent several advisors to the prophetess Huldah to seek her explanation. She delivered God's messages which resulted in reforms.

There are many more Biblical examples of people using their access to policy makers and their resources to influence political and economic decisions, especially in the Old Testament. New Testament examples are fewer, since participatory decision-making was rare in Roman politics. The early Christian community had few rights, resources, and contacts with which to influence officials and their decisions.

Christ, while not directly attempting to influence political leaders, does exemplify the concept of advocacy, or pleading the cause of another. As Christians, we recognize that Christ's advocacy is a central theme of our faith. "We have an advocate with the Father, Jesus Christ the righteous" (I John 2:1). If Christ can advocate for us, we can certainly advocate for our hungry brothers and sisters.

The third way to approach the issue of religion and politics is to look at the history of the churches in the United States. The Christian community has always been involved in public policy issues. Historically the U.S. churches were vocal (sometimes on both sides) about social issues such as slavery, child labor, temperance, and civil rights. Recently, U.S. churches have been very active in the debates over liquor by the drink, abortion, and school prayer.

Interestingly enough, sometimes the same church that has been actively fighting pornography on television, or lobbying elected leaders to halt certain activities, questions whether Christians should be involved in public policy work against hunger. It would seem in such cases that the issue is not really separation of religion and politics. Either those in the church question whether hunger is an issue they should be concerned about, or they question whether Christians can influence public policies on hunger.

The answer to the first question is clearly yes! Based on private church giving for hunger relief, most Christians do believe that they should help hungry people. The answer to the second question — whether Christians can influence public policies on hunger — is also a resounding YES, but fewer Christians would respond in the affirmative. Christians are unaware of their power in this arena. Thus, part of our work in introducing public policy advocacy on hunger into the life of our churches is convincing people that public policy advocacy can help hungry people. It is helpful to be aware of a few examples where Christians clearly have made a difference in the outcome of hunger legislation. Bread for the World is not the only advocacy group working on hunger issues, but it is the one with which I am most familiar; therefore, these examples are drawn from legislative actions which Bread for the World helped orchestrate.

My favorite example of Christians involved in public policy work is the Fithian amendment. In 1980, there was a famine in Somalia. The United States government had originally pledged to contribute $142 million to the relief efforts. When the money was actually appropriated, the amount was reduced to $100 million. At this time, a "supplemental appropriation" was being considered. A BFW staff person located a large item in this supplemental appropriation for furniture for government offices. Questioning the dire need for more furniture, this staff person drafted an amendment calling for cutting $100 million from the furniture category and adding $42.8 million for the famine relief efforts.

Representative Floyd Fithian of Indiana agreed to introduce the legislation, thus giving the amendment his name. Introducing an amendment and passing it are two different things. The amendment was unknown and the vote was scheduled to come up quickly. Bread for the World staff called Christian advocates all over the country. Those who had legislative telephone trees activated them. Others got members of their congregations to write letters urging support of the Fithian amendment.

Within a few days, thousands of calls were placed and letters were sent to representatives, apprising them of an important piece of legislation that would save the government money and help hungry people. A few days later the amendment came up for a vote. It passed by a fairly wide margin. It could never have passed without the calls and letters from concerned Christians.

A few years later, a number of African countries were facing famine. Bread for the World worked with congressional leaders in January, 1984, to introduce a bill calling for $350 million in additional food assistance. When introduced, some people laughed at the size of the request and the recommendation that the legislation be dealt with immediately. Letters were mailed and phone calls placed notifying Christian advocates of the upcoming votes. Many wrote and called their elected leaders. In the committee, the bill was cut back to $150 million, less than the hunger groups wanted but far more than skeptics on Capitol Hill expected. As with much legislation, this bill's legislative history was not straightforward. Part of the bill was passed quickly and another part delayed because of military aid attached to the bill. Eventually, however, the $150 million was all appropriated for Africa, and used to save lives.

U.S. foreign aid is not the only important international area where hunger advocates can work, but it is a very tangible arena for measuring our effectiveness. The sum total of all private giving for food and development in 1983 was $1,320,000. This includes the money we give through our churches and to private groups like UNICEF and CARE. Compare that figure with the $7,992,000 that the U.S. spent on official development assistance in that same year. How foreign aid is spent is a matter which Christians can influence. At this stage in the hunger movement's history, foreign policy analysts assess that Christian advocates can probably influence the allocation of several hundred million dollars a year. Even if the figure is not precise, it is clear to those who work on foreign aid legislation that Christians can increase dramatically their influence on public policy by developing strong, organized legislative efforts.

Similarly, Christians can and do influence public policy on domestic hunger. Administration proposals over the last few years have suggested turning the federal food programs into block grants (lump-sum grants to states without federal standards) and cutting funds for the programs significantly, both of which would have hurt low-income Americans. Bread for the World has worked with a number of other groups in trying to get calls and letters sent to congress. In addition, church groups have highlighted the local hunger problems in the media and in visits with respresentatives and senators. As a result, the programs have not been turned into block grants, and the funds for the programs have been increased modestly, instead of decreased dramatically.

These kinds of public policy "victories" are achieved district by district, or state by state. They are achieved because small groups of people organize a campaign to influence an elected leader on a particular issue. The longer I've worked with legislative advocacy, the more convinced I am of the power of citizen advocacy. Too many people underestimate the impact of calls, letters, and visits.

Writing Letters

Let us look at some techniques of advocacy that are appropriate for churches. The simplest way of communicating with your elected leaders is by letter. Writing a personal letter is effective, and takes but a few minutes.

One of the most frequently asked questions is "Do letters make a difference?" Indeed they do. Although not every single letter will necessarily be read by the elected leader, they do make an impression in one of several ways. Sometimes the sheer number of letters on a particular issue is important. Repeatedly, BFW staff have been told by legislative aides in Washington, D.C. that their offices have been "swamped" with letters on a particular issue. When asked how many were received, the aides replied five or six. Five or six letters and they're swamped!

On issues like hunger, or many others, elected leaders receive far fewer letters than you might imagine. Legislative aides claim for every letter written, they assume that at least a hundred people share the letter's views but didn't bother to write. Because people in general do not write elected leaders, those who do write are more influential than their numbers might indicate.

One time Bread for the World was working on a fairly complicated amendment to legislation on the International Monetary Fund. Bread for the World had been urging people to write their representatives on the issue. Unfortunately, few people had done so because they did not feel they understood the issue adequately. I was asked to contact a number of legislative offices and inquire as to how the representatives were planning to vote. In doing so, a number of aides told me, "We haven't gotten one letter on this issue. If we just got one letter, we'd probably vote for it."

The truth was that the representatives and their aides didn't really understand the issue either. Because the issue was inconsequential to them — having no electoral impact — they didn't really care if they voted for or against it. Had they received one letter, many representatives would have voted for it.

Most issues require more than one letter to influence a vote, but it is generally far fewer letters than one might expect. Consequently, it is very important that you find ongoing ways to incorporate letter-writing to elected leaders into regular church activities. Perhaps your hunger group could write letters once a month. Even those most committed to hunger forget to write on a regular basis. Monthly letter-writing in a group ensures a steady flow of letters and helps people gain confidence in writing about hunger issues.

Perhaps there are other groups meeting within the church who would be willing to write letters once a month. Women's groups and older adult groups are often willing to undertake the responsibility. Some churches have letter-writing tables set up once a month during the coffee hour after service. One church instituted a "letter-of-the-month club." Members of the congregation who pledged to write one letter each month on hunger issues were given a card certifying them as members of the club. This may sound silly, but it really worked.

Offering of Letters

Early in its history, Bread for the World began urging churches to hold Offerings of Letters. An Offering of Letters is a campaign to get many people in a congregation to write letters to their representatives and senators on a specific piece of hunger legislation. In many churches, an Offering of Letters has become an annual or biannual event. Here is how it works.

First, the hunger committee presents the idea to the appropriate church council or committee for approval. Once the topic and the date are approved, the hunger committee must begin preparing the congregation. Announcements should be made, notices put in the bulletin, and posters hung in the foyer or vestibule.

There are at least three ways the letters can be written.

1. Letters can be written at home and brought to the Offering of Letters service. This produces the least number of letters because people forget to write them or forget to bring them to the service. In addition, there is no support for people who have never written a letter before.

2. Letters can be written during the service. Paper, envelopes, and pencils are distributed and time allo-

cated during the service. Usually large charts with the proper addresses are placed in the front of the building. This works very well in some churches. Others find it disruptive. This method generally produces a lot of letters.

3. Letters can be written at tables set up before or after the service. This is the most popular manner for writing the letters. All the information and tools for writing are placed on letter-writing tables. People are encouraged to stop and write a letter. This works well during a coffee-hour time.

One variation on letter-writing tables is to have typing tables. One church did this very effectively by recruiting people who typed and had typewriters. The typists were asked to bring their typewriters to church on a designated Sunday. They were given special training on the Offering of Letters issue and how to advise people about writing letters to elected leders. A dictating chair was set up next to each typist. People from the congregation sat down and "dictated" letters. Everyone had a great time and many letters were mailed to Congress.

The letters should be collected in an offering plate during the service or set on a table. Where appropriate, the letters should be collected alongside the money collection to stress the fact that our citizenship is also a gift from God that should be used to the glory of God. Following the collection of the letters, they should be mailed to the appropriate legislative offices.

One church in California decided they preferred their letters hand-delivered. They sent a woman from their congregation to Washington, D.C. to personally deliver the letters to their representative. Few congregations can afford to do that, but it is a good approach if you are near Washington, D.C. or your state capitol.

Many churches include Offering of Letters as part of a special hunger Sunday. Each year Bread for the World provides an Offering of Letters kit which includes a bulletin insert, worship ideas, a brief sample presentation, and background information on the targeted legislation. Because of the helpful resources, the BFW Offering of Letters is a good one to begin with in your congregation.

The basic idea of an Offering of Letters can be used with a variety of hunger legislation, both state and national. It is important, especially for the first time, that you select an issue you think you can influence. Picking "definite losers" will not be motivating to people who are writing their first letter to an elected leader, and consequently they may never write again. Choose an issue that will be empowering to your congregation.

After the offering, keep the congregation informed about the progress of the legislation. It may be months before the legislation is actually passed. People need to know that their letters played a role, especially when the process drags out.

An Offering of Letters is an excellent organizing tool. It offers a concrete project for a group to plan and conduct. It is an event which requires general support and approval from the church leadership, thus raising the issue of hunger as a responsibility of the church. It gets a lot of letters written which helps pass life-saving legislation, and it gets many people to write their first letter to an elected leader. Writing the first letter is the hardest. And once a person writes a letter about something, s/he is often interested in finding out more about that issue. The process of writing a letter is an educational experience in itself — education through action.

If the offering is well received, try doing an Offering of Letters once a month during coffee hour. It is easy to organize on a regular basis. Make a poster with a sample letter and information explaining the outcome of last month's issue. Make your advocacy ongoing!

Telephone Trees

As described in further detail in the chapter on lobbying elected leaders, telephone trees are often necessary to influence legislation because the legislation is scheduled to move quickly either at the committee or floor level. There is no time for groups like Bread for the World to get a newsletter out to people. Thus, telephone trees (Bread for the World calls them Quicklines) must be set up to communicate quickly about upcoming legislation.

You can set up a branch of a telephone tree within your congregation. It may connect just those on your hunger committee or there may be others who understand the importance of public policy and would be willing to serve on a telephone tree. Messages that are sent via telephone trees are usually very brief. Therefore, it is important that people on the telephone trees receive printed materials which provide greater detail and background to issues. People need to be able to refer back to newsletters or issue papers when messages are brief.

Be sure the local Bread for the World leader or local state hunger organizer knows of your telephone tree. If you are not sure who to contact about connecting your telephone tree to a larger information network, call the national or state office of the hunger advocacy group whose work you wish to support.

Inviting Elected Leaders to Speak

The simple act of inviting your representative or senator to speak at your church about hunger issues is lobbying. It tells the person that hunger policy is something that concerns your congregation.

Check with your congregation's leaders to see what times would be most suitable. Seek the widest range of options possible. The more flexible your invitation, the more likely the elected leader will be to accept. If you give hmr one or two dates, s/he is likely to have previous commitments. It is unlikely that s/he will have commitments for "any Sunday in the spring." You want to be able to invite the elected leader for the widest range of dates and times you can have approved by the church leadership.

Ask the person to speak about what s/he is doing in Congress or the state legislature to end hunger here and abroad. If s/he is not doing much, hsr aides will investigate legislation and may even have the person cosponsor special pieces of legislation prior to the speaking engagement.

You might want to work with the hunger committee from neighboring churches and offer a joint invitation to the elected leader. Doing so will demonstrate widespread concern for the issue and will help you get to know your neighbors with similar concerns.

The program should be friendly, but the hunger committee members can be prepared to ask about particular pieces of legislation. If the elected leader is not familiar with them, you can send more information to hsr office after the meeting.

It is always a good idea to have a backup program prepared in case the elected leader cancels at the last minute. It is not unusual for elected leaders to have unexpected crises. Also, elected leaders are frequently late. Thus, you might want to have some special music or entertainment in case the group has to wait for a half-hour or so.

Voting — Them and You

Let people in your congregation know how their elected leaders vote, whether or not they cosponsor antihunger legislation, and if they take leadership on hunger issues. Such information can be placed in the church bulletin, newsletters, or on a bulletin board. You may even want to post copies of responses received from elected leaders concerning hunger legislation.

A number of groups prepare voting records. Bread for the World prepares one each year on national representatives' and senators' votes on key hunger issues. State advocacy groups do the same thing. This public information should be made accessible to members of the congregation.

Prior to elections, some groups compile responses of questionnaires sent to candidates. If one is done on hunger issues, it would be good to make its results known. Always acknowledge that people make voting decisions based on a range of issues, but suggest that hunger is one issue to consider when voting.

If people in your congregation are not registered to vote, encourage them to register. Depending on your state's voter registration laws, you might set up a registration table before and after church. Check with your Board of Elections for advice. Encourage people to vote. The U.S. has one of the lowest voter turnout rates of any democracy in the world. Being able to vote is both a right and a responsibility, and Christians need to make sure their voices are heard.

There is no need to hide the fact that you are watching how elected leaders vote on hunger issues and that you encourage people to vote. Send your elected leaders copies or pictures of information placed in bulletins or on the bulletin board. Let your leaders know that you care about hunger, are watching their votes, and are praying for them as leaders. Never forget that elected leaders have difficult jobs, with many temptations and lures of power. The Bible tells us to pray for our leaders. We must not forget to do so.

If your congregation has never undertaken public policy advocacy on hunger issues, it is important to start slowly and build support through the work. Consider the public policy suggestions that have been made and select one or two which seem possible for your church or parish.

To know what hunger legislation is pending, you must work with at least one advocacy group. Most hunger legislation is enacted at the national level. Bread for the World, as the only Christian citizens' movement working solely on hunger, is a key group to join. There are several other excellent groups you might want to consider that work on a broader range of policy issues. They include Interfaith Action on Economic Justice, Friends Committee on National Legislation, and Network. (See Appendix D.) There are usually statewide hunger advocacy groups in each state, or statewide Impact groups working on a range of statewide legislation. You should affiliate yourselves with both a national and a statewide policy group so you can stay informed of current legislation. Make your voice heard!

11. ORGANIZING ON CAMPUS

Organizing and developing a hunger group on a college campus involves the same general principles of group development and maintenance as organizing and developing hunger groups in other environments. There are, however, some unique features of organizing in a college setting. This chapter assumes you understand the basic concepts of group development and maintenance presented in earlier chapters, and focuses on the unique challenges created by the university environment.

Transitional Leadership

Leadership in all hunger groups changes and develops, but leadership in campus groups is particularly transitional. Student leaders constantly graduate or transfer. Leadership skills need to be developed in new members long before existing leaders leave. Nonetheless, many college hunger groups are composed primarily of juniors and seniors, with seniors dominating the leadership positions.

In many campus groups, one or two people take on all the work. Those one or two become burdened by the responsibility, and new leadership is not developed. Other members feel less committed to the group because they are not responsible for parts of its work. Involving first- and second-year students in the group's work and leadership responsibilities is critical to its continuance.

I recommend that by midterm of the final semester or quarter the group select people to serve in key leadership positions for the following school year. The new leaders can be trained during the last few weeks of the term and take possession of important files. More importantly, the group will have its leadership established and be able to "hit the ground running" in the next school year. Filling all the leadership roles is not necessary because the group will attract new student leaders the next year, but having a core group of at least three or four ready to go is important.

If possible, the group should set the date and time of its first public meeting for the coming school year. This will allow a room to be reserved and an announcement submitted to the school newspaper, so the meeting will be publicized in the first newspaper of the year. The core leadership group should meet before the first meeting to plan an agenda, and arrange last minute details.

Short Time Spans

Campus groups function within much shorter time spans than community or church groups. Students are only together about thirty of the fifty-two weeks a year. Of those thirty weeks, a week is lost at the beginning of each quarter or semester, as well as time during midterm and final exams. This short time span influences how campus groups function and the types of projects they can undertake.

Most campus groups meet weekly or biweekly, unlike church and community groups that usually meet monthly. If college groups met monthly, they might meet only two or three times during a term. That is not often enough for the group to develop. Even meeting weekly or biweekly, the group must develop its goals and projects quickly. The group does not have time to spend many of its meetings on sorting out its direction. Projects must also have short time frames.

Campus groups must also be flexible in scheduling around school breaks and exams. They must take these factors into consideration and be prepared to make changes as needed.

Institutionalizing

It is helpful, but not absolutely necessary, for campus hunger groups to "institutionalize" themselves. Institutionalization helps campus groups cope with the short time spans and transitional leadership characteristic of campus groups. The two most common forms of institutionalization adopted are becoming a program of a campus ministry and becoming an official student organization.

Becoming a regular program of a campus ministry is the easiest way for many groups to gain institutional status. This only occurs, however, when one or two key campus ministers are committed to the work of a campus hunger group. The campus ministers provide leadership and continuity, and help the group develop quickly and use its limited time effectively. Some of the longest continuing campus hunger groups I have seen are affiliated with campus ministries.

The other main means of institutionalizing a campus group is making it an official student organization. This usually requires submitting to some formal approval process by the student government. The group benefits from the public recognition, publicity, and often from some appropriation of funds accorded to official student groups. The allocated funds, although generally modest, can greatly help the hunger group plan and advertise its programs.

Less Study, More Action

Many community and church hunger groups spend their first six months studying hunger issues together. This is a poor strategy for a campus group. Students' primary occupation *is* study. They do not want to join a group whose main focus is more study. The hunger group should explore ways to help students study hunger issues as part of their ongoing course work, and give group projects a strong action focus.

The first step in helping students study hunger issues as part of their course work is to prepare a list of all courses that relate to hunger concerns. About ten years ago, I compiled a book on the hunger-related curricula offered by colleges across the country. Hundreds of courses were offered in many different departments. Check your catalogs carefully when compiling your list — you may find hunger courses in unexpected places. If you don't find sufficient course work on hunger, you may be able to persuade some professors to incorporate a section on hunger into their existing course outlines. Alternatively, your group could approach several professors about offering an interdisciplinary course on hunger. If offered, your entire group could take it together to increase your understanding of hunger issues.

You can also encourage members to research and write term papers on hunger issues, when appropriate. Students may be able to get credit for more extensive research by arranging to conduct an independent study. For example, a special study on hunger in your community that investigates why food stamp participation is low, might be approved by a political science, sociology, or economics department. *Hunger Watch, U.S.A.* would provide a useful guide for conducting such a study (see Appendix A).

Internships are another way students can gain understanding of hunger issues. Many national hunger organizations, like Oxfam America and Bread for the World, and many local relief agencies accept interns. Find out if your school awards course credit for internships. Encourage group members to apply for internships even if your college does not give credit for them. Internships can be excellent educational experiences and are considerably more interesting than the average summer job.

These are a few ways a campus hunger group can encourage members to study hunger issues without making study a large part of the group's activities. A healthy church or interdenominational hunger group may well spend from 30 to 40 percent of its time in study. A Christian campus program should downplay study, spending 15 percent of its time on worship, 20 percent on other community-building activities, 10 percent on study, and

55 percent on action. Students have lots of energy and want to be a part of groups that are active. Some active projects that work well on college campuses are discussed below.

Projects and Ideas that Work on College Campuses

1. HUNGER WEEK. On many campuses, student groups sponsor several days or a week of activities on hunger. Speakers, fasts, fundraising, letter writing, and worship services are generally included. Many groups schedule their activities to coincide with Oxfam's Fast for World Harvest in November. A hunger week should occur about two-thirds of the way through a term — far enough into the term that the organizers have time to plan, but sufficiently before final exams that people will participate.

2. HUNGER CONCERT. Organize a concert or other entertainment to benefit a hunger organization. Ask the performers to donate their time. You might even consider a schoolwide talent show. (Most music, dance, and acting students never get enough performance opportunities, and can be counted upon to fill the audience with at least a few of their friends and relations.) You can charge an admission fee or ask for a meal ticket (if you can arrange to be reimbursed for it). As an alternative, you can require each person to bring a letter on hunger to hsr congressperson. Organizing a concert can be fun and educational, and will yield the group money or letters.

3. HUNGER DORM. Some schools permit students to form special "theme" dormitories or dormitory floors. Consider organizing a dorm floor around hunger. Occidental College in Southern California, for example, had a hunger floor in one of its dorms. This hunger dorm institutionalized Occidental's hunger group and strengthened the individual members' commitment to hunger action.

4. DORM PROGRAMS. Are resident hall directors required to

provide dorm or floor programs? If so, offer to sponsor a dorm or floor program on hunger. Any dorm leader who is required to offer programs on a regular basis will be delighted with your assistance, and you will be able to introduce hunger concerns to a broader campus community.

5. WORLD HUNGER COLUMN. Approach the school newspaper and offer to write a weekly column on hunger. If you are concerned about having enough timely information, you can write Bread for the World and ask to be added to their press release list. You will be sent up-to-date information regularly about hunger issues before Congress. Your articles should briefly explain an issue and then urge students to write letters about those issues.

6. FASTS. Given the weight consciousness of today's student bodies, getting students to fast is not difficult! Make arrangements with your school food service before the fast to donate a certain amount of money for each meal skipped. Your cafeteria director may at first say it is impossible, but it is not. Fasts happen on hundreds of college campuses across the country, and the majority of them receive the cooperation of their food services. You will not be able to get the full cost of the food service, because the staff must be paid whether or not you eat. If you can estimate the number of meals that will be skipped, however, you should be able to recover the cost of the food unused.

Fasts must be well publicized. If possible, get various organizations on campus to agree to sign up participants. You may want to encourage a little competition between dorms, sororities, or fraternities. Fasting is well grounded in Christian tradition, although it is not often practiced. When planning a fast, don't forget to schedule activities for participants that will link the fast to hunger concerns, and will provide opportunities for prayer. Treat the fast as an educational opportunity for participants as well as a means of raising money.

7. WALKS. Students usually participate in community hunger walks, rather than sponsoring their own. There is, however, no

reason that students could not sponsor their own walk. CROP walks are the most common community hunger walks. Usually, students ask friends and relatives to pledge a few cents per mile or kilometer walked. Make presentations to dorm councils or clubs to solicit their support. As with fasts, you may find that a little competition between dorms or social clubs will spur interest in participating.

8. VOTER REGISTRATION AND EDUCATION. Too few students vote. Your hunger group can register fellow students to vote and provide them with information on the candidates' positions on hunger. A Bread for the World group or other local hunger organization may have prepared the candidates' evaluations. If not, you can develop one yourself. (See the chapter entitled Making Hunger an Election Issue.) You can also invite candidates to speak on campus, and ask them to discuss what they have done or hope to do to alleviate hunger. Asking candidates to address hunger has the dual benefit of educating students in attendance about the candidates' positions on hunger and emphasizing to the candidates that hunger has political (electoral) consequences.

9. CHAPEL PROGRAM ON HUNGER. Most religiously affiliated schools have either a voluntary or a mandatory chapel program. Such programs can provide excellent opportunities for reaching lots of students. Talk with the person who schedules chapel programs about inviting speakers to discuss Christians and hunger. Offer to make arrangements for a speaker or series of speakers from hunger organizations. Most hunger groups are happy to send speakers if you can cover their transportation expenses. (Your school may provide money for chapel speakers' transportation.)

Arranging for a chapel speaker may permit your hunger group to bring someone to campus that you might otherwise be unable to afford. Take advantage of it! Line up a smaller group of students for the speaker to meet. Consider sponsoring a coffee and doughnut time after chapel for interested students to meet the speaker. Schedule hmr to talk with a few small classes or other student groups. Most importantly, be sure the person spends time with your hunger group. S/he can offer encouragement, new ideas, and information, and can discuss career choices related to hunger and development with group members.

10. HIGH SCHOOL PROGRAMS. Students from campus hunger groups can offer programs on hunger to high schools in the community. This allows college students to gain experience speaking publicly and leading groups, while educating the high school students about hunger. If the sessions are concluded with the high school students writing their congressional representatives about hunger legislation, they will be object lessons in civics as well.

11. LETTER-WRITING TABLES. Set up a table at which people can write their elected leaders about hunger issues. The table should be set up in a central location or near the cafeteria line. It should contain informational material about current hunger issues, sample letters, and instructions on letter writing, as well as paper, pens, and places to write. Have the table set up for more than one day so that people can become accustomed to the idea of writing letters to help the hungry, and can become familiar with the issues.

12. ORIENTATION PROGRAM. The best time to interest new people in a hunger group is when they first get to campus. Therefore, a "recruitment" project should be undertaken early in the school year, geared to first-year and transfer students. If the school holds a special program for new students try to give a presentation or host a booth. At one school, the hunger group conducted a hunger simulation game for all new and transfer students. This activated students' concern about hunger while simultaneously advertising the hunger group.

13. SCHOOL BREAK PROGRAMS. Arrange "hands-on" educational programs for students during semester or quarter breaks.

A number of southwestern schools, for example, send students to work at Los Ninos, a direct aid program working with people of Tijuana and Mexicali, Mexico. For more information write to Los Ninos, 1330 Continental Street, San Ysidro, CA 92073 or call 619/691-1437/1441. Such programs both educate and motivate the students who participate.

14. LOCAL VOLUNTEERING. "Hands-on" experience with hunger is available in nearly every community. A campus hunger group could volunteer to work in a soup kitchen, to deliver meals to homebound elderly people, or to assist people applying for food stamps. Most communities have many hunger relief programs that can be supported by a campus hunger group.

15. LEGISLATIVE ALERT SYSTEM. Establish a system on campus for alerting students to upcoming state or national legislation on hunger issues. You will need, first, to contact a state or a national lobbying group that can notify you of fast-breaking legislation. Have the message directed to a telephone that is attended for certain hours each day, such as a campus ministry office or a member's work telephone. Then photocopy the message and place copies in the mailboxes of students who have expressed their willingness to call or write their elected leaders.

Additional Tips for Organizing on Campuses

Set regular meeting times and places. No time is perfect for everyone, but a set time is better than a variable one. Meeting once a week in a reserved room over lunch or supper is often good. Avoid meeting in classrooms — the classroom atmosphere is not conducive to good group dynamics.

Invite other Christian groups to work with you on specific projects. On some campuses, for example, the entire Fellowship of Christian Athletes has participated in fasts, CROP walks, and food delivery programs. Other specialized groups, such as the Christian Law Students' Fellowship, the Asian Christians' Fellowship, or the Black Students' Prayer Group, are also likely allies. Be sure to approach groups from across the denominational spectrum, e.g., the Wesley Foundation, the Newman Center, and the Baptist Student Union.

Contact the Inter-varsity chapter on your campus, also. During the last few years, Intervarsity groups have become increasingly active in hunger work. The chapters are encouraged to perform mission activities, so some groups are seeking projects. The Intervarsity chapter may be willing to assume joint responsibility for planning a fast, organizing a benefit, or handling part of some other project you would like to accomplish.

Take advantage of the presence on your campus of people from Third World nations. Invite them to be part of your group. Ask them to discuss the causes of hunger in their countries. Students from Third World countries have much to offer, but are rarely asked to share their experience.

Finally, never demean the size of your group. Campus hunger groups will rarely attain the popularity of tennis or aerobics. Nonetheless, a small core of people can affect a large college campus. Equally important, those involved in campus groups develop skills and gain experience which are used in later life. A high proportion of hunger organization staff members became involved in hunger work through a campus organization. Campus organizing is excellent training for future, long-term hunger work.

12. SPEAKING ON HUNGER

Are you nervous about speaking in public? If so, you are not alone. A recent survey found that many people fear public speaking more than death! Even experienced speakers get nervous, but they have learned to cope with their nervousness. Being prepared, mentally and vocally, and familiar with your group and your outline eliminates much of the discomfort of speaking before others. The remaining anxiety can be disguised by learning how to deal with the expressions of nervousness.

Mental Preparation

The key to public speaking is preparation. The most important preparation is mental preparation. Think through what you have to offer your audience. Try to develop a positive, constructive attitude toward your speaking. Finally, decide what you want to communicate to your audience and organize it carefully.

Few of us are famous celebrities. Few of us are "experts" on the issues we are discussing. Nonetheless, people want to hear us because we are concerned Christians who have found a way to express our faith in actions. They will listen because we can share our experiences and suggest ways to involve our friends and neighbors.

Developing a constructive attitude toward speaking makes it less frightening. If you think of presentations as "sharing yourself" rather than "showing yourself" you will feel less embarrassed and intimidated. Recognizing that everyone wants you to do well is also important. Think about when you have gone to hear a speaker, or an outsider has come to your group to speak. Haven't you always wanted hmr to do well? You want the presentation to be interesting and the person to do hsr best. Just as you hope the best for speakers, so others hope the best for you. Audiences want you to do well.

The other important part of developing a constructive attitude is spiritual. We should seek God's will for our work against hunger, and understand that God has promised to be with us when we speak on behalf of our brothers and sisters. Public speaking is much less threatening when we make ourselves vehicles for God's message rather than carrying the burden alone.

Group Preparation

Find out as much as you can ahead of time about the group to which you will speak. Usually the contact person who arranged for you to speak can tell you everything you need to know. S/he will be willing to talk with you about the group. The kinds of questions you might ask include:

- How many people should be expected? What is the racial mix and the male/female mix? What is the age range?

- Does the group meet together on a regular basis? Will people already know one another?

- What background do people have on the issues I will discuss?

- How would you describe the political orientation of the group? Are there particular concerns or questions that you know the group would like me to address?

- Are there special people in the group that you think I should know about ahead of time?

- What is the room like? Is there a blackboard or a screen?

● What would you like to see as an outcome from the presentation?

The answers to the first question help you visualize the group ahead of time and allow you to prepare the correct number of handouts and visual aids for the size of the group. You will also get some indication of how realistic the contact person's expectations are.

The answer to the second question helps you plan the beginning of your presentation. If the group is relatively small and people do not know one another, you should allow time for them to become acquainted. If the group is large, you still can plan for people to meet one another, but you will need to use another technique such as asking people to introduce themselves to the person sitting beside them.

Knowing the background of your group helps you determine the level of sophistication suitable for your speech. You can also find out about the audience's current activities against hunger, for which they can be commended. You should plan to speak at the level which will reach the majority of the people in the group. In most cases, this will be an introductory level. You can invite the more experienced people to offer additional thoughts as a means of involving them in material with which they are already familiar.

Knowing key concerns of a group helps you address their questions directly in your presentation. You might even want to say, "Ms. Jones, my contact, told me that this matter was a concern for many of you. I would like to address that question because I too feel it is important." This helps you focus your talk as well as prepare for issues that might be difficult to answer spontaneously.

The open-ended question about special people is important to ask. If a person in the group is unusually difficult, the contact person will often mention hmr in answer to this question. There are several benefits to knowing about a difficult person ahead of time. First, you can give extra attention in preparing for hsr concerns and how you might handle awkward situations. Second, when someone is difficult, it is reassuring to know that you are not causing the problem behavior. Knowing that others find a person difficult gives you confidence in handling disruptive behavior.

The other kind of person you want to know about is an expert in a related discipline, so you can draw on hsr knowledge when appropriate. For example, if someone in the audience works for a federal feeding program or volunteers in a soup kitchen you can ask hmr to answer technical questions about the program.

Finding out where you will be speaking helps you visualize the presentation. It gives you the opportunity to request certain equipment and, if necessary, a different room. Program planners frequently have unrealistic expectations. One of the main ways you will hear about these expectations will be in the answer to your question regarding the room.

Assume, for example, that you have been asked to speak about hunger in Central America on a week night at a church. It is not part of an ongoing program with a regular attendance. The contact person tells you, "You will be speaking in the main sanctuary of the church, because we are hoping a hundred people will come." Unless there is some recent media coverage of the issue, it is unlikely that a hundred people will attend. More likely, ten people will show up. Ten people would be great! But if the contact person is expecting a hundred, s/he — and the ten people rattling around in the sanctuary — will be disappointed. From your first conversation with the program planner, help hmr establish realistic goals and expectations. If for some reason, fifty or a hundred do show up, you can always move to a larger room.

The question about desired outcomes is designed to elicit the objectives for the presentation. If the contact person expresses an interest in seeing a group formed or additional volunteers for a hunger ministry, you can stress it in your presentation and use hsr interest as the action component of your presentation. Sometimes, you may hear a general response such as, "I'd like people to learn more." While learning more is good, it is not a measurable objective that you as an organizer want for your presentation. Based on your knowledge of a group, you should ask people to make specific responses.

An example of a realistic objective for a church group which has never been involved with hunger might be to form a six-week study group using materials you recommend. You could stress the importance of forming a group in your presentation. It would not be realistic to stress something like organizing a community-wide voter registration drive. While forming a study group might be realistic for a church group, it would not be reasonable for a ministerial association. More realistic objectives might be getting a hunger contact person in each church, or publicizing upcoming events in church bulletins. The contact person for the ministerial association can help you discern what is realistic to ask for and what is not.

Outline Preparation

With answers to these questions in mind, you are ready to prepare an outline. The outline gives focus and direction to your talk. It saves you from researching extraneous material and enables you to focus on the important issues. Begin by thinking through the purpose of your talk. Your purpose may differ somewhat from the purpose implied by the official title or topic supplied by your contact person. Your purpose in speaking is to involve people in hunger issues and empower them to take action. In addition, you want concrete, measurable results for your time with people. Thus as you prepare your outline, consider how you will convey your main purpose. Determine how you will inspire and empower people to become involved.

Be sure to work some success stories into your outline. Stories of how "ordinary people" have been able to make a difference are empowering. You might tell how a few calls or letters influenced a congressional vote, how a well-placed letter-to-the-editor affected a community problem, or even what motivated you to become involved in hunger issues. Think ahead about designing your outline to include true, motivating stories.

Your first outline should reflect your main purpose and contain four or five other important points. It should be simple and easy to use. I like to make a rough draft and then go back to fill in the specific points and illustrations. If I were asked to speak on hunger in the U.S., I would probably use a basic outline like this:

   I. Introduction

   II. Who is hungry in the U.S.?

   III. Why are people hungry?

   IV. How have concerned people made a difference?

   V. What can you do?

   VI. Closing

As you can see from the outline, at least half my talk would be concrete and action oriented. Sections IV and V would be full of examples, success stories, and opportunities for people to get involved.

If I were asked to speak on foreign aid, I would use a similar structure. At least half my presentation would be spent discussing how to influence foreign aid, recounting stories of people who have affected foreign aid legislation, and describing what people can do immediately about current foreign aid issues. I would meet the group's educational goal, and my goals as an organizer of empowering and inviting people to become involved.

Supporting the Main Points

Once I have developed the basic outline which I think will be empowering, I go back to work on supporting the main points. In doing so, I keep in mind several principles of public speaking.

PRINCIPLE I. Examples are better than statements. People will remember and understand examples and stories better than statements of fact. Each example or story should be true, unless it is clear to everyone that the story is a parable with a clear message. Logical points and complex arguments, delivered term-paper style, are dull.

PRINCIPLE II. Statistics are inherently boring. Use only statistics that are critical to your presentation and find ways to make those statistics come alive. For example, several years ago, I was asked to give a talk entitled "The Causes and Dimensions of World Hunger." I wanted to show that the national debt affected hunger in the U.S. and in Third World countries. At that time, the amount spent on servicing the national debt was about ten times the amount spent on the food stamp program. Therefore, instead of saying that the U.S. spends X billion dollars annually to service the debt which could be spent on the elimination of hunger, I said that the U.S. spends ten times the annual cost of the food stamp program just on servicing the debt each year. This comparison, which was easy to calculate, strengthened my point and was easy to understand.

PRINCIPLE III. Short is better than long. Audiences rarely mind if a speaker's presentation is a few minutes shorter than the allotted time. The same is not true about presentations that run too long. When in doubt, make your presentation shorter, not longer.

These three simple principles can aid you greatly in developing talks.

Starting and Ending the Presentation

Once you have your outline well developed, think carefully about the beginning and end of your presentation. People attending your talk will decide within the first few minutes whether they are really going to listen to you or not. Thus, it's important both to capture their attention and to gain their affection right away. There are a number of ways to achieve this.

Some people like to start a presentation with a joke. This is a good technique if you tell jokes well. However, if you are not good at telling jokes, *don't*. I can't tell prepared jokes, so it's far better for me to use other beginnings.

I prefer to share a personal experience that motivated me in some fashion or raised my awareness of hunger. These stories allow the audience to know a little bit about me as a person, making me more human. I try to share experiences which have been important for me or which will help illustrate the basic theme of my talk. The stories need not be monumental happenings. They do need to be stories with which people can identify.

Many personal experiences, at least many of mine, have some humorous elements to them. I have found I must be careful that the funny part of my story does not overshadow the main point. For example, one time I decided to begin a talk with a description of a visit I had made to a rural village to help weigh babies and vaccinate children. The vaccinations used were supplied by UNICEF, and Bread for the World had lobbied successfully for $25 million in additional UNICEF funding. I was trying to demonstate that the lobbying effort had produced tangible results.

However, at the beginning of the story, I briefly described the mule ride up to the village. I made a passing joke about preferring my car. At the end of the talk, a number of people commented that the mule-riding must really have been an experience. The way I had told the story, the mule ride was more interesting than the illustration that lobbying on foreign aid can benefit poor people. I have since reworked this story so the funny part does not obscure the main point.

A third way to begin a presentation is to use a theme sentence. The theme sentence can be repeated throughout the talk, and at the close to end the talk. Such a theme approach has the advantage of giving structure to your talk and helping to assure that people leave your talk knowing the main point. Art Simon, the executive director of Bread for the World, has an excellent presentation entitled "Hunger is a Public Policy Issue." He begins the talk with the title, which is his theme statement. At the end of each major point, he reiterates the theme statement. At the close of the talk, he again says, "Hunger is a public policy issue." It may sound very repetitive, but it is an effective presentation. As people leave the program, you hear them repeating the theme. People repeat it, and remember it.

If you want to use a theme approach, write a sentence which clearly states your point. You may want to use a quote or a statement you have read which succinctly, and perhaps poetically, captures what you want to say. This is particularly helpful when you are subject to pressing time constraints.

One time I was asked to fill in for someone who had become ill, and I only had a couple hours to prepare a talk on the "Causes and Dimensions of World Hunger." I remembered a phrase I had heard in a filmstrip, that "Hunger is an immense and complex issue, but to do nothing is to despair, and despair is unbelief." I used this as my theme sentence. It conveyed the point which I made in my talk that hunger is a complex issue, but it is also an issue which calls us to move beyond the complexities and try to do something about it. The theme gave me a good lead into talking about how our faith can sustain and motivate us for involvement over the long haul. I used the phrase at the beginning, at several transitional points in the body, and then again at the end of the talk.

The theme approach, although certainly not the most creative, is an easy way to begin a talk. Jot down good theme sentences when you hear or read them. It will save some searching when you need one.

Another way to begin a presentation is to ask some questions.

They can be rhetorical questions such as "How many of you have wondered how you could help hungry people?" Alternatively, they can be questions that you want the group to answer. If you are speaking with a large group, you will need to ask questions to which people can respond by raising their hands. In a small group, you can call on a few people to answer, or even go around the room and ask everyone to respond.

Questions for a large group might be:

- How many of you have given money for famine relief? (Ask people to raise their hands.)

- How many have ever written a letter to your member of Congress about any issue?

- How many have written to your member of Congress about a hunger issue?

The response to this set of questions will give you a sense of how involved your audience has been in hunger issues, and asking questions will capture their attention. The questions are also a good introduction to the connection between letter-writing and hunger issues. Similar sets of questions can be developed to open presentations on a wide range of hunger issues.

In small groups, I often begin by asking people to introduce themselves and answer one question. I select a question that relates to my topic and will elicit some information about people in the group. For example, if asked to speak with a small group about hunger in the U.S., I might ask people to tell me briefly how they became concerned about hunger in their community. The answers give me a sense of what experiences and backgrounds people have. In many cases I will identify people upon whom I can call during the presentation for specific examples or people who can assist in anwering questions at the end. After everyone else has answered the initial question, I answer it also and then continue with the rest of my presentation.

I would discourage you from beginning a talk by telling shocking stories or overwhelming people with statistics. Both techniques are used frequently in hunger presentations. Many speakers believe that shocking stories get people's attention. This may be true, but there are better ways to capture people's attention. It is very difficult to seem "human" and compassionate when you are trying to shock people. By telling shocking stories you imply that you are better or more concerned than others and they must be "shocked" into responding. Hunger activists also frequently begin a presentations by rattling off statistics on hunger such as "There are 500 million people living in absolute poverty and forty million children die each day of hunger and hunger related diseases." Such statistics, though true, are overwhelming and do not help people to understand the problems. They do not empower people in any way.

In addition, never begin by apologizing for your presentation. Nothing loses an audience's attention faster than starting a presentation with an apology about lack of preparation time or inexperience in public speaking. If you were asked to fill in at the last moment, express this in a positive way without apologizing. For example, you can say, "When Tom asked me last night to fill in for Maria Inez, I was honored. I am pleased to be with you today to share my experiences with the Downtown Food Bank." That asks everyone to make allowances for your short preparation time without apologizing.

Similarly, don't use an apology to communicate that it is your first time to speak in public. If you wish people to know it's your first time, try saying, "It's really good to be here with you today. This is my first opportunity to share with people about my experiences with the Downtown Food Bank. As you might imagine, I'm a bit nervous, but I'm so pleased to be able to talk with concerned people like you." Then smile and look at people!

The end of your presentation is almost as important as the beginning and you can use similar techniques. Close by telling a story, asking a rhetorical question, reading a poem, or repeating your theme. End firmly and with conviction. Memorize your closing few sentences so you can take your time, look slowly around the room, and make your closing statements. Sometimes speakers have trouble stopping. Have your ending memorized so you can stop when you are through.

Style is Important

Think back on a presentation you heard more than a year ago. What do you remember from it? Very likely, you don't remember much about the content. If you enjoyed the talk, you probably remember things like the warmth, enthusiasm and sincerity with which the person spoke. If you didn't like the talk, you may recall the person's argumentative or "superior" attitude. People are likely to remember the feelings you evoke when you speak long after they have forgotten the exact content of your speech. If people remember any specific content, it will probably be your stories or examples. Thus, in preparing for public speaking, you must give *at least as much* attention to style as to content.

What do hunger organizers want to convey in public speaking? I'd say we want to project honesty, sincerity, compassion, enthusiasm, and joy, and as Christians, we want to express our faith. We need not, nor should we try, to convey that we are particularly intelligent or that we are "experts" on hunger issues. Of course we should not try to hide our intelligence, but we needn't concentrate on displaying it either. Those who seek to demonstrate their intelligence usually end up doing just the opposite.

We are best able to convey the right "style" when the characteristics we wish to project are truly part of our lives. However, if they are to show, we must also take time to incorporate them into our presentations. Make sure your outline contains opportunities for you to share your joy and compassion with others. Find ways to fold your personal thoughts and feelings into your talk. Think about how you first became interested in hunger.

Recount that experience or another that was influential in cementing your commitment to hunger. Many of the suggestions covered under outline preparation contribute to the style desired. Telling stories and avoiding statistics, for example, will add warmth and humanness to your presentation.

Body language contributes to the overall impression people have of you. Be conscious of smiling, walking with confidence, extending your hands to greet people, and looking at people as often as possible when you speak. Feedback about body language is especially important because we are seldom aware of our own. Ask your friends for impressions and suggestions.

Question and answer times test our ability to project an open, warm style. Following the guidelines below will help you convey the desired style:

ALL QUESTIONS ARE GOOD QUESTIONS. You must believe this. If someone has a question, it is a good question. If the question conveys a lack of understanding, then be glad the person had the courage to ask the question and you have the opportunity to clear up the misunderstanding. If one person was willing to ask, others were probably wondering the same question. Even if you have heard the question many times before, convey to the person asking the question that you are glad the question was asked.

Of course, there are people who ask questions for reasons other than genuine interest. Regardless of why you think someone may be asking a question, always respond as if s/he were truly concerned about the answer to the question.

NEVER WING IT. If you do not know the answer to a question, say you don't know. Do not try and discuss a matter about which you are unsure. See if someone else in the group can answer the question. Otherwise tell the questioner that you will look up the answer and get back to hmr. If you promise to follow up, do so promptly.

IDENTIFY WITH WHAT YOU CAN. There is something you

can agree with in almost any question. If you can find the point of agreement, agree with it, and then go on to make additional points. For example, if asked "What about people cheating on food stamps?" respond "Yes, that's a problem. I am concerned about people cheating on food stamps because it means there is less money for those who need the program and it gives the program a bad reputation. According to the statistics, less than 2 percent of those who participate in the program in anyway misrepresent their need, and yet that small minority of people endangers the program for all those who really need it." If asked "doesn't U.S. foreign aid just prop up corrupt dictators?" answer "there definitely is some truth in what you are saying. Too much U.S. foreign aid has gone into the hands of people other than those who truly need it, and yet that's not the whole picture. Our goal as advocates is to identify the projects and programs which are helping poor people, support them, and find ways to redirect funds or reform other less effective forms of foreign aid." There is almost always something you can agree with. Do your best to identify it, but do not agree with something untrue.

ANSWER BRIEFLY. Most people do not want a lengthy response to a question. You need not feel you are answering an exam question that requires an exhaustive response. Frequently, people are as interested in finding out if you are open-minded as they are in the actual response. People who have not previously been involved in social justice issues sometimes perceive hunger speakers as dogmatic and not willing to admit problems; and sometimes they are correct. Answering succinctly and honestly, and freely admitting problems, will gain you credibility.

If someone pursues a question a couple times after you have responded, ask to talk with the person after the meeting. It is unfair to the rest of the group to allow one person's concerns to dominate the group's time. Politely ask, "These are really good questions, but I feel it's important to allow time for other questions. Could you and I talk some after the meeting?" Im-

mediately after the meeting, approach the person and ask if s/
he could stay around until you can greet people. If the person
cannot wait, arrange to meet another time. It is important not
to get tied up in one conversation immediately after your talk.
You need to allow others the chance to ask you quick questions,
and for you to seek out group members who seem like potential
leaders.

YOU ARE YOUR ORGANIZATION. If you are representing an
organization, anything you say becomes the organization's position. If you are asked for a position on an issue which the organization has not addressed, simply reply, "I'm sorry, but we do not
have a position on that issue." You may want to explain the
criteria used in choosing issues and the process used to take positions. Do not, under any circumstances, give your personal
opinion if the organization does not have a position. No matter
how you distinguish it, your position will be heard as the organization's.

RESPECT PEOPLE. Treat everyone with utmost courtesy. Go
out of your way to cover up for someone when s/he asks a question that could embarass hmr. Thank people for asking questions and listen intently to their concerns.

Each person who speaks develops hsr own style. Part of your
style will be a natural outgrowth of your personality. However,
a large part of what is called style can be developed. It is a conscious choice of subject material, method of presentation, and
delivery. Developing a style that conveys your values may take
some time, but it merits as much attention as developing the
content of your presentation.

Voice Preparation

Voice preparation for public speaking should begin as soon as
you think you might want to speak in public. Improving voice
and speech patterns takes time and practice. It cannot be accomplished overnight. If you are preparing a presentation

within the next few weeks, ignore voice preparation. Focus on the content and style of your presentation and return to work on your voice later.

I have observed two prevalent vocal problems about which every speaker should be warned. Among women the most common voice problem is talking in a high pitched, "little girl" voice. It sounds silly and does not project well. Women's voices lower a few steps about the same age as men's voices change. To discover the true pitch of your voice, relax your jaw and speak in a serious, but natural, tone of voice. This will probably be close to your natural speaking pitch. Each time you hear yourself raising the pitch, consciously lower it.

The most common voice problem among men is the tendency to growl in the throat rather than project sound through the front part of the face. The growling is uncomfortable and projects badly. To understand what it feels like to project the sound through your face, hoot like an owl or yell "yoo hoo" to someone across the street. Your nose should resonate. Try to match this resonant feeling when you speak.

Both men and women often need to work on breath control and projection. Practice taking deep breaths and exhaling slowly. Try these exercises:

- Stand up with your back to a wall. Make sure your shoulders touch the wall. Breathe slowly. This is how you should breathe for public speaking.

- Lie with your back on the floor. Place a book on your lower abdomen. Breathe slowly. This will help you build up muscles for speaking.

- Find a tree outside your window. Pretend you are speaking to it. Attempt to project your voice to the tree. Take a deep breath and begin counting, 1...2...3...etc., about one per second. Keep the flow of air even. Women should be able to reach thirty-five or forty on one breath. Men should be able to reach almost fifty. This is a very useful exercise in helping you conserve air for speaking. Beginning speakers often lose a great deal of air on the first part of a sentence, and the latter part becomes inaudible.

One of the hardest skills to develop is the ability to speak in complete sentences. Our minds are not accustomed to composing thoughts in complete sentences, and thus we must alter our pattern of thinking for public speaking. The best practice I have found was speaking my thoughts aloud, attempting to speak in complete sentences. Driving alone in a car is a great time to practice. For example, "Why is this light so long. I wish it would hurry up and change so I am not late for class. My teacher is displeased when I am late for class." Once you are in the habit of thinking and speaking in complete sentences alone, it is easier to do so in public. This exercise can also be used to help eliminate "ums" and "ahs." Consciously speak sentences without these additional sounds, pausing in silence.

Dealing with Nerves

All public speakers have experienced nervousness. Most continue to experience some nervousness, although less than when they first began speaking publicly. It is unrealistic to think you will completely eliminate nervousness. Learning how to disguise and diminish your nervousness is achievable.

One of the first ways to deal with nervousness is through mental preparation, as described at the beginning of the chapter. Thinking through what you have to offer and recognizing that you do not have to be an expert is reassuring. The goal in speaking about hunger is not to give a polished speech, although you may do that. Rather, the goal is to involve more people in actions to end hunger. Eliminating a few "ums" and "ahs" is far less important than seeking ways to motivate and empower people. Understanding your goals in public speaking makes it less intimidating.

Prayer is effective in calming nerves. Pray ahead of time for guidance on the content and direction of the talk. A few seconds before you begin a talk, say a silent prayer. If you are at a podium, you can look down at your notes. People will assume you are collecting your thoughts. God supported Moses and the prophets when they were nervous about speaking, and has promised to be with us when we speak.

Unfortunately, even with good mental preparation, and a strong prayer life, most of us still have visible signs of nervousness. So what can we do? In general, we must prepare for nervousness. Prepare for whatever is your greatest fear.

Select a system for notes with which you are comfortable. If you like your notes in sketchy outline form, prepare them that way. If you like a detailed outline, do that. If you want to write out the entire talk, you can do that. However, you should practice enough that you do not have to read the talk. Underline key phrases with a bright colored pen so you can locate your place quickly. Practice delivering the talk out loud and in front of a mirror. It is especially important to practice aloud because written sentences may be too long for a spoken presentation.

If you find that your body tenses, you may want to visit the restroom and do some relaxation exercises. Avoid strenuous exercises that will make you sweat. Sticking your tongue out as far as it goes helps relax jaw and face muscles, which are likely to be the first to tighten. Rotating your head in circles is good for neck muscles.

I practice deep breathing before a presentation. I breath in on the count of ten, and out on the count of ten. This is an excellent exercise when people are able to watch you. The breathing occupies your mind so you think less about your fear. You look the essence of calmness since no one can tell what you are doing. The other advantage with deep breathing is that it sets a pattern of inhaling enough air. Too often, when speakers are nervous, they take quick shallow breaths. They don't take enough air to think or project. Good breathing helps you project and think.

If time permits, it is calming to test out the place from which you will be speaking. Stand at the podium, place your notecards in the place you expect to put them, try the microphone, and get a general feel for the room. Talking to people in the audience before a presentation is also helpful. Wander around and talk to whomever you can find. Talking with people makes the audience more human and less like an unfriendly crowd.

Most of us have nervous habits. I chew on pens or rattle things in my pockets. Therefore, whenever I get up to speak, I make sure that I am not holding a pen and that my pockets are empty. Otherwise, these habits take over without me knowing. If your hands shake, make sure you have a place to set your notes. If your knees knock, try to speak behind a full length podium. If your mouth goes dry, have water handy. Completely eliminating nervous habits is very difficult. It's far easier to prepare for the nervousness and disguise it as best you can.

Instant In Season and Out

The Apostle Paul wrote in II Timothy about being "instant in season and out." He is talking about being ready at any moment for whatever happens. Like the Apostle Paul, we can begin preparing ourselves for unexpected speaking opportunities by jotting down ideas and stories you think would be good in a talk. Clip articles that tell interesting stories or give useful data. I have a simple system for clippings and ideas using four manila envelopes, categorized by domestic hunger, international hunger, advocacy, and other ideas. Develop a system that works for you.

Instant in season and out applies not only to saving ideas for speaking, but to our entire outlook on public speaking. Who would have thought that God would have called Paul to reach out to the Jewish community and spread the Gospel? And yet, God called and used Paul. You may not feel called to speak and yet there may be times when you are asked to do so. Know that God will be with you as you speak about hunger in our world.

13. FORMING A SPEAKERS' BUREAU

Forming a speakers' bureau is a good way to communicate your concern about hunger to the community at large. A speakers' bureau is a publicized group of people who offer presentations on specific topics. A speakers' bureau on hunger provides the community with easy access to people who can speak and lead programs on hunger.

You do not need a large group of people to form a speakers' bureau. Most small groups of people, if properly trained, can organize and maintain an effective speakers' bureau. Forming a speakers' bureau is often an educational and community-building project for a small group to undertake.

Getting Started

The first thing you should determine is the target audience for your speakers' bureau. Do you want to speak with community church groups, or with Presbyterian churches throughout the synod, Catholic churches in the diocese, or both religious and secular groups? Focusing on a particular audience helps you tailor your presentations and direct your publicity efforts.

Once you have decided on your target audience, you can begin thinking about the kinds of presentations you want to offer. The most important determinants are what presentations are most needed and which are the most likely to be requested by your target groups. In most cases, you will find that basic, introductory presentations are the most popular.

You will also want to assess the expertise available in your group. For example, does someone in your group have particular experience or knowledge of Africa, or of agricultural issues? If so, consider offering more specialized programs using their expertise. You can also draw on people in the community who are not part of your hunger group if they are willing to participate in your speakers' bureau. You will, however, want to make sure that outside speakers will use some of their presentation time to involve people, and not simply to give a technically good presentation.

Compile a list of presentations that the group thinks are the most important. Narrow the list down to a handful of presentations. You only need two or three basic presentations in order to publicize your speakers' bureau. Offering others is fine as long as you stress the presentations your group feels are most important. Some of the basic presentations other speakers' bureaus have chosen to offer include:

- The Biblical Basics on Hunger

- The Causes of World Hunger

- Hunger and Public Policy

- Christians and Hunger

- Hunger in the U.S.A.

- An Introduction to Bread for the World

- The Presbyterian Hunger Program (or other denominational hunger programs).

You may want to include some of these topics among your initial set of presentations.

Training Speakers

Once your group has selected the main presentations, you

should set up a speaker training series. This will enable all your speakers to feel adequately prepared when they travel about with their presentations. First ask people in your group to suggest topics they would like covered in a training program. Next, draft a training program outline. Ask the group to look at it and see if it meets their needs. Make revisions as needed.

Bringing an outside trainer in to help with the initial sessions is often beneficial. You probably will be able to find someone who will work with you free of charge. Possibly the group can identify someone who makes effective presentations on hunger concerns. (S/he may not teach public speaking, but is quite proficient.) Ask that person to work with you. Most good speakers enjoy helping others improve their speaking ability.

The ideal trainer has spoken on hunger issues. If your group doesn't know such a person, the second best choice is someone who teaches speech at a local college or university. If you explain what your group is doing, and that you have limited finances, you can usually find someone willing to work with you without charge.

A typical training program will meet four to eight times during a one or two month period. Each meeting should last approximately one and a half to two hours. It is possible to shorten the training program into fewer sessions, perhaps on several Saturday mornings, although it is not advised. Be sure to allow enough time for each person to practice hsr presentation before the entire group.

A typical training program might consist of the following sessions:

Session I   *Introduction to Public Speaking*
              A general presentation by the trainer
              which deals with style, nervousness,
              and generalprogram objectives.

Session II *Designing an Outline*
This session should help each person prepare the outlines for hsr presentations.

Session III *Working with Videotape*
Each person comes with a five minute presentation prepared to be videotaped. This videotaping helps people see themselves as others do.

Session IV *Answering Questions*
An entire session is spent answering difficult questions that are likely to arise.

Session V *Sharing Presentations*
Each person or group should share their presentations. If time permits, over a series of weeks, listen through all the presentations. At the end, give feedback, both positive and negative, to encourage and help the presenter.

The tone of the training time should be supportive and encouraging. Most people are much better speakers than they think they are. An important facet of the training therefore is building confidence.

The outline provided above allocates an entire session to videotaping. Video cameras are excellent training tools. Many churches have the videotape players, but not the cameras. You may be able to borrow one from a friend or a local school. If not, they can be rented. Ideally, each person will have a chance to work with the video camera and screen on hsr own. (This may require someone to show people how to use the equipment.)

Practicing an entire presentation on videotape, and watching it several times, is extremely helpful and will be worth the extra effort required to obtain the equipment.

Using Audiovisual Resources

A speakers' bureau need not offer only spoken presentations. It can also offer special programs that use selected audiovisual resources. These resources can be a major part of certain programs and should be listed in your brochure.

You should test any audiovisual materials you may use. A number of sources from which to rent or purchase audiovisual resources are listed in Appendix B. Once you've selected the resources, make sure that they are readily available to your bureau. You may want to purchase some of them. Perhaps you can get a denominational office or church library to purchase a few of the more expensive ones and allow you to use them.

Since most speakers' bureaus are asked to provide one to one-and-a-half hour presentations, audiovisual resources can add variety and provide a break (for speakers and listeners alike) in a primarily verbal session. Many audiovisual resources last between ten and thirty minutes. Adequate time is thus available for a brief spoken presentation and discussion following the audiovisual materials.

The number and variety of audiovisual resources available to hunger groups has increased dramatically in the last few years. In addition, many churches have invested in audiovisual equipment, makng it more readily available to hunger groups.

Videotapes have become popular recently because they are inexpensive to purchase and reproduce, and videotape players are widely available. Unless you can use several monitors or a large screen, however, they are only effective for small groups. Suitable videotapes are available from hunger organizations. In addition, you may be able to tape hunger-related television programs.

Films are excellent to use, but they are usually expensive. Churches and civic groups are also less likely to have a film projector than they are a video machine or a filmstrip projector. Nonetheless, if your denominational resource service can provide you with a film projector and films, by all means review and use films.

Filmstrips are good, functional audiovisual resources. Most filmstrips come with accompanying tape cassettes. Although filmstrips never move quite as quickly as films, they are more widely used because they are inexpensive to purchase and filmstrip projectors and tape recorders are widely available. There is a large selection of filmstrips available on hunger. If you expect to use one often, it's best to purchase your own copy.

Slide shows can also enhance your presentation. Like filmstrips, projection equipment is widely available. Prepared slide shows on hunger, however, are less available than filmstrips or films. Slide shows are the easiest type of audiovisual resources to prepare yourself. Taking pictures and reproducing slides is a fairly expensive proposition. Thus, if you plan to prepare your own slide show, estimate the costs carefully before you begin.

Slides are available from three main sources. First, check your personal slide collection, and travel about your hometown looking for new pictures. Using pictures of local people and local feeding programs is especially effective when discussing hunger in the United States. Be sensitive to people's need for privacy and dignity when taking these pictures. Your friends' slides are your second source. You may know someone who has travelled to a Third World country. Ask that person if you can review hsr slides and make copies. Finally, some large agencies have slides which can be purchased. Several such agencies and the person to write are listed below:

Clyde McNair, Photo File, Room 4889NS, *Agency for International Development,* Washington, D.C. 20523.

(Borrowers must visit the office in Washington, D.C. Write or call (202) 647-4330 to schedule an appointment.)

Marina Gruenman, Communications, *Catholic Relief Services,* 1011 First Avenue, New York, NY 10022.

FAO Information Office, 1001 22nd Street, N.W., Washington, D.C. 20437.

Photo and Exhibit Service, *UNICEF,* 866 UN Plaza, New York, NY 10017.

Photography Division, Office of Information, OGPA, Room 4407 South Building, *U.S. Department of Agriculture,* Washington, D.C. 20250.

Developing a slide show can be great fun. You can find pictures to explain your basic message, or you can use a slide show to set a certain tone. Some of the most effective slide shows are short "mood setters" showing scenes of people from around the world. They are usually offered with taped background music, and are presented during the first five to seven minutes of a program. Such presentations help people leave behind their day to day concerns and begin focusing on other people.

Overhead projectors are helpful in many presentations. They are particularly useful for explaining technical issues, such as foreign aid. You can place facts and figures on a wall so everyone can look at them together. Some churches and most schools have overhead projectors. Most of the older overheads are big, heavy machines; however, there are several new portable overheads which are quite easy to use. The real plus of using overhead projectors is the ease of preparing overhead transparencies. You can write directly on the transparency with special felt tip markers. If you don't like what you've done, you can erase it. Using a normal photocopying machine, you can copy a chart or graph onto a transparency for use with an overhead projector. Transparencies can be purchased in office supply stores. I have used overhead projectors to show sample letters to members of Congress, charts on U.S. foreign aid, and outlines of the main points to a presentation.

The last audiovisual resource I'd like to mention is audiotapes, used with a simple tape recorder. I would strongly advise against using audiotapes for a group presentation. Audiotapes are excellent for individual use, but are poorly received by groups.

Team Approaches

Team approaches to public speaking are fun and can be very effective. Instead of having one person assigned to a topic, have two, or at most three people. Each person should be responsible for a specific piece of the program. If possible, teams should be as diverse as possible — an older and younger person, a white and black person, a man and a woman — to appeal to a wider audience and to express different perspectives.

Teams are especially good for new speakers. Novice speakers can be paired with more experienced speakers, allowing the newcomers to overcome their initial anxiety and gain experience in a supportive environment.

Team speaking is enjoyable, but not quite as easy as it sounds. Each person has to clearly define the section for which s/he is responsible. The people on the teams must be careful not to interrupt one another. There is always the tendency for team members to correct one another during a presentation. This makes team members appear competitive. The other tendency is to amplify what the other person has said. This makes the presentation longer than it should be and boring. Teams must be especially careful not to add too many details to another team member's response to a question.

The fun part of teams is being able to help one another handle difficult questions, and comparing notes after the presentation. What seems like a difficult question for one person on the team may be quite simple for the other person. Sharing questions comfortably puts a group at ease.

Setting aside time after the meeting to critique one another will improve everyone's speaking and group skills. Analyze carefully what worked and what didn't. Make changes as needed. Be careful to give the person talking your complete attention, even if you are occasionally jotting things down to mention after the meeting.

Publicizing the Speakers' Bureau

Technically, you can begin preparing your publicity materials as soon as you decide on your target audience, but it is probably better to wait until you are well into your training and sure about the kinds of presentations your group is able to offer.

Most groups design a speakers' bureau brochure. These are relatively easy to prepare and not too expensive to get printed. Perhaps an artistic person in your group or a friend might be willing to help put it together. The simplest form of a speakers' bureau brochure is printed on 8 1/2 by 11 inch paper folded into thirds. The front cover says something about the speakers bureau, such as "Des Moines Speakers Bureau on Hunger and Poverty . . . programs and presentations for churches in the Des Moines metropolitan area." It's also nice to have some sort of graphic on the front. The inside of the brochure should describe the kinds of programs and presentations you can offer. The back of the brochure should list a name and phone number to call to schedule programs.

The person listed on the brochure should be easy to reach, or should have an answering machine. Some people may prefer to assume responsibility for scheduling rather than giving presentations. This is great, providing the person who coordinates speakers and requests is extremely dependable. There is nothing worse than a group requesting a speaker and having no one return their call.

Once the layout of the brochure is completed, it should be printed on some attractively colored paper. You may be able to get a discount with a printing company if you explain the purpose of your group. It's probably worth spending a few extra dollars to print the brochure on a sturdy paper stock. You should print two to three times as many brochures as you know where to send them. Thus, if you know you will mail to a list of 100 churches, and each bureau member wants a few brochures, bringing your total to 150 brochures, you should probably order between 300 and 450. It is much cheaper to order enough brochures the first time rather than to reorder. Of course, you don't want to have too many extra brochures stacked up everywhere.

Mail or hand-deliver the brochure to the groups you wish to contact. If possible, send the brochure to a specific person in the group, rather than to the group or church in general. In some cases you may want to mail more than one brochure, such as to the priest and the social concerns chairperson of a church.

Wait for a few weeks after you send the brochure to see what kind of response you elicit. If you receive fewer calls than you would like (or no calls), begin step two of your publicity plan. Step two is always calling churches and groups to which you sent your brochure. Ask them if they received the brochure and if they would be interested in scheduling a presentation. Quite often you will find that people have misplaced the brochure and you will need to send them another one. Also, they will need to check with other people about arranging a program. Offer to call them back within a specified period of time.

Step three of your publicity plan should be to get the speakers' bureau listed in various publications and announced on radio stations. The easiest way to do this is to send a news release to publications and stations you think might be interested. See the chapter on using the media for guidelines on preparing a news release.

It's important to proceed with the publicity in stages. You don't want to find yourself overwhelmed with speaking requests. If your group finds you have enough requests, slow down on your publicity for a while.

Sometimes the timing of your publicity efforts affects the number of requests you receive. You may want to send your brochure out more than once, gearing each mailing to different events or seasons. For example, you might want to send the brochure out in January suggesting Lenten programs, or in May suggesting summer programs. Such targeting can be done easily with a cover letter. Don't worry about sending out the brochure more than once during a year. The brochure may mean nothing the first time someone gets it, but may be exactly what s/he is looking for the second time.

Recordkeeping

At the outset you need to establish accurate recordkeeping systems for speaker requests, publicity calls, and presentation results. I suggest you create a form for each to be used by all group members. For example, you will want a form to record speaker requests. It will help the person coordinating requests to get all the necessary information the first time. The form can then be passed to the person who will give the presentation. An example request is shown below.

SPEAKER REQUEST FORM

Name _____   Home Phone: _____
Address _____   Work Phone: _____
_____   Best Time to call: _____
Date Request Received: _____
Group Requesting Presentation: _____
Subject/Type of Presentation: _____
Preferred Day and Time: _____
Alternate Day and Time: _____
Estimated Size of Group: _____
Date Confirmation Needed: _____

You may want to add the questions discussed in Chapter Twelve that the speaker, not the coordinator, should ask the contact person. By listing the questions, the speaker will have an easier time remembering them all.

A publicity call form is also important. It will help you keep track of who was called and the response. The form should reduce duplicative work and assist in timely follow-up. It should look something like the following:

SPEAKERS' BUREAU OUTREACH CALL FORM

Name of Group/Church: _____

Person Called: _____ Phone Number: _____

Please Indicate the Response:

___ Not interested (ever)

___ Not interested right now. Please
call back in _____

___ S/he is not the right person to talk with. Call: _____
at these phone numbers: (H) _____ (W) _____

___ Quite interested. Will need to check with others, so please
call back on the following day: _____

___ Didn't see the brochure. Please send another to this
address: _____

___ Wants to request a speaker. Please fill out the speaker
request form.

___ Other. Please describe. _____

Caller's Name _____ Date of Call _____

Keeping track of those who wish to be called within a few weeks to confirm a date, or at the beginning of the next year or semester is very important. Without good recordkeeping, those follow-up calls don't happen, and good speaking opportunities are missed.

The third important form records what happened at each presentation. This is extremely useful information if a group requests more than one presentation.

MEETING REPORT FORM

Name of Group: _____ Date of Meeting: _____
Name of Contact Person for the Group: _____
Address of Contact Person: _____
_____

Phone Numbers for Contact Person: (H) _____ (W) _____

General Description of the Meeting

Outcomes/New Potential Leaders/Commitments

Needed Followup (check off when completed)

Your Name: _____
Phone Number: _____

Please attach all relevant publicity materials, participant lists, or other background documents.

The forms may seem cumbersome at first, but they help organize material and notes which you probably have elsewhere — on little scraps of paper, if you're like me! Such records enable new speakers to know what has occurred at previous sessions, and helps earlier speakers refresh their memories.

Does the process for setting up a speakers' bureau sound too easy? Well, it really is easy. It's primarily a means for formalizing your presentations and letting people in the community know of your whereabouts. Basic presentations, such as Christians and Hunger, and Hunger and Public Policy, are generally the most requested, and certainly the most needed in our community. By advertising your availability, you encourage people to plan programs on hunger. That in itself is a community service.

Before I close this chapter, I want to add one word of caution. Occasionally someone requests a very technical presentation which is not listed on your brochure. Unless a bureau member is skilled in that particular area, suggest that the person check elsewhere for a speaker or consider having one of your prepared presentations. It is tempting to agree to prepare the presentation. This could well require an enormous amount of preparation, and it may not be worth it. Quite often when a very technical presentation is requested, the contact person, not the whole group, is interested in the topic. Thus, one goes to all the trouble of preparing a complicated presentation, and it's not of interest or suitable for the whole group. On the other hand, if the entire group is interested in a very technical subject, the presenter is likely to get in way over hsr head unless s/he is already knowledgeable on the subject. It is perfectly fine to explain what presentations the speakers' bureau has to offer and decline other invitations.

14. DESIGNING A WORKSHOP

As a hunger leader you may be frequently asked to lead a workshop on a specific hunger issue or aspect of organizing. A workshop is a training session, usually one to two hours in length, that provides information, tools, empowerment, motivation about the workshop topic, and some direction on how to use the information or skills learned in the workshop. If you approach the workshop creatively, it can be fun — for you to design and lead and for others to attend.

First, find out how much time is allotted for the workshop. To a large extent the length of time will determine what can be done. In general, the longer the workshop time, the more creative and enjoyable the workshop can be. The average workshop time is one-and-a-quarter to one-and-a-half hours. That is the workshop length upon which this chapter is focused. If your workshop length is significantly more or less, you will need to adapt your outline.

Think about the purpose of your workshop. It should *not* be to impart everything you know of the workshop topic. If you are convinced of this fact, you will not feel obligated to overload the workshop with information. Overwhelming people with information is the most common problem of workshops. Sharing information is only part of the purpose of a workshop. You should offer an overview or framework for understanding the issue, encourage and empower people to learn more about it, and give them some concrete tools for developing their skills and understanding.

The overview of the issue should be clear and simple. Participants should leave the workshops able to recite the main points. You may want to introduce the main points at the beginning of the workshop and reiterate them again at the end. There should be no more than four or five major points, and fewer is fine.

The empowerment aspect of a workshop is fundamental. People leaving a workshop should feel that they could thoroughly understand the issue if they devoted some study time to it. Hunger issues are complex, but workshops should build people's confidence about their own ability to understand and study the issues, and provide them with a framework for organizing their thoughts.

Often, workshop presenters seem more concerned with impressing the participants with their intelligence than helping them understand and approach an issue. If workshop participants leave saying, "Wow, is s/he smart. I could never learn that," the workshop presenter has not done a good job. The workshop leader must make complex issues comprehensible.

If a workshop leader does not empower people to learn more, their knowledge on the subject will end when the workshop ends. Regardless of how erudite a workshop leader may be, what s/he communicates in an hour or two is limited. Therefore, the workshop leader must empower and enable people to explore the subject further on their own. The majority of people need greater confidence in their ability to grasp complicated issues. The workshop leader's job is to develop that confidence.

The same principles hold true for developing organizing skills. It may be entertaining for a workshop leader to demonstrate that s/he is a great public speaker or adept at using the media, but it is more important for hmr to enable others to speak or influence the media. Empowerment builds a movement. Information alone does not.

The workshop leader must provide the participants with concrete tools so they can study an issue or develop a skill that will help them grow. The framework for understanding the workshop topic or solving the organizing problem is the most basic of these tools. Concrete tools also include further study resources, quickie dictionaries, and handy guides for busy people. Concrete tools help people progress from the knowledge base they have at the end of a workshop to a more thorough grasp of the subject. Concrete tools help participants develop after the workshop is over.

With these overall purposes in mind, let me suggest several rules for developing workshops.

1. DO NOT LECTURE. Workshops are not lectures. Don't treat them as such. The presenter may be able to impart more information by lecturing than by other means. Nonetheless, the participants do not learn more. Information overload is not empowering. It is overwhelming. When in doubt, less lecturing is better than more.

2. PROVIDE STRUCTURE. I have sometimes seen workshop leaders seemingly abdicate all responsibility for directing the session in their efforts to avoid lecturing. They enter the workshop without a formal outline saying that they are going to "let the group share information" on the issue or skill. This approach rarely works. Considerable knowledge and experience reside within any workshop group, but it is not best used in a meandering group discussion. Sharing partial understandings does not provide an overview, empower, or supply concrete tools. Workshops require the same amount of intense preparation that formal presentations do. The workshop leader must provide a structure and format for drawing out the group's knowledge and experience in a way that achieves the purposes of the workshop.

3. BE CREATIVE. Designing a workshop can be an enormously creative endeavor. The length and format are ideal for trying new methods of nonformal education. Being creative is risky. A new "creative" workshop may not work completely. That's fine, but try it. The experience should improve your next workshop. The best workshops I've lead or participated in have been creative. They are fun to be a part of and fun to design.

4. USE VISUALS. Visual aids are often difficult to use in a for-

mal presentation. They always can be used in workshops. Educators tell us we learn more when we both *hear* and *see* something. Take advantage of the ability for people in a workshop to see things. Put information on flipcharts or chalkboards. Write your main points on transparencies and project them onto the wall using an overhead projector. Place posters reinforcing your main points around on the walls.

Audiovisual resources are good for workshops. Films, filmstrips, and slide shows all offer hearing and seeing opportunities. Obviously, not all audiovisual resources are good. Choose carefully the resources you show in workshops.

Unless the audiovisual resource is one that you have personally designed and cannot be rented, people will not want the workshop to consist solely of the audiovisual resource. People will feel that they could have watched or listened to the material on their own time. I recommend using an audiovisual resource *to supplement* the workshop, rather than *to be* the workshop.

5. MAKE IT "HANDS-ON." If at all possible, find ways to make the workshop a "hands-on" experience. We learn more by hearing and seeing. We learn the most by hearing, seeing, *and doing.* Is there a way to allow people to do something as part of the workshop that will help them learn the issue or skill? It requires creativity to make a workshop a "hands-on" experience, but it's worth it if people can learn more and be empowered.

6. MEET PARTICIPANTS' NEEDS. Different participants are helped most by different kinds of information and experiences. Thus, you must find out as much as possible about the people who will participate in the workshop. For example, if the workshop topic is on organizing a group and you find out that most participants will be college students, you should focus on organizing a group on a college campus.

7. OFFER HOPE. There is nothing worse than a workshop which leaves people feeling hopeless. Many hunger related issues are very bleak, but you can focus on the areas where people

can and are making a difference and less on the areas that seem hopeless. Highlight the facets of the topic which offer hope for the future.

Any workshop you lead needs an outline. Think carefully about your purposes, main points, and ideas for creative learning experiences, and organize them into an outline. The following is the kind of outline you should begin working with:

Generic Workshop Outline

I. *Overview* — a lecture (fifteen minutes)

II. *Discussion* — all participants involved in questions and responses (fifteen minutes)

III. *Learning Activity* — all participate in the "hands-on" learning experience (thirty minutes)

IV. *Discussion* — all participants discuss the activity (fifteen minutes)

V. *Conclusion* — a lecture summarizing the main points and suggesting resources for further involvement and study (fifteen minutes)

The following are some ideas you can use in workshops to make them more creative and "hands-on." The suggested exercises and roleplays should meet the basic purposes of your workshop and help you target one or two of the main points. You can expand on these ideas or use them to spark your own ideas.

"Hands-On" Ideas for Issue Workshops

A. HUNGER IN THE U.S.A. If your workshop is designed to help participants understand the many problems low-income people face, you might design a role-playing exercise of a person trying to obtain and use food stamps. Be sure to include the food stamp caseworker, the cashier at the grocery store, and the person making condescending comments in the grocery store checkout line. This exercise could be used to explain the eligibility requirements and the process for applying for food stamps or the workings of the food stamp program.

Another approach would be to assign each workshop participant to a low-income person's actual situation in which the person's poverty causes hmr to go hungry at times. Ask the group to discuss the person's options. Particularly poignant are examples of single heads of households who work, but remain poor because of high childcare, rent, and transportation costs. This exercise demonstrates that poverty is the major cause of hunger.

If you want participants to understand the tradeoffs between food and other necessities, assign each workshop participant a family. Describe each family's income, family size and ages, and special situations on index cards or separate sheets of paper. Give workshop participants a copy of the newspaper and ask them to find places to live, jobs, and childcare given their family's income. Ask them to make family budgets based on the information they received. At the end of the allotted time, ask participants where the family would live, where they would shop, and how they would handle unexpected financial obligations.

Another simple experience that helps people understand more about food stamps is to ask each participant to fill out a food stamp application form and determine if s/he is eligible. People generally have a greater appreciation of the complexity of the forms and documentation required after completing one.

If time permits, another way to illuminate a federal food program is to visit a WIC clinic or a food stamp office. Talk with both clients and program administrators. Ensure time for debriefing and group discussion after the visit. Depending on where you are located, it may also be possible to visit a migrant camp, Indian reservation, soup kitchen, or other place where workshop participants might have a direct experience with low-income people. These on-site visits must be carefully arranged to avoid paternalism. Make sure that workshop participants have a chance to interact directly, and as equals, with program recipients.

The workshop ideas listed above are recommended for middle- and upper-income people who have limited experience with hunger and poverty in the U.S. Many of the exercises help participants understand the frustrations and problems that low-income people face. The models are not appropriate for low-income people who are well aware of the problems, or those with extensive experience with hunger in the U.S.A. As a workshop leader, you must assess the composition of the participants, before using one of these exercises.

B. U.S. AGRICULTURE POLICY. If your workshop concerns agricultural policy, you may want to design your learning activity to explain the political forces that shape U.S. agriculture policy. Design a role-playing exercise of the markup of the Farm Bill. ("Markup" occurs when a bill is revised in committee.) Assign roles similar to those on either the Agriculture Committee in the Senate or the House of Representatives. For example, someone can be Jesse Helms. Give people some background information about their options as legislators and ask them to mark up the bill. Discuss the exercise, identifying the various interests that affect the legislators' decisions.

C. INTRODUCTION TO WORLD HUNGER. If you want to give people an overview of the key issues they need to understand, consider giving a multiple choice quiz on hunger facts at the beginning of the workshop (see Illustration 1). Follow up the quiz with a discussion of why those facts have occurred. Do not ask people to reveal their answers. Use the quiz to focus participants' attention and give structure to a difficult topic.

An introduction to world hunger is a difficult workshop to lead creatively, because the subject matter is so broad and the purposes of the workshop are difficult to identify. I recommend using an introductory film or filmstrip to assist with this workshop if the time is too short for the "quiz" approach.

D. TAX POLICY AND HUNGER. If your workshop explores the relationship between tax policy and hunger, assign each person to an income situation and ask hmr to fill out a mock tax form. Using selected scenarios, demonstrate the relationship between taxes and poverty. You can also easily demonstrate the inequities in the tax system using alternate scenarios.

E. DEBT AND TRADE. If you want to help a group understand the importance of debt and trade issues to hunger, gather basic balance of payment and trade information on a Third World country. Provide some additional data about the country such as the population, gross national product, and type of government. Divide the workshop participants into three groups. Group one is international bankers from the International Monetary Fund. Group two is governmental representatives of the country. Group three is poor people who live in rural parts of the country. Ask each group to design three or four steps of a trade and debt plan for the country. Ask all workshop participants to approach the planning as their respective groups would. Discuss the different results.

F. FOREIGN AID. One learning activity frequently used by Bread for the World staff to explain U.S. foreign aid is to make small placards with the names of the parts of a foreign aid chart written on them. Each participant is asked to choose one or two placards randomly. The placards are then used to build a chart of foreign aid (see Illustration 2). Building the chart helps people remember the various parts of foreign aid. This is a good technique if the main purpose of the workshop is to provide an overview of the composition of foreign aid.

If you wish to demonstrate the predominance of military and

security related aid in U.S. foreign aid to Third World countries, select and examine aid to one particular country. Provide participants with actual background data on a Third World nation, such as Pakistan, including general economic information, and a description of potentially hostile neighbors. Tell participants the total amount of bilateral U.S. aid which is given to the country. Ask each participant or small groups of participants to allocate that total amount between categories of aid such as food aid, agricultural assistance, general economic support, and military aid. The participants will need to understand or be given brief explanations about the types of aid which can be offered. Compare the allocations made by participants with the actual allocation from the U.S. government.

"Hands-On" Ideas for Skills Workshops

A. PUBLIC SPEAKING. In a workshop intended to help participants develop public speaking skills — do it! Use the workshop time to have each person write and deliver a brief presentation. If time permits and the group is small, videotape each presentation and let the speaker watch it. Most people have never seen themselves on videotape. Many people remark, "I didn't sound as dumb as I thought." Frequently people realize how serious they look and are encouraged to smile more and tell more stories. Others discover distracting habits that the group can help them find ways to hide or overcome.

B. USING THE MEDIA. Like public speaking, the main purpose of many media workshops is to overcome people's fear of the media. There are a number of confidence-building learning activities for use in a media workshop. Consider role-playing an interview by a reporter. Divide people into pairs, with one being the reporter and the other being the interviewee. Give the reporters sample questions to ask. Make sure each participant gets a chance to be interviewed.

If the workshop centers on writing a news release, have participants write one. Distribute model news releases which can be used as a pattern. Ask each person to select a topic and then help hmr write a news release about it.

If letters-to-the-editor are the workshop's main focus, bring some outrageous articles written on hunger issues. Divide the participants into groups of two or three and allow them ten minutes to draft responses to the articles in the form of letters-to-the-editor. Discuss the resulting letters.

C. LOBBYING ELECTED LEADERS/LEGISLATIVE PROCESS. Most workshops on lobbying elected leaders are intended to explain how the legislative process works, and how to lobby elected leaders, given that process. One logical learning activity in such a workshop is to have participants "act out" a bill going through Congress. One person is the "bill" which goes from subcommittee to committee to rules committee to the floor and so forth. Different people act as subcommittee members and the other parts. Although this sounds silly, people enjoy it, and they remember the process better than if it had been presented in a lecture. The legislative process can be a very dull subject!

Don Reeves, a hunger activist in Nebraska, leads an excellent lobbying workshop for people who have some experience with lobbying. He distributes a form that looks as follows:

1. I am (name) _____, (description in ten words or less) _____
_____,
(from) _____

2. My representative in the Nebraska legislature is
_____. She (he) serves on the _____
_____, and _____
_____ Committee(s).

3. Complete one sentence.
I am a good lobbyist (because) (whenever). . . .

(or) My lobbying seems effective when. . . .

4. Complete one sentence.
I am a poor lobbyist (because) (whenever). . . .

(or) My lobbying effort seems counterproductive when. . . .

Each person is given a few minutes to fill out the form. Then each person is asked to introduce hmrself by reading what s/he wrote. Not only do participants meet one another, but they learn from one another in a structured fashion. Participants leave the workshop realizing the importance of committee assignments and knowing lots of tips on lobbying.

Frequently, the main purpose of a lobbying workshop is to build people's confidence about their ability to lobby elected leaders. A good way to do that is to divide participants into pairs. Ask them to take turns being the citizen advocate and the legislative aide. Have the citizen advocate call the aide and talk briefly with hmr about an upcoming hunger issue.

If you are fairly sure that most workshop participants have never written a letter to an elected leader, doing so during the workshop demonstrates how easy and simple it is. Give participants a little background on a particular piece of legislation and then distribute paper, pens, and envelopes. Ask people to write their own elected leaders so the letters can be mailed after the workshop. This exercise emphasizes that one need not be an expert to write an effective letter.

D. ORGANIZING AND MAINTAINING A HUNGER GROUP.
Marlene Kiingati, a regional organizer for Bread for the World,

designed one of the best workshops on maintaining a hunger group that I have ever seen. She has written a role-playing exercise about a group interacting. Following an overview of group-process theory, various workshop participants are given background descriptions of group members. They are then asked to accomplish certain tasks within the group. Marlene videotapes the group. Following the role-play, she plays back the videotape and participants stop it at various points to describe the group interaction and how they might have dealt with situations differently. People learn both how groups interact and how they personally act within a group setting.

E. BUILDING A HUNGER MINISTRY IN YOUR CHURCH. If your workshop is to encourage and strengthen an existing hunger ministry, consider using the "Assessing Your Church's Hunger Ministry" form found at the end of Chapter 8 in a learning activity. Ask each participant to fill out the form about hsr congregation. Ask all the participants to indicate in which area their congregations are the weakest. Use much of the remaining workshop time developing ideas for strengthening the weaker areas.

* * *

The examples above are only a sample of ideas that are creative, empowering, and educational. Some of the exercises take the entire workshop period. Others use only a small portion. Begin by testing sections of your workshops using creative learning methods. Once you feel comfortable using them, you can test creative models for the entire workshop period.

You will find that developing a creative workshop can take a great deal of time. Scripts, case studies, and role-playing exercises take a lot of time to develop. But once a model is created, it can be reworked and developed into a workshop that you can use successfully many times.

Illustration 1

Dimensions of World Hunger

1. How many people live in absolute poverty (are chronically hungry)? _____

2. How many people die as a result of hunger and starvation? _
   _____

3. What percentage of those who are hungry are children? ____

4. What continent has the highest percentage of hungry people? _____

5. What continent has the highest number of hungry people?
   _____

6. Fifty percent of the world's hungry people live in just five countries. What are they?

   a) _____

   b) _____

   c) _____

   d) _____

   e) _____

7. What is the poorest country in Latin America?
   _____

8. What is "per capita GNP" and why is it a poor indicator of the

standard of living for many people? _____
_____
_____

9. What is the "Infant Mortality Rate"? _____
_____
_____

10. Are there any positive signs about hunger or is everything getting worse? _____
_____
_____

11. What are some hunger related causes of death in children?
_____
_____
_____

Bread for the World, 802 Rhode Island Avenue, NE, Washington, D.C. 20018 (202) 269-0200

AN OVERVIEW OF U.S. FOREIGN AID

Illustration 2

FOOD AID	DEVELOPMENT AID

FOOD AID

"Food for Peace"
"P.L. 480"

$1 billion

Title I
Concessional Sales
Self-Help Measures

Title II
Grants
Distributed by PVO's
CARE
WORLD VISION
CRS
CWS

Title III
"Food for Development"
Forgiven Loans

DEVELOPMENT AID

Multilateral
through int'l
institutions

United Nations   MDB's

(U.S. makes separate contribution to each agency and multilateral bank.)

UNICEF
health, educa-tion, nutrition
Child Survival Fund

World Bank
IDA "soft loans"

UNHCR
refugees
UNDRO
disaster relief

Regional Dev. Banks

IFAD
Int'l Fund for Agriculture Development

Illustration 2

"SECURITY AID"

Bilateral from U.S. to a country	Economic Support Fund (ESF)	Military Aid
U.S. Development Aid $1.9 billion	Large-scale economic aid to "strategic" countries	Foreign Military Sales Credits (FMS) concessional sales
Agency for International Development (AID)	Israel and Egypt receive most	Military Assistance Program (MAP)
Health Account Child Survival Fund	Pakistan El Salvador Turkey Sudan Philippines	Grants of Military Equipment Dorgan Amendment Pryor Amendment?
Targeted Development Aid New Directions (1973)	Not Poverty-Oriented $2.9 billion	International Military Education and Training Internal Police

15. USING THE MEDIA

Throughout most of 1983 and 1984, hunger relief and development organizations and religious leaders tried unsuccessfully to focus public attention on the famine in Africa. Finally, on October 22, 1984, NBC aired the first film footage on the famine in Ethiopia. People were shocked, and the U.S. public responded generously. Groups that had been working on Ethiopia were bombarded with phone calls. If I had not already been convinced of the power of the media, I would have been at that time.

In September of 1983, I spent a short period of time in Addis Ababa, the capital of Ethiopia, interviewing relief workers and trying to develop the public policy approach Bread for the World would pursue in Congress. Upon my return, Bread for the World issued news releases, organized a briefing on Capitol Hill, and sought media interviews to publicize the problem. Local BFW members wrote letters-to-the-editor and sought news coverage of the famine. We were told "no one's interested." Several reporters told me, "it isn't news."

Once NBC broke the story, we could do virtually nothing else besides respond to media inquiries. National affiliate TV crews turned up at local BFW meetings, BFW volunteer leaders were interviewed on TV and radio stations, over thirty press conferences were well attended, and numerous BFW members assisted reporters in writing stories. The situation in Africa was not qualitatively different between late 1983 and late 1984, but the interest of the media was; thus, our ability to get our message publicized was changed dramatically.

Clearly, media coverage is important in furthering work against hunger. Obtaining media coverage is not an end in itself, rather it is a means for achieving goals. Media coverage can

190

educate the general public about hunger and can influence elected leaders. The coverage of Africa made people aware of the famine and caused a general outpouring of money. BFW members tried to focus media coverage on topics that would influence legislative decisions made in Washington, D.C. Finally, media coverage can provide visibility for your hunger group and its programs. Such visibility makes your community outreach and advocacy work easier. It adds credibility to your group, and publicizes programs to a broad audience.

The media can assist in work against hunger. To use the media, however, we must understand a bit about how they work, cultivate contacts, and develop media skills. The biggest obstacle to using the media is fear. The best way to overcome that fear is to find out how media operate and then take a stab at working with them. As with many areas of life, the best way to develop skills in using the media is through practice. Many hunger leaders have become experts in their local media in just a few months.

Although we can learn to use the media relatively quickly, we will not be able to control it. As with the media coverage on Africa, the hunger community did not have the resources or power to dictate the timing of the coverage on Africa. Nevertheless, if we are prepared, we can take advantage of the media's interest in an issue (like Africa), and find regular opportunities to convey our concerns and publicize our programs.

Set Priorities

Eventually, every hunger group needs or wants to use the media to convey a concern or publicize an upcoming event. There may be one, or two people in your group who would like to be the group's media coordinators, or the entire group may be interested in working with the media. Whichever way you choose, the whole group should participate in establishing priorities for your media efforts. Without priorities, working with the media will become a full-time job, and few people or groups have that kind of time to devote to media work.

A firm grasp of your group's overall goals is needed to determine what kind of media are appropriate to use. Set priorities based on the kind of media coverage you need to meet your goals. For example, if your group primarily wants to publicize its monthly meetings, then a priority for media work is finding and learning how to use all the community calendars. It is not important to develop relationships with news reporters. On the other hand, if one of your group's major goals is to influence public policy, you may need to develop relationships with news reporters, especially those who cover national legislation. Your media work should support the overall goals and objectives of your group. Again, media is a means for meetings your goals, it is not the goal in itself.

Selecting media that reach your target audience is important. If your hunger group is designed for Southern Baptists or you want to include more Southern Baptists, you should target the Southern Baptist stations, statewide papers, or local church newsletters and bulletins. If your group is predominately white and wants to broaden its racial diversity, you should target non-white media. Many towns have black or Hispanic newspapers and radio stations. Your media priorities should reflect your group's desire to embrace diversity.

Following are some questions to ask in setting your media priorities. Some of the answers may be difficult to reconcile. For example, the medium which is easiest to get into may have the least outreach potential. Set aside adequate time for your group to discuss the following questions on how best to focus its media efforts.

- Which media reach the most people?

- With which media are contacts worth developing for future work?

- Which media are most likely to cover your issues?

- Which media reach your target audiences?

- Which media best help you meet your group's goals?

The major media in your community, the large secular newspapers, television stations, and radio stations, reach the most people. Their wide reach makes considering ways to approach the major media important. Needless to say, papers like the *New York Times* are difficult to approach. The same is true for national major network television shows. Thus, in setting priorities, these probably should not be your first choices. In most parts of the country, however, you should devote some attention to the major media. Religion editors or socially concerned reporters are often good contacts. Radio and television talk shows on the major stations that cover community concerns are worth pursuing.

As you read the paper, listen to the radio, or watch the television, you may identify media representatives who seem worth "cultivating" for the future. For example, is there a reporter who has written occasionally about hunger in your community? Who covered the African famine in late 1984? Did any of the reporters travel personally to Ethiopia or another famine-striken country? If there are key media persons with whom developing relationships seems worthwhile, make getting to know these people a priority even if there is no immediate result.

Small, local media are much more likely to cover local activities. A weekly, community newspaper or a college paper probably will use most news releases they receive that have a local angle. Small radio stations, especially Christian stations, are likely to be interested in hunger and justice concerns. Denominational publications are also likely prospects for coverage. Do not forget about the small media. Your chance of coverage is higher than in major media, and your coverage of your target audience (such as community groups or Christians concerned about social justice) may be quite high.

Develop a Media List

Once you have set your priorities, you need to develop a media list. There are several ways to find out about the media in your community. First, check the Yellow Pages under "radio stations and broadcasting companies," "television stations and broadcasting companies," "news services," "newsletters," and "newspapers." If you know another social justice group in the community which works effectively with the media, ask them if they would share their media list with you or assist you in compiling your own. Sometimes advertising companies compile and sell media lists.

The local public library will have reference books on media. Ask the reference librarian for assistance. The following are a few books to consult (most are published annually):

Armstrong, Ben, ed. *The Directory of Religious Broadcasting.* Morristown, NJ: National Religious Broadcasters.

Beacon's Publicity Checker. Chicago: Beacon's Publishing Company.

Cable TV Publicity Outlets — Nationwide. Washington Depot, CT: Public Relations Plus, Inc.

Gebbie Press All-In-One Directory. New Platz, NY: Gebbie Press.

The IMS Ayer Directory of Publications. Fort Washington, PA: IMS Press.

National Directory of Weekly Newspapers. Brooklyn, NY: American Newspaper Representatives, Inc.

National Radio Publicity Outlets. New Milford, CT: Public Relations Plus, Inc.

TV Publicity Outlets — Nationwide New Milford, CT: Public Relations Plus, Inc.

Select the names, addresses, and phone numbers of the people that seem most appropriate, given your media prioritities. Before you mail materials, call to check that you have the correct names. The reference materials *and your media list* will become out-of-date quickly. Update your media list regularly. If your group has access to a computer, organize the list on the computer so it can be revised easily.

News Releases

The most standard means for communicating with the media is the news release. A news release is a story or announcements (news) written in a format that is easy for the media to use. Your message has its best chance of being reproduced if it's presented in the desired fashion. News releases are sent to newspapers and radio and television stations.

Use a news release to announce the formation of your hunger group or speakers' bureau, including quotes from group members on its future plans. Send news releases to announce special programs and events, such as a slide show or candidates' forum on hunger. Issue a news release announcing the results of a new study on hunger in your town or explaining the local aspect of recently published national statistics on hunger. If you find that twice as many people are using the services of a soup kitchen this year as last, interview people to discover why its use has increased, and write a news release about it.

News releases can be used to express shock, concern, or support. For example, if the mayor makes an outrageous statement about low-income people, reflecting an insensitivity to their difficulties, your group may want to issue a statement expressing concern and calling on the mayor to learn more about hunger and poverty in the community. On the other hand, if the mayor initiates a special program to provide additional food to low-income people, issue a news release congratulating the mayor for showing such compassionate leadership. News releases of this sort must be closely timed to events covered by the media.

News releases are very important in advocacy work. With a few exceptions, the media generally cover public policy issues after they've been voted on, or in such general terms that the general public has difficulty being involved in the legislative process. Your news releases can provide a public service, if they educate the public on upcoming legislative issues so that concerned citizens can participate in the decisions.

You can also send news releases reporting on your elected leaders' votes, statements on hunger, and leadership on hunger issues. Elected leaders, at both the national and state level, need to be commended when they vote for or support legislation aimed at reducing hunger. Similarly, the public needs to know when they are supporting policies which will increase hunger, or opposing efforts to reduce hunger. If your group is in contact with a public policy group such as Bread for the World, you will be better informed about hunger legislation than 99 percent of the reporters in this country. You will be offering a service to reporters on such news items.

Your group will also gain political leverage by demonstrating ability to use the media. The staffs of elected leaders closely monitor newspaper articles about their bosses. Elected leaders are more careful about votes and positions on hunger issues if they know a group is watching and prepared to report on them. Evaluate how to present issues in the media so that elected leaders receive support for taking what you consider to be the best position. Make sure that your news release is polite and considerate even if you disagree with a vote or position. Address the issues rather than questioning the person's motivations. Conflict with elected leaders may be unavoidable and may be instrumental in changing their positions, but avoid alienating them unnecessarily.

The kind of news release you are sending will determine the proper recipient. If your message is about legislation or other hunger "news," send it to reporters who cover legislation or that kind of news. If you are unsure to whom it should be sent, address it to the City Editor at the major daily paper, the Managing Editor at weeklies, and the News Director or News Assignment Editor at radio and television stations. Do not send a news release to more than one person at a newspaper or station.

If you are announcing the formation of your group or speakers' bureau, you should send the release to the Religion Editor at the daily paper and the Managing Editor at denominational publications, local community papers, and other targeted print media. If you are inviting people to join your group or seeking invitations to speak, send the news release to informal publications like church bulletins and church newsletters. For example, send the release to the Editor, Church Bulletin, St. Gertrude's Church.

If you are publicizing an upcoming event or meeting, direct your news releases to the community calendars. Look through past papers for the correct address. Many radio and television stations have community bulletin boards as well. Generally, these news releases must be short and follow the guidelines recommended by the paper or station.

News releases are used to announce events or press conferences which you want the media to attend. Do not expect the media to attend every event. However, if you think your event or press conference is newsworthy, send the news release to the editor of the appropriate department (e.g. religion) or the general editor (City Editor for dailies, Managing Editor for weeklies, and News Director for radio and television stations), and then follow up with a phone call.

In some major cities, AP and UPI publish daily listings of upcoming events in what is called a daybook. Send a news release to the daybook for events you would like the media to attend. The day before your event, call to check if the daybook received your news release and if the event is listed for the next day.

There is a standard format for a news release. It should be

typed, doublespaced, on legal or letter size white paper. The margins should be wide on all four sides. If you have letterhead paper for your group, put the first page on letterhead stationery.

In the upper left hand side (or right hand side) of the release, single space the name and address of your group, and the name and phone number(s) of a person who can be called for further information. On the opposite side of the page, give the date on which you wrote the release. A few spaces below the date, give the time at which your story can be released. Most often, your news release will read "For immediate release," but it can give a specific date and time.

The headline for the story should be catchy if possible, but more importantly, it should summarize the contents for the reporter or editor. Type the headline in all capital letters and center it. Begin the story below the headline.

The first paragraph of the news release has to be crammed with facts. It should tell who, what, where, when, and sometimes why. Put the most important information at the beginning of the release. Editors tend to cut from the bottom of the release.

Write the release in an objective style. Give short statements of facts. Only include a few sentences in each paragraph. The standard way to get your group's opinion into the release is to quote members of your group. You may feel silly at first doing this, but it is standard procedure.

Information about your group is usually placed in the last paragraph, and unfortunately is frequently cut. If there are special documents, letters, or statements that seem important for reporters to have in full, they can be sent as attachments.

If the release is longer than one page, type "more" at the bottom of each page except the last. On the second and following pages, type the headline and the page number. Type "-30-" at the end of the news release. This is a tradition which comes from early printing days, but continues as standard notation for the end of a news release. Try to keep your news release to two pages or less.

The easiest way to prepare a news release is to follow a sample. Several are included ·

SAN FRANCISCO SUN-REPORTER
San Francisco, CA
January 22, 1986

Marie Pierce, Local Media Coordinator in San Francisco, regularly writes a newspaper column focusing on the Black community of San Francisco. In this column she also shares information about Universal Child Immunization.

From The
Desk Of
Marie Pierce

Mrs. Marie Pierce

Bread for the World has almost three-hundred members in the 5th Congressional district, of which San Francisco is a part. We have very fine cooperation from our elected officials. In the year almost ending, we have worked hard to get legislation passed that would assure longer lives for babies and children in Third World countries. Therefore, I think this information would be of interest to many of your readers.

COST OF IMMUNIZING WORLD'S CHILDREN DECREAS-ING

The cost of immunizing the world's children by 1990 will be far less than originally estimated because of technological advances and economics of scale, the House Select Committee on Hunger was told late November.

In 1984, UNICEF estimated the additional cost for the five years accelerated campaign at $1.25 billion, according to Stephen Joseph M.D., Special Coordinator for Child Survival. The current estimate is now $750 million. India and China were cited as countries where economics of scale have cut the cost of immunizing.

Dr. Wm. Forge, Centers for Disease Control, who heads a Task Force of international organizations working on child survival, said increased stability advances which lower the cost and improve the prospects of immunizing the world's children against measles, polio, pertussis, tetanus, tuberculosis and diptheria.

Senator Bill Bradley, author of Senate Concurrent Resolution 78 in support of the goal of immunizing the world's children by 1990, told Rep. Mickey Leland, Chairman of the Select Committee on Hunger, Rep. Sala Burton, member, and others present at the hearing, that every day 11,000 children die because they are not immunized, bringing greater human loss than the Mexico earthquake and other public tragedies.

FOR IMMEDIATE RELEASE

IFAD SURVIVES! U.S. AGREES TO 60/40 FUND-ING FORMULA

WASHINGTON — A new $500 million budget for the International Fund for Agricultural Development (IFAD) was approved last week in Rome after more than two years of negotiations.

The United States finally made a long-delayed financial pledge to IFAD that ensures the survival of the multilateral agricultural development organization. IFAD was established in 1974 by the United Nations' World Food Conference. It specializes in providing loans to peasant farmers in the poorest countries of the world to help them increase food production.

IFAD was the focus of Bread for the World's national "Offering of Letters" campaign last year. That effort produced more than 100,000 letters to Congress and to Reagan Administration officials in support of IFAD's programs. Arthur Simon, executive director of Bread for the World, called the agreement a critical step in the right direction.

"We're pleased that IFAD is still alive and will continue helping the world's poor farmers produce more food," said Simon. "IFAD's work is very important if we want to help break cycles of food dependency in developing countries."

Simon also gave credit to the scores of daily newspapers which informed the public about IFAD's funding problems.

(more)

IFAD SURVIVES

"Television helped stimulate a strong U.S. Africa famine response last year," said Simon, "but the nation's daily newspapers and religious media helped save IFAD. It just made too much good sense to a lot of people."

The 32 OPEC and Western nations that fund IFAD agreed to provide $500 million for IFAD's previous $1.1 billion three-year budget. Under the new agreement, the 20 participating Western nations will contribute $300 million while OPEC nations will give $200 million — a 60/40 ratio. The United States, which fought the 60/40 ratio, has pledged $85 million over the next three years to IFAD, 17 percent of IFAD's budget.

This year, Bread for the World will continue efforts in Congress to gain passage of a U.S. contribution to IFAD's Special Africa Fund. This special fund was approved last year by IFAD to help drought and famine-stricken countries produce more food. The special fund is also designed to protect hard-hit African nations from cuts caused by IFAD's reduced budget.

Thus far, more than 10 countries have either pledged contributions or have shown interest in the special fund for Africa.

Letters-to-the-Editor

Many people who are unwilling to work on any other kind of media coverage will want to write a letter-to-the-editor, because it looks so simple. Indeed, it is simple, and because the letters-to-the-editor are widely read, they are a good source of coverage. Letters are printed which respond to articles that have appeared in the paper. Thus, this is not a good vehicle for announcing general activities of your group. It is a good vehicle for public education and sometimes for advocacy. Any time an article about hunger or a related issue "misses" the hunger angle, recruit someone in your group to write immediately. Timeliness is very important. You must send or hand deliver your letter within a day or two of when the article first appeared. Here are a few examples of ways to use letters-to-the-editor to further your public education and advocacy goals:

The Original Story	Your Letter-to-the-Editor
General story on the famine in a poor nation.	Points out pending legislation in Congress which would help alleviate the famine.

Story outlining abuse of the food stamp program.	Expresses concern that the article implied that there is widespread abuse despite the facts demonstrating otherwise. Include important facts that the story omitted.
Story attributing unrest in a developing country solely to communism. Recommends only increased military assistance.	Demonstrates that hunger and poverty are a major source of unrest in that country. Suggests that aid given to relieve hunger and poverty will be more effective than military aid in achieving global stability.

If you want the letter-to-the-editor to give visibility to your hunger group, ask the person who writes the letter to give hsr association with the group. For example, it can be signed Susie Smith, President, Holy Trinity Episcopal Hunger Committee; or Renee Ortega, member of the Interchurch Alliance Against Hunger. Such an identification offers visibility, but it also tells the paper that the writer has authority for writing on the issue.

Newspaper Interviews

An interview with a reporter is a good way to get newspaper coverage. It is also much easier that you might expect. Generally, you get greater coverage than you would with a news release.

The hardest part of an interview with a reporter is arranging it. You can either schedule the interview yourself, or get someone else to do it for you. I prefer to schedule interviews for others and have others schedule them for me. By having a third person schedule the interview, the scheduler can forthrightly tell the reporter how wonderful the interviewee is. It's difficult to use that approach yourself!

If possible, identify the reporter with whom you should speak ahead of time. If your group is religious, I recommend the religion editors. They are seldom as busy as news reporters. Consequently, they can give you more time for an interview and may spend more time writing the article. I'm convinced, in addition, that religion editors frequently write about boring topics, so when an issue like hunger is more interesting, they may cover it more thoroughly.

If there is not a religion editor and you're not sure with whom to speak, call the newspaper and ask for the "city desk." The "city desk" is responsible for assigning reporters to stories. Give the person at the city desk a brief picture of what the interviewee has to offer for a story, and ask if there is someone with whom you could speak. Let's look at how this might be done.

Assume that your group, the First Church of God Hunger Committee, has just completed a study of food services for hungry people in the community. The head of the committee or the writer of the report are potential interviewees. If you are going to schedule the interview, find yourself a title, such as the media coordinator, or director of public relations (sounds impressive!). Your call to arrange the interview might go as follows:

Ring, ring.

Newspaper switchboard: Hello, this is the *Jolly Town Gazette.* May I help you?

You: Yes, I would like to speak with Ms. Brown, the religion editor.

Newspaper switchboard: Just a minute please, I'll connect you.

Ms. Brown: Hello, Ms. Brown speaking.

You: Hi, Ms. Brown. My name is Betty Lawrence. I am the media coordinator for the First Church of God Hunger Committee. One member of our committee, Mr. Thomas Eward, has recently completed a study of the food services provided for hungry people in our community. He has discovered some very interesting information. I was wondering if you would care to spend a few minutes talking with him about his study. He is knowledgeable about what is going on in our community, as well as about the plans our hunger committee has for improving food availability in the area.

Ms. Brown: Well, yes, I might be interested in that, but I'm working under a tight deadline right now.

You: Well, Mr. Eward is willing to stop by your office with the study at your convenience. He has time available tomorrow afternoon and Thursday morning. Is either one of these times good for you?

Ms. Brown: Thursday morning looks good. How about nine?

You: Great. I will confirm the time with Mr. Eward. If there are any problems, I will get right back to you. Otherwise, he will be there at nine on Thursday. If you need to change the time for some reason, why don't I give you Mr. Eward's number so you can reach him directly. It is 456-7890. Thank you for your time.

Ms. Brown: You're welcome. Goodbye.

That's all there is to it. Adapt the initial comments for various situations. In general, you should seek to interest the reporter over the phone, but not give the whole story. The key to obtaining an interview is offering interesting, up-to-date information that has local impact. Think through the "local angle" on your story, and be prepared to discuss it briefly.

Once the interview is arranged, make sure the person to be interviewed is prepared. S/he should practice responding to likely questions. Think of some pithy statements which are good to quote. Reporters appreciate good quotes. Make copies of materials that should be left with the reporter. Sometimes the reporters will read carefully all the materials left, and excerpt additional points.

The person being interviewed should arrive at the appointed place on time. If the interview is conducted at the press office, a photograph is usually taken. Therefore, the person should dress appropriately. (If you like the photo, you can usually purchase the original if you ask within a month or so.)

When I'm being interviewed, I usually take a few minutes at the beginning to get to know the reporter. I ask hmr how long s/he has worked at the paper and where s/he is from originally. I try to establish some personal rapport with the person. I figure that if the person feels positively toward me as a human being, s/he is more likely to write a positive story. Most reporters are nice people.

Despite their friendliness, however, be careful what you say in an interview. Assume that comments will be taken out of context so think before you speak. Anything you say may show up in print, even if you say, "Please don't quote me on this." That is not a fair request to ask of a reporter. Just don't say it if you are not willing to see it in print. Sometimes a reporter will ask you something "off the record." Again, unless you know the reporter well, be careful. Even if your exact statement is not quoted, the tone may be communicated and reported.

Towards the end of the time with a reporter, s/he generally will ask if there's anything else you'd like to say. At that point, the person being interviewed should ask to have your group's name, a contact person's name, and phone number included in the article. There is nothing worse than having a wonderful article published about your group, but no way for people to get in touch with you in order to join. If you do not ask to have the information listed, it will not be. If you do ask, about half of the time it will be included.

At the end of the interview, I ask the reporter if s/he would like to receive our press releases on a regular basis. Reporters almost always say yes, and they are much more apt to use them once they've had a personal contact with the group. This is a good way to build your media list.

Do not ask to see the interview before it is printed. This is not standard practice and reporters find it insulting.

When the interview is printed, I write the reporter a personal thank you note, even if the interview is not perfect. In fact, most interviews contain inaccurate statements or material that I would have stressed differently. Expect that the article will not be how you'd like it. Unless the interview is really awful, I do not correct the errors. Rather, I use the thank you note as a way to build a relationship with a reporter and to offer my assistance in future hunger related articles s/he might write. If a reporter knows s/he can call you, s/he might call for additional information, or a quote responding to a current situation. The reporter should view you as a helpful source of information for the future.

Meeting with an Editorial Writer

One hunger group, *Results,* has been extremely successful in getting positive editorials written about pending hunger legislation by arranging meetings with an editorial writer. Occasionally they meet with the editorial board (several people), but generally they meet with the editorial writer who comments on issues related to hunger and poverty.

If you wish to meet with an editorial writer, select an issue which could be well served by an editorial and is possible given the past editorial stances taken by the paper. Assuming the issue needs an editorial and that it is the kind of issue about which the paper writes editorials, ask for the name of the correct editorial writer. Most legislative issues and local policy matters are appropriate for editorials.

Next, the group that plans to meet with the editorial writer should rehearse what they will say and how to respond to questions. If questions arise, research the answers by calling a hunger organization or other sources of information.

Then, when the group feels ready, make an appointment with the appropriate writer. Talk with hmr about the importance of the issue. Give additional background information and places where s/he might call if s/he has questions. Far more often than one might think, this process works! Meeting with an editorial writer can produce an editorial supporting or opposing an issue about which your group is concerned. Such editorials are read by elected leaders and the public at large; and consequently, can influence public opinion in general, as well as specific votes and decisions. In this way, editorials can serve as a means for working against hunger.

Radio and Television Interviews

Arranging interviews on radio and television talk shows is similar to arranging newspaper interviews. The main difference is that radio and television interviews usually need to be scheduled farther in advance, although this is not the case with a particularly timely (and usually controversial) issue. Under normal circumstances, send a letter of inquiry to the person who arranges the program for which you (or someone else) wishes to be interviewed. This person is usually the program manager. The correct name can be obtained by calling the radio or television station and asking. Explain whom you would like to be interviewed, what issues the viewers would find of interest, and indicate that you will call the program manager within five to ten days. Expect that s/he won't have received your letter and that you will have to send another one.

When you talk with the program manager, be prepared to explain why the person should be interviewed and how the issues are of concern to the viewers. If possible, give examples of presentations that the person has done which were well received. No program manager wants to schedule someone on hsr show who will be an embarrassment.

Once an interview is scheduled, send a confirmation letter. In it, include possible questions the interviewer might ask, as well as the group's name and address. The name and address are particularly important for television so the station can prepare a message to be flashed on the screen when you tell people how to get involved.

Television preparation is similar to preparation for a presentation or a newspaper interview. Practice answering questions calmly and succinctly. If you have anticipated and practiced answering terrible questions, the real thing is bound to be easier. Summarize your main points in a handful of well-phrased themes. Reiterate these themes during your interview. Make the themes simple and easy to remember.

Even when a confirmation letter containing recommended questions has been sent, I carry a small notecard with sample questions. If it appears that the interviewer is not fully prepared, I ask hmr if s/he would like to use the questions I brought along. Television interviewers usually don't need them. Radio interviewers frequently do. It works nicely to have an interviewer asking the questions you want to answer!

Obviously, dress doesn't much matter for a radio interview, although I recommend that you look professional. It does matter for TV. In general, wear a simple outfit, such as a solid colored suit. Solids are better than prints. Bright colors usually film well; neutral shades do not. Refrain from wearing much jewelry because it is distracting. Some makeup, especially powder, is good. The program manager can advise you on which colors look best on hsr station.

Arrive early to the station, especially if the interview is live. There may well be forms to fill out and releases to sign before being interviewed.

Many people are very nervous about speaking on radio or television. It is similar to giving a presentation, but with more equipment and fewer people at hand. Basic principles of public speaking, such as telling human stories and using statistics sparingly, should be followed on radio or television. In addition, let me add the following pointers:

1. STRESS SIMPLE THEMES. Return to the themes you prepared, especially when a question seems to take the discussion way off track.

2. AVOID NO-WIN QUESTIONS. Sometimes interviewers ask extremely controversial questions that are impossible to answer in a short amount of time. Don't try. Explain that you think the interviewer is not asking the right question. The right question is. . . . whatever you think is better and proceed to answer it. Sometimes interviewers wish to spark a debate. Debating may produce a lively show, but it rarely encourages people to join in work to end hunger.

3. INTERRUPT IF NECESSARY. Normal rules of etiquette tell us never to interrupt. That rule does not hold for radio and television interviews. Obviously, you should not interrupt often, and it must be done nicely, but sometimes it should be done. If the interviewer is getting far afield, or is asking a series of extended questions, or is babbling incorrectly about an issue, feel free to interrupt. Use a phrase like "Excuse me, but could we get back to the point that. . . ." and make the point you believe is important.

4. TELL PEOPLE HOW THEY CAN HELP. If a main reason for being interviewed is to get others involved, make an opportunity to explain how they can help. Too often, the time gets away and the chance to invite people to get involved is missed. Repeat an

address or phone number several times. Don't expect the phone to ring off the hook as a result. Few people get involved as a result of a talk show, but one or two may.

5. WATCH THE CLOCK. Make sure you get the chance to reemphasize your main points near the end of the show. With a minute left, quickly wind up the current questions and say, "before our show ends, I'd like to remind people. . . ." Radio stations always have a big clock on the wall where you are being interviewed. Television stations are good about giving five minute and one minute warnings on flash cards.

Before you leave the station, ask if there is a news director who should be contacted about receiving your group's news releases. The interviewer is seldom the appropriate person to receive such material. Make a follow-up call to the person recommended and ask if s/he would be interested in receiving your group's news releases. If s/he would be, add hmr to your media list.

Send the interviewer and/or the program manager a personal thank you note. Offer yourself as a resource for future shows on hunger. You may want to suggest some program topics that you think would have broad community appeal, and offer your group's assistance.

Radio and Television Editorials

Some radio and television stations air editorial statements. If your group disagrees with the editorial statement, consider replying to it. If your group is mentioned by name, you have a very good chance of getting your reply aired, because the Federal Communications Commission stipulates that stations must provide equal time for different viewpoints.

If you are interested in responding to a radio or television editorial, call the general station number and ask how to get equal time for responding to the editorial. Your response will need to be prepared quickly.

Inviting the Media

Sometime you may plan an event which seems particularly newsworthy, and you may want to invite the media. As recommended earlier, send everyone on your media list a news release. Call all the reporters the day before the event to remind them, and give them any last minute information which indicates how newsworthy the event will be.

A candidates' forum on hunger issues would be an excellent event to which to invite the media. A hunger awareness tour visiting local feeding programs might interest the media. Depending on the size of the town, you might get a few reporters to attend a seminar, educational program, or offering of letters in a church.

If you expect members of the media to attend, set up a media table with media packets. Media packets are simply folders containing relevant documents such as fact sheets, news releases, and background information. Be careful not to put too many items into the packets. Less is better than more. Assign one person to greet reporters and assist them as needed. Be sure to get the names and affiliations of reporters for future contacts.

If your event is going well, but few (or no) reporters are present, equip someone with coins and call reporters from the nearest phone. Tell the reporters, "Things are really going well down here. You should hurry and send someone so you don't miss the story." Sometimes those extra dozen calls at the last minute will produce reporters.

News Conferences

A news conference, frequently called a press conference, is an event called solely for the purpose of releasing important news to the media. Sometimes news conferences are called in conjunction with an event, but the news conference itself is designed for the media.

Until 1984, I had discouraged groups from holding news conferences. Most I had heard of were a lot of work and not very successful. In 1984, however, I changed my mind. Despite considerable media coverage of the African famine during the fall of 1984, little attention was paid to public policy and how the U.S. government could assist. People were responding generously as individuals, but pressure on elected leaders was needed to assure additional governmental assistance.

The national BFW staff decided to see if news conferences could be organized around the country to call on our government leaders to take extraordinary measures against the famine. The organizing staff called BFW volunteer leaders across the country and asked them to organize news conferences. We called people on Tuesday and Wednesday and asked them to organize the conferences for the next Tuesday. Thirty-five groups decided to organize press conferences, although only a few had done so previously.

First, denominational leaders were asked to speak at a news conference. They were requested to support an interdenominational statement of concern on Africa, as well as to prepare additional comments to deliver orally at the news conference. Many denominational leaders were willing to help.The local organizers were careful to gather a diverse group of church leaders — Catholic, Protestant, Evangelical, black, and white. The panel of speakers usually had four or five church leaders plus a BFW spokesperson.

Sites were selected for the news conferences. Some were held in churches, some at council of churches' buildings, and some at press clubs. No one had difficulty finding space, although some folks had trouble lining up microphones.

The biggest job was inviting the media to the news conference. News releases were sent to as many reporters as possible. Some groups were able to mail them on Saturday. Other groups had to hand deliver them on Monday. Some groups sent an initial news release announcing the news conference and a follow-up one once the speakers were confirmed. Depending on the scheduled time of the news conferences, reminder calls were made to key media representatives on the day before or the day of the news conference.

At the news conferences, volunteers distributed packets containing the interdenominational statement, additional written statements by the church leaders, brief biographies of the speakers, and background information on the famine in Africa.

The news conferences were a great success. In all but a few cases, many reporters attended. At some news conferences, all the major newspapers and television stations participated. The stations that sent television crews used clips on the evening news. The newspaper coverage — in such diverse cities as Boston, Los Angeles, St. Louis, and Birmingham — was outstanding. At the few conferences reporters did not attend, the organizers proceeded without them and delivered the results to the papers. Some covered the news conferences without attending.

News conferences are not the easiest form of media work, but they can be successful. The keys to success are the timeliness of the issue, the importance of your message, the speakers delivering the message, and well organized logistics. If your group has never worked with the media before, don't start with a news conference. With a little experience, however, a news conference can be used to communicate an important message to a wide variety of media.

*   *   *

For better or worse, the media play an increasingly important role in influencing how people in the U.S. think *and* in decisions made by our elected leaders. To ignore the media is to ignore some of the most powerful communicators in our society. Our concerns *are* newsworthy.

The only way to learn to use the media is to try it. Find a person or two in your group who are interested in media work, and ask them to coordinate your group's media efforts. The immediate fruits of your work are easy to measure — whether or not you get coverage. The long-term benefits of increased awareness and influence on hunger issues, although harder to measure, are immensely important to ending hunger.

16. LOBBYING ELECTED LEADERS

The importance of public policy advocacy on hunger issues and ideas for integrating advocacy work into your church's hunger ministry have been stressed in previous chapters. This chapter will address the basic forms and techniques of lobbying.

The word lobbying often conjures up negative images of closed door meetings and under-the-table finances. Webster's dictionary defines a lobbyist as "a person who tries to get legislators to introduce or vote for measures favorable to a special interest that he represents." More broadly, lobbying includes trying to influence all public officials. Elected leaders are usually easier to influence than appointed ones. Elected leaders are more sensitive to constituents' concerns, because they will be facing those same constituents in the next election. As Christians concerned about hunger and living in a democracy, we want to share our concern about hunger, our "special interest" if you will, with our elected leaders.

Some people make a distinction between advocacy and lobbying. They stress that advocacy is speaking out for others and lobbying is speaking out for one's self. If we consider "interest" to be only immediate self-interest, then the entire hunger movement is an advocate for hungry people overseas. When the hunger movement works against hunger in the United States, however, it is both advocate and lobbyist because the hunger movement includes low-income people speaking out for themselves.

I am a bit uncomfortable with the distinction between advocacy and lobbying, because I believe working against hunger is in everyone's economic self-interest. Moreover, as Christians, working against hunger is in our spiritual self-interest. We know that as we have "done it unto the least of them" we have done it unto Christ. Having said this, if you prefer to use the term advocacy rather than lobbying, by all means use it.

Whether we are lobbying or advocating, we will sometimes find the political process confusing and messy. We must be prepared for this reality. Bills which began as excellent pieces of legislation change. Questions as to if, when, where, and how to compromise are difficult to answer. Our overall goal is to alleviate hunger, and thus being effective has high value. How to be the most effective, however, is often a judgment call. We do the best we can given the information we have, but we are probably wrong sometimes. Thus, people of conscience can take different positions. The "Christian" position on legislation is seldom as clear as we would wish. There is no room for moral superiority and self-righteousness in work on public policy.

Persistence is strongly needed in lobbying work. One of my favorite Biblical characters is the importuning widow. As described in Luke 18, the widow continually pled her case before the judge, whom the Bible describes as one who "feared not God, nor regarded man." The judge finally succumbed to the woman's request because he got tired of hearing from her. She won her case because of her persistence.

I wish I could say that hunger legislation would always prevail because of its moral rightness or the strength of our arguments. Unfortunately, this is not the case. We certainly need to present the clearest case and the strongest arguments possible. Nonetheless, we cannot count on them to make the difference. Like the widow, we must add persistence and continual pressure.

While we must proceed as if all elected leaders were deeply concerned about hunger and will be moved by the power of our arguments, this simply is not the case. Many politicians will be moved to act because they feel it is in their best political interest, either because many constituents have expressed concern or because the media may cover the issue and hsr work. We move some to act because they get tired of hearing from us.

Because the hunger movement has limited resources, we must target our lobbying efforts as carefully as possible. Most legislative work is performed at the committee level, so targeting resources at the committee level is wise. Identify the committees on which your elected leaders serve.

The easiest way to find out is to write and ask them. Then discover which of these committees deal with hunger legislation. Work with your elected leaders on the hunger issues dealt with by their committee assignments. For example, assume your national elected leaders' committee assignments look as follows:

Leader	Committee Assignment
Representative	Post Office
	Ways and Means
Senator One	Agriculture
	Appropriations (Agriculture Subcommittee)
Senator Two	Judiciary
	Environment and Public Works

The Post Office Committee does not deal with hunger legislation. The Ways and Means Committee deals with trade legislation and tax legislation, both of which affect hunger. Thus, your group should study trade and tax issues so you can communicate your concerns effectively to your representative.

Senator One serves on two committees which affect hunger. Senator Two's committee assignments are not as influential on hunger matters. Therefore, you should focus more efforts on lobbying Senator One than Senator Two. The Agriculture Committee has jurisdiction over food aid, food stamps, U.S. agriculture policy, child nutrition programs, and grain reserves. The Agriculture Subcommittee of the Appropriations Committee has jurisdiction over the funding of these programs. Senator One's committee assignments offer direction and focus for your group's study and lobbying efforts.

If one of your elected leaders is a committee chairperson on a committee that deals with hunger legislation, s/he is even more important to lobby. Committee, and sometimes subcommittee, chairpersons have a lot of power. They can influence their colleagues, schedule the legislation for times helpful or harmful to legislation, and usually have extra resources for developing legislation and lobbying.

An additional factor in targeting your efforts will be your group's assessment of the responsiveness of each elected leader. Generally, the higher up the political ladder and the further away from elections, the harder an elected leader is to influence. Thus, your state representative is likely to be the most responsive. Influencing your U.S. senator can be difficult, especially if s/he has just won reelection by a wide margin.

Nonetheless, finding ways to influence your senators is important, especially if one or both of your senators are on committees which deal with hunger issues. Join with other groups around the state in developing joint lobbying campaigns.Target your calls, letters, visits, and media work in such a way that even senators with safe seats will hear your message. Be persistent.

The lobbying techniques discussed below — letter-writing, calling, and visits — are appropriate for elected leaders at any level, whether local, state, or national. Since all international hunger policies and most domestic hunger policies are determined at the national level, I want to encourage your group to work primarily, but not exclusively, on national public policies. Lobbying just those local elected leaders who are more accessible and less intimidating may be tempting, but decisions made by U.S. representatives and senators affect the lives of many people.

Letter-writing

Letter-writing is the most basic form of lobbying, and it works. As discussed in Chapter 10, letters make a difference. Although not every letter is read individually by the elected leader, a legislative aide who is responsible for advising the elected leader on positions to take and constituents' interests does read and respond to each letter.

Congressional offices, and I'm sure other legislative offices, are overwhelmed with the number of issues that come before them. Letters are extremely helpful in providing additional information on issues, bringing upcoming votes to the leader's attention, and giving the leader a reading of how constituents feel about issues. If an elected official does not hear from anyone on an issue, s/he assumes that no one cares about that issue. On the other hand, if s/he hears from many people on an issue, s/he will consider that issue more carefully.

Most letters should be brief and to the point. They should ask the elected leader to take a specific action, such as to cosponsor a bill or vote for or against specific legislation. If you have the bill number or name of an amendment, include it, but don't delay writing because you don't know a number. Some bills may not have been assigned numbers at the time you are writing. Furthermore, staff people can find the appropriate bill number if you describe the bill.

Be polite and reasonable in your letter. Never threaten not to vote for the person in the next election or anything else. Share your Christian motivation for writing on the issue, but avoid sounding (or being) judgmental.

Hand-written or typed letters or postcards are fine, as long as they are readable and personal. Staff do not take form letters as seriously. A petition carries about the same weight as one letter. Two or three personal letters is far more effective than a lengthy petition, unless you have plans to get media coverage about the petitions. Word-processed letters should only be used if they look personal.

Occasionally you may want to write a somewhat longer letter explaining your concerns on an issue in detail. You may even want to enclose some background information for the elected leader and hsr staff to read. At times this is very helpful. However, do not think that you have to be an expert in writing to express your opinions, nor that your letters need to go into great detail.

Asking selected questions about a bill or amendment may encourage a legislative aide to study the issue in greater depth. In addition, it may mean that your letter will require an individual response which will focus the legislative aide's attention on the issue. You can also request from your elected leaders copies of bills or congressional studies that interest you. Asking for a particular bill may prompt a legislative aide to read the bill.

Thank the elected leader for past action when possible. A separate thank-you note following cosponsorship of a bill, a vote you appreciate, or a leadership action in committee or floor discussion is encouraging to elected leaders. They need to hear words of thanks as well as requests.

If the response you receive from your elected leader does not answer your questions or address your concerns, write another letter. Thank hmr for the letter but indicate that it did not respond to your letter. Most likely, you will get another letter which responds more directly. Sometimes this happens because the elected leader would rather not address your questions or concerns. Other times the letter is placed in the form-letter response pile when it should not have been.

Receiving a form letter, in itself, is not a bad thing. It is an indication that the elected official is receiving so much mail on the issue that s/he had to write a general response. A form letter is a good sign of the quantity of mail generated on the issue.

No firm guidelines exist on how many letters to write your

elected leaders. A letter a day is too many! One letter a month during the legislative sessons is not too many. Obviously, there is a point at which your letters will be dismissed because of their volume, but most of us have not reached that point. A target of three letters a month, one to your U.S. representative and each U.S. senator, is a healthy target which certainly will not tax the congressional staff. You should also write regularly to your state elected leaders when your state legislature is in session.

Father Charlie Mulholland, a priest from the eastern part of North Carolina, is an avid letter-writer. He writes his U.S. representative almost every month, sometimes more often. His representative's office refers to him as "Representative Jones's penpal." Indeed, they have almost become penpals. Nonetheless, the aides pay attention to the letters.

Find ongoing ways to incorporate letter-writing into your group's plans and your personal habits. A basic letter to an elected leader probably takes ten minutes to write and address, and yet so few of us set aside that time. We need to find ways of making this important form of lobbying happen consistently.

Calling Elected Leaders

Telephone calls to elected officials' offices are an effective way of communicating about an issue which is coming up quickly. You will seldom speak with the elected official, but rather with an aide who will deliver the message and recommend responses. The call brings the issue to a legislative aide's attention, both by the content of your call and the fact that s/he is interrupted from hsr work to answer the call. Legislative aides do not enjoy taking lots of calls on a particular issue, and yet the calls make a point which is then passed on to the elected leaders.

It's useful to become acquainted with the legislative aides responsible for hunger concerns. In congressional offices there are usually different people for federal food programs and foreign aid issues. Once you know who they are you can talk with them regularly and begin developing a relationship with them. State and local officials may only have one aide.

Usually the addresses and phone numbers for elected leaders are in the telephone books. If not, you can get them by calling the League of Women Voters in your town. The general switchboard phone number for U.S. House or Senate offices is (202)224-3121. It will add only an extra fifteen seconds to your call.

Here's an example of a typical lobbying phone call:

(Receptionist)	Hello. Representative Smith's office.
(you)	Hi. I'd like to speak with the aide who works on foreign aid issues.
(Receptionist)	Oh, that's Bob Wilson. Hold on just a moment and I'll put you right through.
(Bob)	Bob Wilson speaking.
(you)	Hi. This is Kim Jones. I'm from Little Town in the Representative's district.
(Bob)	Yes, I'm familiar with Little Town. What can I do for you?
(you)	I am concerned about the foreign aid bill that Representative Smith will be asked to vote on in committee next week. I think the bill number is HR 1234. I don't feel like the balance between security and development aid is in the right proportions. We need to place a greater emphasis on food and development aid to poor countries. In that regard, I would like to urge the Representative to vote for

	the Cole Amendment and vote against amendments to increase security aid.
(Bob)	What is the Cole Amendment?
(you)	I believe it proposes increasing funds for UNICEF, a agency which is worthy of support.
(Bob)	Is there anything else you'd like me to tell the representative?
(you)	No. I'd appreciate it if you could get back to me about how he votes.
(Bob)	I'll be happy to, and I know he will take your concerns in mind when he votes.
(you)	Thank you very much. Have a good day.

(end)

Most conversations are similar to this. They are almost always short. Occasionally an aide will ask you a question you can't answer. That's okay. You should feel fine about saying you don't know. It is the aide's job to get the information on the bill. If you know of a resource group in Washington, D.C. working on the issue, you might give the aide the phone number to call. For example, if you know that Bread for the World is working on the legislation, you can suggest that the aide call the Bread for the World office if s/he has additional questions. If you have the time, you can offer to get the information and call back, but that is not necessary.

Some people find phone calling easier than writing letters. If you prefer the phone, use it. Congressional offices usually answer the phone from 9:00 A.M. to 6:00 P.M. If you live in the Mountain or Pacific time zones, you can call before the rates change at 8:00 A.M. Some people in Central Time call at 7:50

A.M. their time (8:50 A.M. Washington, D.C. time) and find congressional staff available.

U.S. representatives and senators have offices located in their districts, as well as in Washington, D.C. The staff who work in those offices deal with constituent matters; they are not responsible for legislative matters. If you call them, they will merely relay the information to the Washington, D.C. office. They will not make recommendations on policy to the representative or senator. Therefore, if you can afford to make the long-distance call, it is more effective. Nonetheless, calling the district office is better than not calling at all.

Meeting with Elected Leaders

An extremely effective means of lobbying is to have a group meet with the elected leader. Hunger groups often put off such a meeting because they "aren't ready." That is nonsense! Almost as soon as your hunger group is formed it is worthy of meeting with an elected leader, if only to inform hmr of your existence and offer your assistance with hunger issues.

The hardest part of meeting with a member of Congress is getting the appointment. First send a letter to the person's appointment secretary. Ask for a thirty minute appointment at the congressperson's convenience. Suggest times/days that would be good for your group, but emphasize that you are flexible. Ask if you could meet during an upcoming recess and mention when it is, if you know. (Congress takes breaks for *all* holidays. They are off a good part of January and August during a nonelection year.) The elected leader will probably want the meeting to be held in hsr local office. This enables the person to see a number of groups during the course of one day.

Call the appointment secretary a few days after s/he should have received the letter. Ask if s/he has had time to schedule an appointment for your group. If not, find out when you could call back to schedule an appointment. Sometimes it is difficult to pin down a date. Persistence is needed here — the widow's tactics. Call before each recess to see if they can fit you in during the recess. Eventually, you will get an appointment.

The meeting is important. It fixes your group in the elected official's mind, and gives you the opportunity to demonstrate your concerns and offer your assistance. Establishing a dialogue and rapport with the representative is the most important outcome of the meeting — although concrete commitments are always nice!

Once the appointment is confirmed decide who will participate in the meeting. Think about the composition of your group. It is good to have a diverse range of people, men and women, blacks and whites, different professions, and young and older people. It is also good to have a person or two that you are fairly confident will identify with the elected leader in some fashion. For example, if the person is Christian, invite a minister or priest from hsr denomination to join you. If the person is Jewish, you might invite a rabbi. Of course, you want to be sure that the person invited agrees with your group's positions.

A group of four or five is a good size. It's hard to have much diversity with fewer, and many more can become overwhelming and cumbersome. If you are meeting with a U.S. Senator, try to have people from across the state.

If possible, the group that is to meet with the elected leader should gather a few days before the meeting to clarify people's roles and how the time should be used. One person should serve as the meeting coordinator to ensure that time is spent well. It is the group's opportunity to ask the elected leader questions and to make a few points. A standard "political" tactic is for the elected leader to ask the group questions in order to get members of the group discussing something among themselves. When this happens, precious time is lost. Determine your questions ahead of time and avoid getting side-tracked.

Practice responding politely to differences of opinions that may emerge in the meeting. Your group can anticipate most of these differences. It is far more important that your group appear composed of reasonable people and concerned community residents, than that you cover all issues in great detail. Remember that building rapport is key, because if the meeting goes well you have an opening for future discussions. You can disagree politely, just don't debate.

When the day arrives for your meeting, make sure your group arrives early, but be prepared for the meeting to begin late. Elected leaders often have tightly packed schedules which get behind.

At the beginning of the meeting, the coordinator should introduce everyone in the group and present briefly how the group would like to use the time. S/he might say, "We'd like to spend the next few minutes telling you a bit about our group, and then asking you some questions on hunger so we can better understand your positions. Then we'd like to save a few minutes to tell you about the proposed Jones amendment to the foreign aid bill which we think sounds excellent. Does that sound all right to you, Representative Blackwell?" The coordinator should be courteous and respectful, but should take control of the time.

One person should bring a camera and take a picture at the meeting. The picture should then be enlarged, framed, and given to the elected leader. It will serve as a reminder of the group. It may even be hung on a wall in the office (along with pictures of the Boy Scouts). It can also be sent, along with a news release, to the local paper.

Leaving some information or a special book with the person at the end of the meeting is nice. Present the materials at the end so the person will not be tempted to flip through it while people are speaking. A number of Bread for the World groups have had Art Simon autograph copies of his book, *Bread for the World,* which were then presented to the elected leaders. Who knows how many elected leaders actually read it? Perhaps a few did, or almost as good, perhaps their legislative aides read it.

If your group asks the elected leader for a specific commitment — cosponsorship, voting, introducing legislation, or whatever — the elected leader is likely to hedge making a decision. This is perfectly reasonable if s/he is unfamiliar with the issue to which you are referring. Express to the elected leader that you respect hsr need to study the issue further. Ask if you might provide information to a legislative aide. If you give the information to an aide, ask when you might call back regarding the elected official's decision.

Following the meeting, your group should evaluate the meeting. What went well? What do you wish had gone differently? What would you do or not do next time? Be sure to record these comments so people can review them prior to the next meeting. Then, if the composition of the group changes, the experience gained will not be lost.

Someone in your group should send a formal thank-you note to the elected leader. Express the group's desire to work with hmr on hunger issues. Offer the group as a resource for information on hunger. If you promised to send special background materials, do so immediately. Research answers to questions the elected leader asked and your group could not answer, and send responses as soon as possible.

Report back to your entire hunger group about the experience. Act out what happened to help others share in the experience. Next time an appointment with the elected leader is scheduled, one or two people from the first meeting should participate for continuity, but the rest of the group should be different people. This will allow more people to experience and grow from the meetings.

Invitations to Speak

An invitation to speak on hunger is often a good means of lobbying your elected leader. Assume the elected leader is concerned about hunger. Invite hmr to speak on "Legislation to

Help End Hunger in America" or "The U.S. and Hunger in Africa." What will then happen is that an aide will be assigned to draft a speech. S/he will look up current legislation on hunger and hsr boss' position. If the elected leader is supportive and not already a cosponsor, s/he will become one so it can be mentioned at the presentation. Sometimes the aide learns about unfamiliar hunger legislation and is then in a position to recommend support from the elected leader.

Several years ago, Representative Doug Barnard, Jr. was asked to speak at a church in Augusta, Georgia. While drafting the speech, an aide learned about the proposed Food Security Reserve. The more the aide learned, the more reasonable the idea sounded. When the representative spoke, he thanked the church for inviting him to speak on hunger. He told them that as a result of researching the talk, the aide had learned about the proposed Food Security Reserve and brought it to his attention. He announced at that meeting his decision to cosponsor the legislation. Representative Barnard was one of the first Southerners to cosponsor the legislation and was key to getting others on-board — all because of an invitation to speak!

The questions asked following a presentation can also influence an elected leader. If asked about legislation with which s/he is unfamiliar, an elected leader will often respond that s/he will look into the legislation. That alone is a good thing. The kinds of questions asked also help the elected leader judge the community concern about an issue. Most elected leaders are very concerned about their constituents' interests.

The question and answer time should be handled in a respectful manner. Questions should not attack or express hostility towards the elected person. A strong meeting facilitator will be needed.

Inviting the person to speak at a regularly planned church function is the easiest to organize. A Wednesday night family supper or an adult forum immediately after the Sunday service would be a good time. Make sure the structure allows time for questions and answers.

A special community meeting can be organized at which the person would speak, but more work is involved. You would need to print announcements, arrange space, send publicity notices, and recruit an audience. With a general public event, you are also never quite sure who will attend. People may well come who are antagonistic towards the elected person, and so the question and answer time must be carefully controlled.

If at all possible, you want the elected leader's experience speaking about hunger to be positive. Ideally, you would like the person to feel that hunger is an issue s/he would like to adopt as one of hsr primary issues. Most elected officials have three or four areas of main interest. The hunger movement would be well served by more elected leaders making hunger a key, or even a minor, issue.

Meeting with Legislative Aides

Legislative aides who work on hunger issues, especially those in Washington, D.C., are almost as important to build a relationship with as elected leaders. Respected legislative aides have enormous amounts of power and responsibility.

If you have recently met with your elected leader, or if you are having trouble getting an appointment with hmr, invite a legislative aide who works on hunger issues to meet with you. If the aide is to be in the district, or state, s/he will generally accept. Aides are seldom invited to meet or speak with groups, and thus are pleased to be invited.

If hunger is of special interest to the aide, s/he may be well-informed and could be helpful to your group. An aide may be willing to meet with your group for an hour or two and explain how the legislative process works or answer questions about certain pieces of legislation. If the aide is concerned about hunger, s/he will be pleased to know of your group's existence and will appreciate your support.

If the legislative aide has not been particularly concerned about hunger, the meeting is an opportunity to educate the aide on hunger problems and what can be done. At the very least, the meeting will emphasize to the aide that there are constituents in the district or state who are concerned about hunger. The aide will remember this when s/he recommends positions to the elected leader.

Another means of building a relationship with a legislative aide is to invite hmr to a hunger seminar. S/he could come as a participant or possibly to lead a workshop on hunger or the legislative process.

Town Meetings and Public Forums

Most elected officials have some sort of town meetings or public forums where they meet with constituents and answer questions. The number of meetings usually expands around election time. Members of your hunger group should take turns attending these various meetings. Ask specific questions on hunger issues. Elected leaders judge community concerns by the kinds of questions that are asked.

In 1985, Senator Sasser (D-Tenn.) scheduled a series of town meetings across the state of Tennessee. A number of BFW members attended the meetings. At several meetings, he was asked his position on the International Fund for Agricultural Development (IFAD). The first time he got the question, he said he was not familiar with the agency. After the second or third time the question was raised, he was determined to find out more about the agency and consider his position. Upon returning to Washington, D.C., he became a cosponsor of the pending legislation in support of IFAD.

Such forums offer good opportunities for lobbying by asking

well-thought out, targeted questions. Ask questions that require concrete responses and that can elicit positive media coverage. For example:

- Do you support reforms to target more U.S. foreign aid to the poorest of the poor? If so, will you cosponsor such and such a bill?

- Will you vote for increasing funds for the WIC program so more low income children and mothers in our community will have food?

These kinds of questions will portray the elected leader in a favorable light if s/he answers the way you would like. In addition, the question should elicit concrete responses of which you can remind the elected leader later if necessary.

Following a town meeting or public forum, write the elected leader. If you agreed with hsr positions on hunger issues, express your appreciation and offer your support. If you disagreed with the positions, write asking for clarification on the positions and state your opinions. If hunger questions did not get raised, write asking the questions you had planned to ask.

Encourage Personal Experiences with Hunger

We all learn the most from our personal experiences. The same is true with elected leaders. Therefore, assisting or encouraging elected leaders to have personal experiences with hunger and hungry people will help them learn about hunger.

A number of years ago, Senator Hollings (D-S.C.) visited the homes of low-income people in his own hometown of Charleston. It radically changed his attitude toward hunger and prompted him to work more diligently on hunger legislation. Consider inviting your elected leaders to visit a soup kitchen or food pantry. Arrange ways for them to gain a better understanding of hunger in the communities they represent.

Encourage your U.S. representative and senators to participate in investigative trips to famine-stricken nations. (Such trips are sometimes arranged by the Select Committee on Hunger, the Foreign Affairs Committee, and the Appropriations Committee.) Representative Roukema (R-N.J.) went on one such trip to Ethiopia. The trip made a great impression on her. Soon after her trip, she took leadership in Congress to see that adequate assistance was sent. Few representatives are so calloused as to see starving children and not be moved to respond more generously! Encourage your elected leaders to experience hunger personally.

Media

Using the media to lobby elected leaders has long been effective. Elected leaders are very sensitive about their public images, and the media plays a large role in determining that public image. Effective media coverage can focus on an elected leader's position, the content of an issue, or your group's position on an issue. See Chapter 15 on how to use the media. As discussed there, hunger groups can use the media to lobby their elected leaders.

Election Work

Almost any election activity focusing on hunger is a form of lobbying. The activities influence both the incumbent and the challengers. Since election work on hunger will be covered extensively in the following chapter, I will not discuss it here except to note its importance as a form of lobbying.

Prayer and Fasting

I am not sure I want to include prayer and fasting as forms of lobbying, but I do think they need to be an important part of our lobbying work. First, we should pray for ourselves in discerning issues. Secondly, we should pray for the outcome of legislation (which may not always be exactly as we expect), and finally, we should pray for our elected leaders. Being an elected leader in our complex world is extremely difficult. The number of issues leaders are expected to understand and vote upon is overwhelming. The temptations of money and corruption are great. Those in public service need our earnest prayers.

One BFW coordinator, Beverly Phillips, told Representative Crane (R-Il.) when she met with him that she prayed for him daily. Imagine his surprise! And yet, later, when he had a chance to reflect on it, I'm sure he was pleased to have a constituent praying for him daily. We should all follow Beverly's example and regularly pray for our elected leaders.

I would like to add fasting to prayer, knowing full well that this is an area in which I personally need to grow. The Biblical tradition of fasting and praying in times of decision and difficulty is one which the hunger community should follow. It certainly seems fitting for those of us concerned about hunger to be hungry ourselves occasionally.

17. MAKING HUNGER AN ELECTION ISSUE

Why should people concerned about hunger want to involve themselves with elections? They may not want to, but they need to become involved. Elections are an integral part of our political process. Being involved with elections makes us more effective public policy advocates for and with hungry people. Election work entails both direct benefits to your public policy advocacy work, and indirect benefits to your hunger group and your community at large.

Direct Benefits to Election Work

Your election work can force candidates to address hunger issues. Candidates generally prefer to address popular issues about which they have a personal concern. Hunger often is not one of those issues. Nonetheless, if candidates repeatedly are asked questions about hunger in town meetings, candidate forums, and on questionnaires, they will realize that hunger is an issue they must consider. If they are not already concerned, they may become genuinely interested in legislative options for ending hunger.

Election work can increase media coverage of hunger issues. For months before an election, the media focuses on election issues. If your group can get the candidates to discuss hunger, the media will cover it. Alternately, if you can get the media to investigate candidates' positions on hunger, the candidates will have to address hunger. Either way, the general public will hear or read more about hunger issues. In addition, if your group was the primary force behind the increased media coverage, you will gain the reputation as a group who knows how to use the media. That reputation will increase your clout with whichever candidate is elected.

If you make hunger an election issue, the candidates will likely promise some course of action which you can encourage them to fulfill after the election. Few social justice groups keep track of promises and statements made by candidates during campaigns. You may be sure that business and individual self-interest groups do. Election work can be undertaken that will record candidates' statements on hunger, allowing your group to remind those elected of their campaign promises. This must create a concrete record so you can refer to a candidate's specific response rather than a general recollection of what you think the official indicated s/he would do.

You may explore candidates' past voting record on hunger issues as part of your election work. Sometimes, only one candidate's record, the incumbent's, can be analyzed. Other candidates, however, may have records on hunger from different elected offices. For example, if a U.S. representative ran for the U.S. Senate, s/he would also have a hunger record.

Measures of "hunger performance" include voting records on hunger legislation, public statements on hunger issues, cosponsorship of hunger legislation, and positions on hunger issues expressed in letters to constituents. These measures are particularly important if your group has been disappointed with an official's work on hunger. For example, occasionally, an elected official will cosponsor a piece of legislation, indicating hsr support, and then vote against it when it actually comes to a floor vote. An elected official should be asked about this kind of behavior. Elected officials know that the general public does not know how they voted on most issues. They should know that your hunger group is watching their work on hunger issues. Such watchfulness urges officials to think carefully about their hunger positions.

Election activities such as these can develop contacts and strengthen your influence with elected leaders. You will find getting appointments and discussing your concerns with the elected leaders easier if you become acquainted with their staffs before the election. Many key campaign staff members are placed on the legislative staff after the election. If you assist the staffs in developing the candidates' positions on hunger, they will surely remember you as a source of information on hunger once elected.

Elected leaders are most responsive to their constituents' concerns around election time. You may find elected leaders, such as senators who have six-year terms, more open to your concerns the year or two before the election. If this is the case, by all means take advantage of the opening. Seize the opportunity to build a positive relationship with the hopes that it will continue if s/he is reelected.

I have seen this phenomenon on the national level. A year before a vulnerable senator was up for reelection, his staff called Bread for the World frequently to discuss ways to work together. The senator cosponsored numerous pieces of hunger legislation. He took leadership on hunger issues at many points in the political process. He received one of Bread for the World's Distinguished Service awards for leadership on hunger issues in congress. The following year, after his reelection, his staff would barely return phone calls from Bread for the World staff. There seems to be two lessons in this story. One is that at election time the elected leader's openness to hunger issues should be developed and used to the degree possible while the election opportunity "exists." The other is that you should seek to get the candidate's commitment in a tangible form (i.e. in writing) to use in subsequent lobbying efforts.

Indirect Benefits

In addition to increasing your effectiveness as public policy advocates, making hunger an election issue provides many indirect benefits to your group and to your community.

Election work can help your group understand the political process. One reality of politics is that "elected leaders are always running" — for reelection. This is especially true for elected leaders with two year terms. Election work can increase your group's political sophistication by introducing it to the active political forces in the community and by giving it hands-on experience in a fundamental aspect of political life — elections.

Election work can increase your group's media contacts, skills in working with the media, and name recognition. While none of these results alone would justify election work, they are positive side benefits of getting the media to cover hunger issues during an election.

Your election work can help voters understand the candidates' positions on hunger and consider them in voting. Voters take a broad range of issues into consideration when they make their choice. One of those issues you would like voters to consider is hunger. To do so, the voters need to know the candidates' positions and how those positions affect hungry people. This information is unlikely to be available without election work by hunger groups.

Some election work (e.g., voter registration drives) can increase the voting constituencies for programs that help hungry people here in the U.S. Many low-income people are not registered to vote and, in fact, don't vote. As a result, less of a voting constituency exists for programs that benefit low-income people in the U.S. The constituencies for middle- and high-income programs have higher voter turnout, and thus are of more electoral concern to candidates. If more low-income voters registered and voted, elected leaders would think carefully before cutting low-income program benefits, such as food stamps.

Taking an even wider view, it is important for the society as a whole that low-income citizens play a greater role in the entire political process. Registering, and then voting, can be an empowering process and one step on the road to greater overall political participation and civic health.

Finally, election work makes Christians more aware of the connections between their concern about hunger and their participation in the political process. One of the biggest obstacles hunger organizers face is that concerned people separate hunger from politics. Christians find giving money much easier than writing their elected leaders. In the process of registering voters, helping people to the polls, distributing questionnaire results, or whatever your group decides to do, you have the opportunity to educate Christians about the relationship between politics and hunger.

No one election project would provide all of the direct and indirect benefits discussed above, but each would provide at least a few. Your group should consider which kinds of election work seem most effective and appropriate for your community and most suitable for your group's resources. Set specific goals and steps. Because of the early primary dates in many states, you may need to begin planning by January of an election year.

Hunger Questionnaires

Questionnaires on hunger issues are an easy and effective way to make hunger an election issue. First, develop a set of questions that will require the candidates to define their positions on hunger policies. Five or six good questions are plenty. The questions should elicit specific responses that are more than just a yes or no. Be sensitive to the politics in your community as you develop the questions. For example, if your area has recently had a big scandal with the school lunch program, you might not want to ask a question like, "Do you support increasing funding for the school lunch program?" Candidates concerned about adequate funding levels for the program could not indicate their support without alienating many voters. The BFW Election Kit listed in the resource section suggests suitable questions to ask U.S. congressional candidates for the coming election year.

The questionnaires should be hand-delivered or sent registered mail to the candidate's campaign director. Allow no possibility for the questionnaires "getting lost in the mail." Include a cover letter indicating the date you would like the questionnaire completed and explaining your publicity and distribution plans for the questionnaire. Politely inform each candidate that you will publicize hsr response *or* hsr refusal to return the questionnaire. Do give the candidates and their staffs adequate time to complete the questionnaire (between four and eight weeks).

Most candidates will not complete the questionnaires on time without some prompting. Call the campaign director a week before the due date reminding hmr of the deadline. Be prepared to offer extensions of a week or two if requested.

Once the responses have been received, summarize them in a readable fashion. Quote candidates exactly; do not take phrases out of context. Print a one-to-two page fact sheet or brochure comparing the candidates' positions. Print enough copies to distribute widely to the media and community at large. Send a copy to each campaign director.

Send a news release to the newspapers and radio and TV news programs announcing the results of the questionnaire. Enclose the brochure or fact sheet. If your news release is timely, it will be used. Candidates' positions on hunger issues are newsworthy. If the race is particularly close and the media is covering every angle of the race, you may want to hold a press conference to obtain even broader coverage. Get the maximum media coverage possible from your questionnaire before distributing the results to the general public.

Distribution of the results will probably be limited by the financial resources and time you are willing to invest in printing and mailing. If the questionnaire is well done, you may be able to get some financial assistance with printing and mailing extra copies of the questionnaire from church and community groups.

People associated with hunger groups should be a high priority for distribution of your questionnaire summary. They will be most concerned about candidates' positions on hunger issues. If desired, you can distribute your questionnaire summary at churches, shopping malls, or county fairs. You may want to hand out the summary at voter registration sites, if your state's election rules permit, or distribute it just beyond the legal distance from polling sites.

Perhaps members of your group could help register new voters and hand out the questionnaire results simultaneously. If you want to do this, be sure to check local election rules to see if it is legal to put out materials. If so, let candidates know what you are doing so they will consider your group as one they must "reckon with."

Timing your release of questionnaire results is important. Publicizing the questionnaire results may be more important before the primary than before the general election. This is particularly true in districts which are solidly one party or another. For example, if your district is always won by a Republican candidate, then it is more important to do a questionnaire summary comparing the Republican candidates before the primary than one comparing the Republican and Democratic candidates before the general election. Look carefully at the characteristics of your district to determine the most effective timing.

Keep copies of all questionnaire results and the accompanying press coverage. Later, when a candidate is elected, you can remind hmr of hsr statements. If s/he does not follow through on an important promise or principle on hunger issues, talk with the elected official. If s/he still does not change hsr position, you have the makings for an excellent media story, especially for the media that previously publicized the questionnaire.

Candidate Forums

There are two approaches to using candidates' forums. You can work to get one or two hunger questions included in another group's forum, or you can organize your own forum. The easier of the two approaches is working to get hunger questions included in another group's forum. Groups like League of Women Voters have extensive experience in conducting high quality candidates' forums. It's much less work if you can support their forum.

Another possibility is to work with a coalition of groups to produce a forum. If you do this, ensure from the beginning that your questions will be asked and that you believe the association with the other groups involved is a positive association for your group.

If you decide to sponsor your own candidates' forum, the most difficult part will be securing the candidates' commitments to attend. The closer the forum is held to the election (either the primary or the general, depending on the race), the more media coverage and interest it will generate; however, the closer to the election it is, the more reluctant the candidates will be to commit their time.

Once you have tentative commitments from the candidates, find a site and begin working on publicity. Assembling a large group is not difficult, but you need to publicize the forum widely. Send press releases and follow up with phone calls to assure that all the major media attend. The logistics of a candidates' forum are complicated. You need to figure out how to get the candidates in and out without meeting one another (they do not like to meet one another), how to maintain order, how questions will be asked, how to arrange outlets and space for the media, and so forth. There are some excellent guides on planning an election forum listed in the resource section. Review them carefully before you start.

If you are able to undertake the work involved, a well planned forum will provide many benefits. It will get prominent media coverage, force candidates to address hunger issues, help voters know the candidates' positions, develop contacts with the campaign staffs, and build name recognition for your group.

Town Meetings

Many candidates hold town meetings in their districts. Get a listing of all the meetings from the campaign staff or the newspaper. Organize small groups of hunger advocates to attend each meeting and ask hunger questions. Publicize the meetings to people in churches. Vary the questions somewhat, but make sure that the candidates get the message that hunger is a concern to the voters in the district.

House Meetings

House meetings are similar to town meetings except they are smaller and usually attended by invitation only. Try to get members of your hunger group invited to as many of these house meetings as possible. Ask friends who are active in politics if they know of people hosting house meetings and how you might get an invitation. Use the opportunity to ask the candidate questions about hunger.

Voter Registration Drives

Registrations laws vary greatly between states, and sometimes within states. Your first step, therefore, must be to call the Board of Elections and inquire about voter registration laws. You will also need to know the deadlines for registering voters so you can plan accordingly.

States register voters in four different ways. An easy means is mail registration. About half of the states use this method.

People simply fill out a postcard and mail it in. Some states have cards in both English and Spanish. Other states use deputized or branch registrars. If your state employs this method, you should investigate how to become a registrar. Perhaps a number of hunger organizers could become registrars.

The most complicated procedure is centralized registration. With this method, voters have to go to a certain office, usually during business hours, to register. This is often difficult to do, especially for those with limited transportation or strict working hours. A few states allow people to register at the polls on election day. This is the easiest registration of all. People come to the polls, register, and vote.

Once you understand the voter registration rules for your state, you can decide whom and where you will register based upon your group's goals. If your goal is to register more Christians, then you may want to register people in churches before or after services. If your goal is to increase registration of low-income people, then you should focus on low-income neighborhoods, churches, or centers. Food stamp offices, WIC clinics, and soup kitchens are excellent places to register low-income voters. People participating in federal food programs or receiving private food assistance have a direct interest in candidates' positions on hunger and should be encouraged to vote. Be sure that your state's election rules permit registration at the sites you have selected.

Be sure to invite newly registered voters to join your hunger group and to attend any upcoming candidate forums or hunger education programs.

Voter registration campaigns should be accompanied by "get out the vote" campaigns. Registering people is fruitless if they do not vote. Be sure to record the name, address, and phone number of people you register, then follow up and encourage them to vote. Calling new registrants right before an election to see if they have transportation to the polls is an ideal follow-up.

Arrange rides to the polls if needed. If your group does not have enough people to call newly registered voters, a mailing urging people to vote and listing a number people can call if they need a ride to the polls is second best.

A number of groups are organized to work on voter registration. You may want to join a coalition or volunteer to be part of another group's efforts. For example, a number of denominations joined together to sponsor the Churches Committee on Voter Registration. Approximately 30 areas were targeted for 1986 voter registration campaigns. If you are in one of those areas, it would make sense to work with that group. The NAACP, Urban League, and the League of Women Voters also organize voter registration drives. See the resource section for names and addresses of groups that sponsor voter registration drives.

Campaign Work

If individuals within your hunger group feel strongly about one candidate or another, encourage them to volunteer time or contribute money to the campaign. By working with the campaign, individuals become acquainted with candidates and their staffs. It is fine, even desirable, to have hunger group members working for more than one candidate. The odds of having contacts with whomever is elected are greater. The volunteer should explain to the volunteer coordinator that s/he is working in the campaign because of concern about hunger issues. The volunteer should not hesitate to wear a hunger button and discuss hunger with people at campaign headquarters. Turn over among volunteers is rapid at most campaign headquarters. If the volunteer can stay more than a month or two, hsr responsibility and influence among the campaign staff will increase quickly.

Once a volunteer gets to know the campaign staff, s/ he should ask to read position papers on hunger issues. If there are none on hunger, s/he might offer to draft one. If there is one, s/he should ask to comment on it. Urging the candidates to adopt positions papers on hunger will help them clarify their positions on hunger.

Hunger groups should not endorse candidates. Many legally cannot. They should encourage members to work with the candidates of their choice and not run the risk of being perceived as partisan. Your hunger group should be active in elections, but should not endorse a candidate.

Hunger Candidates

Candidates have access to groups and media coverage unavailable to hunger organizers. Is there a person in your group who is fairly articulate? Consider encouraging that person to enter the race with the sole purpose of raising hunger issues. This is definitely worth considering if there are not too many candidates and an assessment indicates that you could give a respectable showing. Fourth or fifth in most races is still respectable.

A Bread for the World activist, John Hohenstein, ran in the primary for the House of Representatives in the third district of Pennsylvania several years ago and came in fourth in a field of seven. The incumbent won with 20,000 votes. The person who came in second spent $165,000 on the campaign and received 10,000 votes. John Hohenstein gained 4,500 votes with a campaign budget of $2,000. He was able to articulate hunger concerns, and since has been invited to most major political events in the area. He is perceived as someone with a political following who should be heeded. His running gave him better access to those actually elected.

Even with a hunger candidate, per se, a hunger group should not endorse a candidate. As individuals, people may want to work in the campaign, especially in getting the person on the ballot, but the group should not become a political club.

Who knows what the future may hold? As the hunger movement gets stronger, a hunger candidate may even win. But, this is probably a few years down the road. In the short term, a hunger candidate can raise the issues, get broader coverage of the issues, and develop contacts with those who are elected.

Post Election Work

No matter who wins the election, your hunger group should congratulate the winner and start to build a relationship with hmr. Set up an appointment soon after the election to offer yourselves as resources on hunger issues. If the elected official is new to the office, your first meeting should focus only on getting acquainted. Give the person some general information about your group and some background materials on hunger issues. Find out who will be the legislative staff person working on hunger. Arrange to meet with hmr as well. Encourage the newly elected leader to make hunger one of hsr main legislative issues.

Hunger PAC

A hunger PAC has recently been formed to contribute money to candidates with strong hunger positions. If you or others would like more information about this PAC, write to the following address:

> Americans Against World Hunger
> P.O. Box 18364
> Washington, D.C. 20036

While a hunger PAC may help some good candidates, the most important election work is done by groups involved at the local level. The strongest resource of the hunger movement is you — people who are concerned and active.

Elections are an integral part of the legislative/political process. To ignore elections is to ignore a significant part of the U.S. political system. This limits our ability to influence what happens on hunger.

As organizers, we should see elections as an exciting organizing tool. Election work can educate and empower people,making a stronger and more effective movement of people against hunger.

18. JOINING COALITIONS

Hunger groups frequently work with other organizations to achieve mutually sought objectives. They join coalitions, temporary alliances of different groups, to achieve these common goals. I've heard a lot of talk about coalitions, but I've not seen enough groups do some careful thinking about the advantages and disadvantages before joining coalitions. Let us look briefly at some of the pros and cons of joining coalitions, as well as some guidelines, alternatives and priorities for undertaking coalition work.

Advantages

The most important advantage of joining a coalition is that coalitions can achieve victories when hunger groups acting alone could not. Many local, state, and national hunger issues need the support and work of more than just the hunger community. This is especially true for some legislative work. For example, hunger groups have supported the WIC program (Supplemental Food Program for Women, Infants, and Children) for a number of years. This program provides high protein food, such as milk and cheese to pregnant women, infants, and children up to five who have low incomes and are at nutritional risk. The program effectively targets benefits to those who need them. Unfortunately, there are many more people who need the program than can be served, given the program's limited funding. Thus, hunger groups have sought to increase funding for the program. National hunger groups have joined in coalitions with nutritionists and the health community to work for funding increases. Such selected coalition work helps achieve victories which hunger groups could not achieve alone.

Coalitions can allow groups to pool resources for a mutually desired project to which no one group can devote all its resources. For example, most hunger groups support World Food Day, as designated by the United Nations. To sponsor a successful World Food Day event, either one or two groups must do a lot of work, or many groups can each do a limited amount of work. A coalition makes good sense for such a mutually desired project.

Your hunger group may also decide to join a coalition to build contacts among targeted constituencies or to gain name recognition. For example, if your hunger group is not integrated, you may want to consider joining a coalition heavily dominated by other racial groups. Alternately, if your hunger group is primarily composed of one denominational group, such as Southern Baptists, you may want to join a coalition in which other denominations are strongly represented.

Coalitions are important to join or organize when elected leaders are attempting to pit groups against one another. This frequently occurs over budget cuts. For example, if your state's governor indicates that s/he plans to cut back on emergency food assistance or housing assistance for low-income people, you may want to join a coalition with low-income housing groups. Your hunger group certainly does not want to be in the position of encouraging cuts in low-income housing programs to increase food assistance.

Disadvantages

The disadvantages of joining coalitions are more complex than the advantages, and thus are important to analyze carefully. Joining coalitions can be a way to avoid doing the hard, day-to-day outreach work necessary to organize a group. Instead of setting up ways to reach out and broaden the hunger movement by involving new people, groups may join coalitions. Tim Sampson, a long-time community organizer, wrote in an article "From Coalition and Other Relationships" (*The Organizer,*

Fall, 1983), "All the cooperating, coordinating, networking and coalition-building will not organize the unorganized." Joining coalitions should not be done to avoid grassroots organizing. Involving new people is more important than drawing from the existing pool of people involved in hunger work. Be sure that joining a coalition is not a means of avoiding the more difficult, but the more important work of reaching out to people who are not already involved.

Coalitions can drain your group, without directly meeting its goals. Because your hunger group has limited resources and energy, and cannot do everything, you must set clear goals and steps, and make these your priorities. Some groups feel they should join coalitions, whenever asked. Beware: the coalition may require meeting time, publicity, and other limited resources from the group. You should not join a coalition simply because it promotes a good project or a worthy issue. There are literally thousands of good projects and issues. You should join only those that address your group's priorities.

Beware of statements like "We only want someone to meet with our planning group once a month." Group process is such that the person attending coalition meetings will not be able to avoid committing hmrself and the group to additional tasks and responsibilities. Just by attending meetings, the person is bound to do more. This is OK if the tasks are in line with the group's priorities.

Joining a coalition may be an excuse for spending time with like-minded people. Finding support communities is important for all hunger organizers. It is not, however, a sufficient reason for joining a coalition. There are bound to be less time-consuming and more relaxing ways of socializing with supportive people than joining coalitions that do not further your goals.

Joining a coalition can alienate your group from potential participants. One of the advantages of hunger as an organizing issue is that it appeals to a broad range of people.This advantage can be negated if you join coalitions that have a much more limited appeal. If your group joins coalitions with groups perceived as left or right of center, your group will be perceived that way as well. I personally believe that because hunger concerns people of all political stripes, you lessen your effectiveness when you become closely aligned with issues and groups that attract fewer people. You may strongly support the other groups in the coalition, but it may be better for your hunger group if you don't join the coalition.

The coalitions you do join should be selected for the benefits to your group and others, and generally should not be perceived as strongly partisan or biased.

Guidelines for Joining

Each request to join a coalition should be weighed carefully. Usually the approach of social justice groups is to join unless there are specific reasons not to. I recommend the opposite approach. The group should not join unless there are strong advantages to joining. Some questions you should ask before deciding are:

1. How will joining benefit our hunger group? Try to answer this specifically, not just with a response like "other groups will like us better."

2. How will our joining benefit the coalition? Does our group have special resources and approaches which will uniquely benefit the coalition? Joining for joining's sake is not worth much. What can you offer?

3. Will joining the coalition help you achieve the goals you have set for yourselves and get new people involved, or will it take you off track?

4. What resources, financial or human, are expected as part of joining the coalition? Could they be used in another fashion which would more directly meet your goals?

5. Can you support the project (assuming you think it's a good project) without joining the coalition?

6. How are decisions made? Will decisions be made with which you don't agree?

7. Will the coalition make statements or policies without the approval of your group?

8. Will joining the coalition require the group to downplay its faith perspective in a harmful fashion?

Coalitions can strengthen or diminish the work of hunger groups depending on the coalitions' goals and required resources. Take time to carefully weigh the pros and cons of each coalition before deciding to join.

Alternatives to Coalitions

Your group has a number of alternatives to joining a coalition. Offering alternatives will indicate support and interest in others' concerns without the disadvantages of joining the coalition.

You can offer to publicize a certain event, or personally attend a coalition's function. Groups often organize coalitions to increase attendance at specific events. You can assist the group by attending the event without joining the coalition.

You can offer to highlight the hunger dimensions of the coalition's topic without joining the coalition. For example, your group may be asked to join a coalition on Central America. If you decided that joining is not in your group's best interest, you could offer to highlight hunger in Central America in your activities. You could feature Central America in a press release, presentation, or workshop on hunger.

You can endorse a statement or conference without joining the coalition. You will want to be sure how your endorsement will be used, of course, but an endorsement will commit you to less than joining the coalition. Especially if the coalition is expected to require many meetings, providing an endorsement may be preferable.

Priorities for Joining Coalitions

There are times when the advantages of joining coalitions far outweigh potential difficulties, and alternatives are not adequate. In these cases, you should actually seek out coalitions to join. For example, if your group is not well-integrated, joining coalitions with other racial groups may be a priority. It can help your group develop stronger contacts and establish trust with other racial groups in the community. Similarly, if your group does not include low-income people, joining coalitions with low-income groups will probably be a priority.

Your group may set goals it cannot meet alone, and forming a coalition will be necessary to accomplish them. For example, some election projects are difficult to conduct alone. Voter-registration and candidates' forums are two projects which might be priorities for coalition work. In general, ad hoc groups and short-term coalitions are better to join than ones with no definite end. They generally have clearer objectives and require more limited commitments of resources.

Joining a coalition should be done strategically and carefully. You should weigh the advantages and disadvantages. Too many small groups dissipate their time and resources supporting projects that are of marginal benefit to them. You should require the coalition's project to meet your priorities. Never allow your group to be pressured into joining a coalition. Joining coalitions requires us to be "shrewd as serpents, and innocent as doves."

19. INNER STRENGTH AND OUTER WITNESS

We who approach hunger organizing from a Christian perspective view our work as a special ministry to which we are called as part of our Christian witness. We show forth God's love for us and God's love for our neighbors. This expression of God's love is the very core of the Gospel. When Christ was asked what was the greatest commandment, he replied, "Thou shalt love the Lord thy God with all thy heart, and with all thy soul, and with all thy mind." The second greatest commandment, he added, was "like unto it, Thou shalt love thy neighbor as thyself." (Matthew 22: 37-39) Loving our neighbors as ourselves requires that we struggle to eliminate the bonds of oppression that deny food to hungry people.

God calls us to commit our entire lives to the work of justice, not just a passing year or two. Consequently, we must find ways to handle the pressures confronting us, and develop ways to improve our understanding and skills, and nourish our faith for the long haul.

There are certainly many pressures that call us to abandon the struggle. The pressures on Christian people in the U.S. to conform are strong. The constant barrage of the media stressing physical beauty, possessions, and power, are hard to ignore. We read newspapers, listen to radio, watch television, see billboards, and they all transmit the same message — take care of yourself first.

The pressures at the work place, just to keep a job, consume time and energy. Most jobs do not particularly want transformed people. Employers prefer us to conform to the standards of the world, to seek financial rewards, and to care first and foremost for ourselves.

Our families place pressures on us. First our parents and siblings, and later our spouses and children communicate their expectations about how we should act. A little bit of charity work is nice. This constant social justice stuff is going a bit overboard! Seriously though, in most cases, parents, siblings, spouses, and children want us to succeed in traditional terms. Assuring them of our love and affection without feeling pressured to conform is seldom easy.

Perhaps the most distressing, if not the most difficult pressure that Christians face is the pressure within our churches. Sometimes it seems that our churches have accepted the world's values. Buildings become more important than people. Rich people are valued more than poor. Those working against hunger are withdrawn from rather than encouraged and supported. In the very place where we look for help in seeking the kingdom of God, sometimes we experience pressures similar to those found elsewhere.

The largest pressure we face is the issue itself. The human suffering caused by hunger calls us with overwhelming urgency. The root causes of hunger confuse and bewilder us. The elimination of hunger seems far off, if not impossible. The issue of hunger leaves us depressed. We feel frantic to respond, and we despair.

So how do we deal with these pressures? How do we renew ourselves for the long-term work of social justice? I have no easy answers to these questions. I do have a few reflections.

First, I believe we should see how Christ dealt with pressures. At the beginning of his ministry, Christ selected a group of people to work with him. The disciples were a group of people with which Christ could relax, share food, and talk. Those of us working on social justice concerns also need a support community. We need people around us who can encourage us and challenge us to grow in understanding and commitment. We need friends who will help us be transformed rather than conformed to the world.

If you are not part of a supportive group of people, find one or start one. Even if your family is supportive, few people are able to sustain their involvement in hunger concerns without additional friends who share their values.

Christ also took time to pray and reflect. He regularly went to the hills to be quiet. We need to find our own prayer times and places, even if they are not actually in the hills. Set aside time and find a place which allows you to be alone with God on a regular basis. Those with large families may need to make some quiet time early in the morning, or schedule regular walks in the park. Without that time for inner reflection, you will not be able to sort out the pressures of the world or reestablish your priorities.

Journal writing has become a popular exercise for many Christians. People use their journals to develop and strengthen their spiritual lives. Fasting, although not nearly as popular as journal writing, is a spiritual discipline which we should practice more regularly. The Bible consistently directs us to fast and pray. What is more fitting for Christians concerned about hungry people?

Finally, Christ took time to relax. We, too, need to make time to relax. I am not suggesting that we focus our lives on relaxing or being entertained, but rather that we know our own personal limits. If we don't find those limits, and learn to live within them, we will burn out.

Have you ever noticed in reading the Gospels that Christ was regularly found riding in boats? No doubt, boats were a major means of transportation in those days; however, I believe Christ enjoyed riding in boats. Remember the time he slept through a violent storm? One has to like boats to sleep during a storm! An organizing colleague of mine who fishes to relax suggests that Christ really liked to fish!

The majority of Christ's activities depicted in the Gospels are teaching, healing, and prayer. Christ is, however, shown relaxing several times. He attended a wedding in Cana. He ate with his disciples. He accepted the perfume from the woman in Bethany. Most of Christ's relaxing appears to have been done alone, in prayer and quiet. A number of times the Gospels indicate that Christ went off alone or sent the disciples ahead without Him. Different people relax in different ways. It is important that you identify activities you find relaxing and renewing.

I used to believe that burnout was just an excuse and that people did not really burn out. I do not believe that anymore. I have seen committed people burn out. Victims of burnout become so distressed by the problems of the world, and push themselves so hard, that they reach a point where they can no longer function effectively. If we want to work for justice many years, we have to see that we do not overburden ourselves. We need to relax and renew ourselves. We need to take time to pray. And, we need to find people who will support us in our work for justice.

As we develop the support groups, prayer life, and relaxing activities we need to keep our inner selves whole, we must strive to develop the understanding, skills, and faith that make us effective workers. We need to develop the inner spiritual and intellectual strength necessary for a strong outer witness. Only a well-developed inner strength can prepare us for the pressures to conform and the overwhelming nature of the issue of hunger. To nurture our inner strength, we need to study carefully, develop organizing skills, and be lead by faith.

CHRISTIAN ORGANIZERS NEED TO STUDY CAREFULLY. Hunger is an enormously complex problem that has its roots and its solution in economics and politics. Thus, we must strive to understand the political and economic world in which we live. We must attempt to understand the relationships between the U.S. and Third World nations, and the economic and political forces within our own country. We need to comprehend the U.S.

legislative process so we can influence it. I am afraid, that as a community of social justice leaders, we do not study as much as we should. Hunger organizers need to study.

Over the years, I have interviewed a number of candidates for organizing positions at Bread for the World. Most of the candidates have been active with hunger issues for a number of years. One question I have almost stopped asking candidates because of the embarrassed silence it causes is, "What books have you read within the last year on hunger or economics or another related topic?"

A few years ago I was at a hunger seminar that had two session on foreign aid — one basic course and one advanced course. I was one of the workshop leaders for the advanced session. About fifteen hunger activists who had been involved with hunger issues for a long time came to the workshop. As the workshop advanced, it became obvious that most of the participants did not understand the difference between U.S. bilateral aid and aid given by private voluntary agencies. Not knowing these things in themselves is not bad. Not knowing them and thinking one is ready for an "advanced" session is a concern. That these people had been lobbying on aid issues for six or eight years and had not really struggled to learn about them is also distressing.

Do hunger organizers need to go back to school or become experts in one phase of the hunger issue? Certainly not, but they do need to grow in their understanding of the causes and solutions of hunger. We can not be satisfied with simple answers. We need to set up the systems for study — both within our groups and individually — that will provide the analytical tools to confront the complicated problems of hunger in our world.

Studying the issues carefully not only gives our organizing work more focus and direction, it also teaches us to pace ourselves. The more we study, the greater appreciation we develop for the complexity of the problem and the need for us to see our work against hunger as a lifelong commitment, and not one that can end any time soon.

CHRISTIAN ORGANIZERS NEED TO DEVELOP THEIR ORGANIZING SKILLS. Christians working to build a movement of people concerned about hunger need to develop their organizing skills. Like understanding hunger issues, developing these skills requires study and reflection. We need to analyze what works in our communities and what does not. How can we interest more people in hunger concerns? How can we relate the needs of hungry people both here and abroad to our neighbors in ways that reach them? How can we convey complicated issues simply, but not simplistically?

Developing our organizing skills teaches us to deal with people. In the process we are challenged to look at the messages we convey to people, and to reflect on our entire outlook and approach toward people around us, especially toward those who are different than we. Developing organizing skills teaches us about ourselves. Sometimes we learn the strengths we have to offer. Other times, we recognize the sinful, unreconciled parts of our lives.

Until recently, too few hunger leaders concentrated on developing organizing skills. Just by reading this far, you have made a sizable time investment in developing organizing skills, and hopefully you are better equipped to begin or continue organizing on hunger.

CHRISTIAN ORGANIZERS NEED TO BE LED BY FAITH. One of my favorite hymns is "We've Come This Far By Faith." I believe it's true. The hunger movement, in general, and each of us in particular has come this far by faith. The steps we have made toward justice have been accomplished through faith, and not by works alone.

Faith integrates our knowledge of hunger issues with our skills and strategies for organizing. Our faith provides the overall vision of where we are going. We will never have a perfectly clear vision, but our faith allows us to see glimmers of a vision. Without faith, it is difficult to have much hope.

Our faith enables us to work for justice without feeling responsible for curing all the injustices in the world. Our work for justice must flow out of God's love rather than from guilt. The often quoted statement from Mother Teresa is fitting. She says, "We're not called to be successful, we're called to be faithful." This faith will support us while others burn out, because we don't feel responsible for all the problems. Rather, we feel responsible for doing the best we can.

Faith gives us confidence because we know God's grace is available to us. Without faith, we will always feel inadequate. We can never do enough good work. People involved in justice work tend to push themselves too hard. Without the knowledge of grace that comes from faith, we will always find our efforts lacking. Our faith offers us the knowledge that God loves and accepts us despite our shortcomings.

Faith helps us not to judge those around us. People working against hunger tend to be a critical lot. We don't like the state of the world. Its easy for that critical nature to become judgmental. Because we are all imperfect, we must learn to support and encourage one another, and not judge one another.

Finally, our faith gives us courage — good courage. Have you ever noticed the phrase used repeatedly in the Books of Moses and in Psalms that reads, "Be of good courage." I am fascinated by that phrase "good courage." I'm not sure precisely what it means, but it seems reserved for people of faith. It is a phrase which seems apt for hunger work.

We need good courage to study economics even when it seems intimidating. We need good courage to understand ourselves better and learn how to work more closely with our neighbors. Most importantly, we need good courage to take actions to relieve the suffering of hungry people. Many of the actions needed, meeting with elected leaders, giving presentations, or writing media stories, demand courage. We find that courage, good courage, from our faith.

Hunger is a long term problem. It is unlikely to end in our lifetime. To be faithful for the long term, and to be effective witnesses in the world, we must develop our inner strength. We must find ways to deal with the pressures of our personal lives and the pressures caused by the nature of hunger itself. These pressures are unlikely to disappear, so we must find ways to overcome them. Our strategies must include finding friends who share our values, establishing quiet prayer times, and learning when and how to relax.

Beyond maintaining ourselves, we must strive to be stronger and more effective witnesses in the world. We must study carefully, develop our organizing skills, and be led by faith. Only by doing so will we obtain a vision for the future. Organizing on hunger is important because lives matter. Each person is a child of God and is entitled to food. As we work against hunger, we are God's witnesses in the world. To be the strongest witnesses, we must nourish and develop our inner strength. This will sustain us in our ministry when others decide that hunger is a passing fad. Our inner strength undergirds our witness and provides courage for our work.

Go forth. Develop your inner strength. Be of good courage. And organize as if lives depended on it!

APPENDIX A —
PRINT RESOURCES

Christians and Hunger

Freudenberger, C. Dean, and Paul M. Minus, Jr. *Christian Responsibility in a Hungry World.* Nashville: Abingdon Press, 1976. Clear, simple explanation of why Christians should be involved with hunger. The statistics are a bit out of date.

Gonzalez, Justo. "Biblical Handles on Hunger." *Handles for Action.* Vol. 4, #2, Spring, 1984. This edition of the newsletter of the Presbyterian Hunger Program deals with Biblical passages which are perceived as difficult ones, such as "the poor you have always with you." Very helpful for working with Christians. For the newsletter, write to 341 Ponce de Leon Avenue, NE, Atlanta, GA 30365.

Nelson, Jack A. *Hunger for Justice: The Politics of Food and Faith.* Maryknoll, NY: Orbis Books, 1980. A good introduction to the politics of food and development issues.

Sider, Ronald J. *Cry Justice: The Bible Speaks on Hunger and Poverty.* Ramsey, NJ: Paulist Press, 1980. A handy collection of readings from the Bible related to hunger and poverty.

Sider, Ronald J. *Rich Christians in an Age of Hunger: A Biblical Study.* Downers Grove, IL: InterVarsity Press, 1984. An excellent introduction to why Christians should be involved in hunger issues. Written from an evangelical perspective.

Simon, Arthur, *Bread for the World.* Ramsey, NJ: Paulist Press, Revised 1984. A clear and compelling overview of issues and why Christians should be involved. Free to new BFW members.

Organizing (general)

Adamson, Madeleine, and Seth Borgos. *This Mighty Dream: Social Protest Movements in the United States.* Boston: Routledge & Kegan Paul, 1984. A history of selected protest movements in the U.S. Good discussion of the role of conflict in social change. Powerful photographs and historical documents.

Alinsky, Saul D. *Rules for Radicals.* New York: Random House, Inc., 1972. The "classic" in organizing literature.

Hedemann, Ed, ed. *War Resisters League Organizer's Manual.* New York: War Resisters League, 1981. Particularly helpful chapters on designing leaflets, printing materials, and organizing street fairs and theater.

Kahn, Si. *Organizing: A Guide for Grassroots Leaders.* New York: McGraw-Hill Book Company, 1981. A solid introduction to grassroots organizing.

O.M. Collective. *The Organizers Manual.* New York: Bantam Books, 1971. Good information on teach-ins, direct action plans, and constituencies. Unfortunately, this book is out-of-print.

Piven, Francis Fox, and Richard A. Cloward. *Regulating the Poor: The Functions of Public Relief.* New York: Random House, Inc., 1972. Stimulating reading about the patterns of public welfare in U.S. history. Demonstrates the importance of conflict and organized groups in increasing welfare payments.

Staples, Lee. *Roots to Power: A Manual for Grassroots Organizing.* New York: Praeger Press, 1984. Based on Acorn's model of community organizing around neighborhood issues. Instructive for all organizers. Good chapters on the role of organizers, group maintenance, and dealing with details.

Embracing Diversity

Carey, RDC, Loretta, and Kathleen Kanet, RSHM. *Racism: Two Americas and Sexism and Human Liberation.* Two booklets in a twelve-session program entitled *LEAVEN.* Silver Spring, MD: Leaven Office, 1984. Provide a framework for group study on racism and sexism. Each unit designed for a two-hour session. Recommended for groups from five to twelve people.

Cobb, Jonathan and Richard Sennett. *The Hidden Injuries of Class.* New York: Random House, Inc, 1973. Classic study of the internal conflicts suffered by blue-collar workers in the U.S. Offers helpful insights for groups seeking to involve more blue-collar workers.

Kochman, Thomas. *Black and White Styles in Conflict.* Chicago: The University of Chicago Press, 1983. A thought-provoking presentation of style differences between black and white people. Helpful to blacks and whites in understanding possible sources of conflicts.

Men Against Patriarchy. "Overcoming Masculine Oppression in Mixed Groups." *Off Their Backs . . . And On Our Own Two Feet.* Philadelphia: New Society Publishers, 1983. One of the best articles written on the dynamics of sexism in group meeting situations. Enlightening reading for men and women.

Moore, Robert B. *Racism in the English Language.* New York: The Racism/ Sexism Resource Center. An essay looking at the racism in the English language and a five-session lesson plan to help groups look at racism. Good discusssion piece for groups.

Forming and Nurturing a Group

Auvine, Brian, et. al. *A Manual for Group Facilitators.* Madison, WI: The Center for Conflict Resolution, 1985. Best book available for group facilitators working with social justice groups. Helpful ideas for meeting facilitation and setting goals.

Coover, Virginia, et. al. *Resource Manual for a Living Revolution*. Philadelphia: New Society Publishers, 1985. Fine collection of exercises and role-plays on group dynamics, decision-making, conflict resolution, and skills building.

Johnson, David W., and Frank P. Johnson. *Joining Together: Group Theory and Group Skills*. Englewood Cliffs, NJ: Prentice-Hall, Inc., 1982. A classic textbook on groups. Lots of exercises for groups having difficulties with basic communication, controversy, conflicts of interest, and listening to one another.

McCoy, Bob. "Stages of Small Groups". An unpublished paper available from Inter-Varsity Christian Fellowship, 810 S. 7th Street, Minneapolis, MN 55415. Brief, but excellent, introduction to small group theory. Written for use by leaders of Christian small groups.

The Navigators. *The Small Group Letter*. A newsletter for Christian small groups designed to enhance small group life and ministry. Produced ten times per year. Available for $17 from Subscription Services, P.O. Box 1164, Dover, NJ, 07801.

Nicholas, Ron, et. al. *Small Group Leaders Handbook*. Downers Grove, IL: InterVarsity Press, 1981. Geared primarily toward Inter-Varsity chapters, but a good collection of articles on small groups with a faith center. Sixty pages of resources offer creative suggestions for people to get to know one another.

Prince, George M. *The Practice of Creativity: A Manual for Dynamic Group Problem Solving*. New York: Macmillan Publishing Co., Inc., 1972. Excellent suggestions for group leaders on getting the most creativity out of a group.

Working Within Your Church

The Christian Life Commission of the Southern Baptist Convention. *Planning Guide for a World Hunger Emphasis*. Nashville: The Christian Life Commission of the Southern Baptist Convention. Tells when, why and how to plan a world hunger emphasis. Ideas for involving families and children. Worship aids for a Sunday worship service, devotion, meal, and a retreat.

Church World Service/CROP. *Educational Resources*. Elkhart, IN: Church World Service. Designed for use by a CROP recruiter in a church. Provides suggested activities, print and film resources, worship ideas, alternative meals, and a dramatic reading.

Division of Mission Promotion. *How to Reveal the Gift: A Handbook for Mission Promoters*. New York: Presbyterian Church General Mission Board and Support Agency. Delightful handbook on giving a minute for mission, arranging attractive displays, presenting effective audiovisuals, receiving a mission speaker, publishing a mission brochure, celebrating a mission festival, and promoting a special offering.

Fagan, Harry. *Empowerment: Skills for Parish Social Action.* Ramsey, NJ: Paulist Press, 1979. An introductory workbook for undertaking social action in the parish. Practical and nicely designed. Good chapters on social change and leadership. Offers eleven steps for selecting and implementing actions.

Pierce, Gregory F. *Activism That Makes Sense: Congregations and Community Organization.* Ramsey, NJ: Paulist Press, 1984. Makes a good case for local involvement on immediate self-interest issues.

Starting Emergency Food Programs

Arnold, John. *Give Me Your Hungry: Food Pantry Operational Handbook.* St. Louis: Salvation Army. A detailed manual designed for those wishing to start or expand their pantries. Good for those experiencing large demands and needing to improve their agency's functioning.

Maryland Food Committee. *Plain Talk About Emergency Food Centers.* Baltimore: Maryland Food Committee. Designed for people who have already decided to establish a food center and need help in the best way to set it up. Good for sensitizing volunteers to the needs and concerns of people using food pantries.

SEEDS. *How to Start a Soup Kitchen.* Decatur, GA: SEEDS. Well-written, simple introductory piece on starting a soup kitchen.

Wright-Dietelbaum, Dianne. *How to Start a Food Pantry.* Los Angeles: Interfaith Hunger Coalition, August 1984. Put together to assist groups in Los Angeles, but most of the suggestions are applicable for church's anywhere. A valuable seventeen-page booklet for those setting up a food pantry. Write to the interfaith Hunger Coalition, 1010 South Flower Street, Suite 404, Los Angeles, CA 90015.

Bible Studies and Worship Aids on Hunger

Alternatives. "World Food Day/Thanksgiving Bulletin Insert." Ellenwood, GA: Alternatives. A double bulletin insert including words and music for a song based on Isaiah 58.

Bread for the World. "All God's Children." Washington, D.C.: Bread for the World. A dialogue designed to be read by children during a worship service. Compares the lives of young people in rich and poor countries.

Bread for the World. "Behold, I Am Making All Things New." Washington, D.C.: Bread for the World. A two-person dialogue about the relationship between personal religion and social activism.

Bread for the World. *Voices from the Quiet.* Washington, D.C.: Bread for the World. An extremely popular worship aid. A 15-minute chancel drama using two main speakers and the entire congregation as the chorus.

Pohl, Christine, and Martin Fradis. *Hunger and Oppression -Justice and Hope: Seven Bible Studies*. Washington, D.C.: Bread for the World Educational Fund. Each study designed for use with groups in a one hour time frame. Questions included.

Adult Hunger Study/Action Programs

Bread for the World Educational Fund. *Hunger in a Land of Plenty*. Washington, D.C.: Bread for the World Educational Fund, 1985. An excellent study course on hunger in the U.S. Includes background reading, discussion questions, Biblical reflection and action ideas. Leader's manual available. The best study on domestic hunger.

Bread for the World Educational Fund. *A Hungry World*. Washington, D.C.: Bread for the World Educational Fund. A six-session general introduction to hunger. Designed for Christian groups.

Bread for the World Educational Fund. *Land and Hunger: A Biblical Worldview*. Washington, D.C.: Bread for the World Educational Fund. A six-session study course. Each session has a short simulation exercise, background reading materials, discussion questions, and Biblical reflection. Accompanying leaders guide available.

Church World Service Office on Global Education. *Scriptural Poster-Related Curricula*. Baltimore: Church World Service Office on Global Education, 1984. Six 50-minute curricula explore the connections between hunger and children, refugees, water, global security, militarism, and women. Can be purchased individually or as a set.

Dodd, Dee Anne, ed. *Hunger and Militarism: A Guide to Study,Reflection and Action*. New York: American Friends Service Committee, 1984. Good background on the issues. Somewhat limited on reflection suggestions. Recommended for advanced groups.

Fitzpatrick, James and Karen, with James and Kathleen McGinnis. *Those Who Hunger*. Ramsey, NJ: Paulist Press, 1979. A program of prayer and education on world hunger designed for parish use during Lent. An excellent package including a program coordinator handbook, leader's guide, workbooks, liturgy book, slides and cassette, and publicity poster.

Jorgenson, Bonnie, and Arthur Simon. *Too Many Are Hungry: What Can I Do?* Kansas City: Leaven Press, 1985. An excellent Biblically focused six-session study guide. Includes prayers, readings, reflections, discussion questions, and action outreach ideas.

Sapp, W. David. *Bible Studies for a World Hunger Emphasis*. Nashville: The Christian Life Commission of the Southern Baptist Convention. Four short Bible studies. Two designed for individual and family use, and two for group study.

Family and Intergenerational Hunger Study/Action Programs

Adams-Williams, Jan, Judy McMillan, and Milo Shannon-Thornberry. *Those Who Speak for God: Household Studies on the Minor Prophets.* Ellenwood, GA: Alternatives, 1984. Nine Bible studies for use by families.

Dregni, Meredith S. *Experiencing More with Less.* Scottsdale, PA: Herald Press, 1983. An intergenerational curriculum for camps, retreats, and other educational settings. Focused on lifestyle issues, although relates to hunger concerns. Suitable for ages 5 through adults.

Grissom, Harriette, and Milo Thornberry. *A Journey Through Africa.* Ellenwood, GA: Alternatives, 1985. A seven session study guide designed especially for use in intergenerational households. Helps families understand more about the causes of hunger in Africa.

McPortland, Joanne. *The Empty Place.* Los Angeles: Franciscan Communications Center, 1976. A family activity booklet on world hunger. Designed to be used in the home by parents and older children. Ideally, the booklet should be used in conjunction with the filmstrips "A World Hungry".

SEEDS. *Roots of Hope: Miss-a-Meal Meditations.* Decatur, GA: SEEDS, 1979. This small book contains 52 Biblical meditations which are ideal for miss-a-meal programs or for family Bible studies.

Shalom Education Taskforce. *Ending World Hunger: The First Steps.* Nashville: Discipleship Resources, 1983. An intergenerational hunger study. Designed for use in a retreat setting or over several Sundays or weeknight sessions. Includes simulation games, Bible studies, and recommended films. Suitable for senior high through adults.

Sprinkle, Patricia H. *Hunger: Understanding the Crisis through Games, Dramas, & Songs.* Atlanta: John Knox Press, 1980. A collection of creative resources for involving all age groups in hunger issues. Indicates the targeted age groups, preparation needed, special features, and number of players.

Youth and Children's Hunger Study/Action Programs

The Board for Social Ministry Services The Lutheran Church-Missouri Synod. *A Festival of Sharing.* A resource book for conducting a thirty-hour fundraising fast or hunger help retreat. Designed for youth groups.

Campolo, Anthony. *Ideas for Social Action.* Grand Rapids, MI: Zondervan Publishing House, 1985. Best book available on involving youth in mission and service. Not specifically geared toward hunger issues, but many of the ideas relate to hunger. Excellent chapters on service projects that meet special human needs and on raising funds for social action.

Dilli, SSND, Rosemary. *Poverty and Human Development, What is Poverty?* and *Poverty and Justice.* Washington, D.C.: Campaign for Human Development. Three lesson plans for grades 3-5, 6-8, and 9-12, respectively. Include outlines, activities, and discussion questions.

Division for Life and Mission in the Congregation in consultation with the Hunger Program. *Hunger Helps for Children.* Minneapolis: American Lutheran Church Hunger Program. A resource booklet for highlighting hunger over the Lenten, Easter, and Pentecost seasons. Includes children's sermons and activities.

Dykstra, Deb, and Fennetta Raymond. *God's Gift Shop.* Unpublished, 1985. Copies available at cost from Fennetta Raymond, Oakdale Park Christian Reformed Church, 1313 East Butler S.E., Grand Rapids, MI 49507. A four-session vacation Bible school curriculum, with two designs. Design one is for children age 4 through 1st grade. Design two is for grades 2 through 6. Creative ideas and activities in each session.

Foote, Sharon. *Plant a Seed, Begin to Care, Begin to Share,* and *Learning to Care, Learning to Share.* Nashville: Discipleship Resources, revised 1983. Three hunger curricula for preschool, very young elementary, and older elementary children, respectively. Intended for use as vacation church school curricula, but can be adapted for use with children during a church-wide hunger study event. Many creative ideas in each book.

Hendrix, Lela M. *Hunger Alert: An Awareness/Action Guide for Youth and Youth Leaders.* Nashville: Christian Life Commission of the Southern Baptist Convention, 1984. Good collection of youth awareness and action activities. Designed for use in Southern Baptist churches, but can easily be adapted for other denominations.

Impact on Hunger. *Hunger and the Catholic Tradition* and *World Hunger: Learning to Meet the Challenge.* New York: Impact on Hunger, 1985. When used together, these two books offer an excellent religious curriculum for high school students. The first is a religious supplement to the second, a public-school curriculum.

Lersch, Phil and Jean, and Bonnie Munson. *Hunger Activities for Children,* and *Hunger Activities for Teens.* St. Petersburg, FL: Brethren House, 1978 and 1979, respectively. Two of the finest collections of learning activities on hunger available. Written from a faith perspective. The ideas could be adapted for use in Sunday school classes or vacation church school.

Otero, George G., and Gary R. Smith. *Teaching about Food and Hunger.* Denver: Center for Teaching International Relations Press, 1978. Contains thirty-three learning activities for students in grades 6 - 12. Each activity includes directions for the teacher and single copies for student forms.

Pavlenko, Nancy. *Help for Hungry People.* Minneapolis: Augsburg Publishing House, 1977. Five-session study with materials for children and teachers. Separate suggestions for use with children kindergarten age to 3rad grade, and 4th to 6th graders.

Seanor, Tim. *Royal Ambassador World Hunger Relief Manual*. Memphis: Brotherhood Commission, SBC. Geared toward Southern Baptist Crusaders, a boys' organization, although adaptable to many Christian children's groups. divided into two parts, one for grades 1-3 and the other for grades 4-6. Includes meeting suggestions, study ideas, and an excellent cmpilation of hunger awareness games and puzzles.

SEEDS/Alternatives. *All Tied Up!* Ellenwood, GA: SEEDS/Alternatives, 1984. Excellent educational program on hunger for youth for a weekend retreat or youth week event. Clear leader instructions, recommended program schedules, planning guides, simulation materials, posters and certificates. Well designed and easy to follow.

Organizing on Campus

Bread for the World. *Bread for the World on Campus: A Resource Kit*. Washington, D.C.: Bread for the World, 1983. Attractive kit with many ideas for campus organizing. Highlights public policy work. Good sections on events and outreach, publicity, and studying hunger in the university.

Bread for the World. *Hunger Watch U.S.A.* Washington, D.C.: Bread for the World, 1985. A manual of how to survey the hunger needs in your community. Includes timelines and questionnaires. Good independent study project or campus group project.

Church World Service/CROP. *Organizational Guide for a CROP Hunger Walk*. Elkhart, IN: Church World Service/CROP. Helpful guide on how to organize a CROP walk. Includes general information about Church World Service/CROP and hunger issues.

Nutrition Awareness 2005. *Nutrition Awareness 2005 brochure, Nutrition l985 Cookbook,* and *Nutrition l985 Program Kit*. Spokane,WA: Nutrition Awareness 2005. Whitworth College began an innovative dining and education program on hunger a number of years ago, originally called Nutrition l985. The name was then changed to Nutrition Awareness 2005. The brochure ($.50) describes the program in general. The cookbook ($4.50) gives recipes and information on designing an alternative dining program on campus. The kit ($26.25) if for those ready to set up an alternative dining service. It includes menus, recipes, brochures, posters, handouts, and model materials. Request resources from Linda Grandfield, Nutrition Awareness 2005, Whitworth College, Spokane, WA 9925l.

Oxfam America. *Fast for a World Harvest Organizer's Guide*. Boston: Oxfam America. Well-organized information on how to plan and run a campuswide fast, as well as on projects the fast supports.

Public Speaking

League of Women Voters. *Projecting Your Image: How to Produce a Slide Show*. Washington, D.C.: League of Women Voters, 1977. Helpful four-page guide on producing a slide show to accompany a presentation.

Uris, Dorothy. *A Woman's Voice: A Handbook to Successful Private and Public Speaking*. New York: Barnes and Noble Books, 1975. Best book written for women on public speaking.

Zannes, Estelle and Gerald M. Goldhaber. *Stand Up. Speak Out: An Introduc tion to Public Speaking*. New York: Random House, Inc., 1983. A comprehensive guide book for all kinds of public speaking opportunities. Very readable.

Using the Media

Bortin, Virginia. *Publicity for Volunteers: A Handbook*. New York: Walker and Company, 1981. An excellent introduction to all forms of media. Includes many helpful illustrations.

DeVries, Charles, ed. *Religious Public Relations Handbook*. New York: The Religious Public Relations Council, Inc., 1982. Excellent handbook for local congregations. Includes information on church newsletters, press relations, and general community relations.

Fleming, Peter. *Church and Press: Friend of Foe? How to Be Friends*. New York: The United Church of Christ Office of Communication, 1982. Handy eight-page booklet on developing a good working relationship between churches and the press.

Lobbying Elected Leaders

Bread for the World. *Congress in Committee, Guide to Effective Letter Writing, Congressional Committees, and Voting Record on Hunger*. Washington, D.C.: Bread for the World. These four background papers give background on how congress works, how to write effective letters, information about which committees each member of congress sits on, and how representatives and senators voted in the last session on key pieces of hunger legislation.

Bread for the World. "Letters: An Effective Response to Hunger." Washington, D.C.: Bread for the World. An attractively designed bulletin insert ideal for use in a church. Available for $.10 each or $8 per 100.

Bread for the World. *Offering of Letters Kit*. Washington, D.C.: Bread for the World. Gives detailed information about how to plan and conduct an offering of letters in a church. Specific information about one important upcoming piece of legislation.

Fitzgerald, Gloria. *Visiting with Your Member of Congress*. Washington, D.C.: Bread for the World, 1985. Four-page background paper on do's and don'ts of meeting with a representative or senator. Includes information about strategic hunger committees.

Friends Committee on National Legislation. *How-To Series*. Washington, D.C.:

Friends Committee on National Legislation. Helpful set of seven pamphlets on how to write a letter to the editor, work in politics, visit a member of congress, write members of congress and the president, work for the congressional candidate of your choice, organize an action network, and adopt a member of congress. At $.10 each, you can't go wrong!

League of Women Voters. *Making an Issue of It: The Campaign Handbook.* Washington, D.C.: League of Women Voters. A step-by-step instruction book on managing, coordinating, and executing a legislative lobbying campaign.

League of Women Voters. *Tell It to Washington.* Washington, D.C.: League of Women Voters. Helpful guide for citizen action including general information about lobbying effectively by letters, calls, and visits. Written from a secular perspective.

Simon, Arthur. *The Case for Citizen Action Against Hunger.* Washington, D.C.: Bread for the World. A succinct four-page piece on why Christians should be advocates with and for hungry people. Useful in churches concerned about public policy advocacy.

Simon, Arthur. *No Grounds for Divorce: Christian Faith and Public Policy.* Grand Rapids, MI. Eerdman's William B., Pub. Co., 1987. A new book by the Executive Director of Bread for the World on why Christians should be involved in public policy. Best book available on the subject.

Making Hunger an Election Issue

Bread for the World. *Election Kit.* Washington, D.C.: Bread for the World. An excellent packet on how to make hunger an election issue. Contains sample questions to ask candidates.

Bread for the World. "Vote Against Hunger." Washington, D.C.: Bread for the World. A bulletin insert for use in a church around election times. Urges Christians to consider hunger as they vote. Available for $.10 each or $8 per 100.

Cohn, Marlene K., and Mary Stone. *Getting out the Vote.* Washington, D.C.: League of Women Voters Education Fund, 1984. Designed to help groups increase voter participation. Includes sections on registration, voting, nonpartisanship, and looking ahead to secure election reforms.

National Board of the YWCA of the USA. *Your Vote is Your Voice.* New York: YWCA of the USA. A kit for voter registration, education and turnout programs. Available for $3.50 from Helen Parolla, Coordinator of Public Affairs and Public Policy, YWCA of the USA, 726 Broadway, New York, NY 10003.

Understanding Denominations

Frazier, E. Franklin, and C. Eric Lincoln. *The Negro Church in America* and *The Black Church Since Frazier.* New York: Schocken Books, Inc., 1973. These two books are jointly published as one book. Classic books on the black church.

Jacquet, Jr., Constant H., ed. *Yearbook of American and Canadian Churches.* Nashville: Abingdon Press, 1985. Published annually. Contains background information, general organization, officers, periodicals, and other organizations or divisions of hundreds of religious bodies. Useful reference book.

"Major Denominational Families by Counties of the United States: 1980". Atlanta: Glenmary Research Center. This map based on the most recent census data gives a graphic representation of regional denominational strength. Shows counties which are at least twenty-five percent one denomination or another. Fascinating information.

Niebuhr, H. Richard. *The Social Sources of Denominationalism.* Magnolia, MA: Smith, Peter, Pub., Inc., 1984. A classic introduction to why so many denominations exist in the U.S. Well written and easy to follow.

Inner Strength/Outer Witness

de Mello, Anthony. *Sadhana: A Way to God, Christian Exercises in Eastern Form.* Garden City, NY: Image Books, 1984. Fascinating reading for those seeking guidance in meditation and devotional exercises.

Dorr, Donal. *Spirituality and Justice.* Maryknoll, NY: Orbis Books, 1985. A thought-provoking book linking spirituality and justice. Written to challenge Christians to be more involved in justice issues and to strengthen those already involved.

Foster, Richard J. *Celebration of Discipline: Paths to Spiritual Growth.* San Francisco: Harper & Row Pubs., Inc., 1978. Extremely challenging book for any Christian. Includes chapters on the inward disciplines of meditation, prayer, fasting, and study, the outward disciplines of simplicity, solitude, submission, and service, and the corporate disciplines of confession, worship, guidance, and celebration.

Foster, Richard J. *Freedom of Simplicity.* San Francisco: Harper & Row Pubs., Inc., 1981. Most helpful book on "simple lifestyle" because it puts the issue in a broad faith context.

Rainer, Tristine. *The New Diary: How to Use A Journal for Self-Guidance and Expanded Creativity.* Los Angeles: J. P. Tarcher, Inc., 1979. A practical guide on keeping a journal. Not written from a Christian perspective, but helpful for those who want to use a journal to develop their spiritual journeys.

Tutu, Desmond M. *Hope and Suffering: Sermons and Speeches.* Grand Rapids, MI: Eerdmans, William B., Pub. Co., 1984. This fine collection challenges Christians everywhere to develop hope in the midst of a hungry world.

APPENDIX B - SOURCES FOR AUDIOVISUAL RESOURCES

The following organizations will send you complete lists and descriptions of their audiovisual resources on hunger, poverty, and development issues. In addition, all the major relief and development organizations offer audiovisual resources describing their work.

American Friends Service Committee
1501 Cherry Street
Philadelphia, PA 19102
(215) 241-7000
Free loan of a large selection of audiovisual resources. Loans are also made from the AFSC regional offices.

Bullfrog Films
Oley, PA 19547
(215) 779-8226
Producers of filmstrips and slide shows on hunger concerns. Purchase prices range from $50 to $150.

California Newsreel
630 Natoma Street
San Francisco, CA 94103
(415) 621-6196
Producers of films on difficult issues, such as the hidden costs of unemployment. Rental prices range from $50 to $75.

Church World Service/CROP
P.O. Box 968
Elkhart, IN 46515
(219) 264-3102
A good collection of audiovisual materials on hunger. No payment, other than return postage, is required for rentals.

EcuFilm
810 Twelfth Avenue South
Nashville, TN 37203
(800) 251-4097, in Tennessee, call collect (615) 242-6277
A media distribution service that consolidates the film and video resources maintained by the Christian Church (Disciples of Christ), Lutheran Church in America, Maryknoll Missioners, National Council of Churches, Presbyterian Church (U.S.A.), United Church of Christ, and United Methodist Church. A large collection on many topics. Rentals range from $10 to $35.

Franciscan Communications
1229 South Santee Street
Los Angeles, CA 90015
(800) 421-8510
Producers and distributors of audiovisual resources, including a number on hunger and world order issues. Rental fees range from $15 to $150.

Maryknoll Film Library
Maryknoll, NY 10545
(914) 941-7590
Twenty-two Maryknoll films can be rented at $25 per day ($5 for Catholic schools) or purchased on video for $19.95.

Mass Media Ministries
2116 N. Charles Street
Baltimore, MD 21218
(301) 727-3270
Producers and distributors of films and videos on a number of topics. Rentals range from $10 to $100.

Mennonite Central Committee Resource Library
21 S. 12th Street, Box M
Akron, PA 17501
(717) 859-1151
An excellent collection of audiovisual resources primarily on hunger and justice issues. There is no rental fee, but borrowers pay return shipping costs.

Oxfam America
115 Broadway
Boston, MA 02116
(617) 482-1211
A small collection of audiovisual resources on hunger and development. Rental fees range from $10 to $30.

The Resource Center
P.O. Box 450
Albuquerque, NM 87196
(505) 266-5009
Producers and distributors of twelve audiovisual resources on Central America, the Caribbean, and Mexico. Rentals are $25 per week.

U.S. Committee for UNICEF
331 East 38th Street
New York, NY 10016
(212) 686-5522
Distributors of UNICEF films. A nice collection of films for different age groups. Rentals are free, but donations are encouraged to offset costs.

World Bank Film Library
Room D-845
1818 H Street, N.W.
Washington, D.C. 20433
(202) 477-8350
A small collection of audiovisual resources developed by the World Bank. The handling fee for each rental is $25. Discounts available for school teachers.

APPENDIX C - SELECTED DENOMINATIONAL HUNGER PROGRAMS AND AGENCIES

African Methodist Episcopal Church

Missions Department
African Methodist Episcopal Church, Room 1926
475 Riverside Drive
New York, NY 10115
(212) 870-2558

Women's Missionary Society
2311 M Street, N.W.
Washington, D.C. 20037
(202) 337-1335

African Methodist Episcopal Zion Church

Department of Home Missions, Pensions, and Relief
P.O. Box 30846
Charlotte, NC 28231
(704) 333-3779

Department of Overseas Missions
African Methodist Episcopal Zion Church, Suite 1910
475 Riverside Drive
New York, NY 10115
(212) 870-2952

American Baptist Churches in the U.S.A.

Hunger Office
American Baptist Churches in the U.S.A.
Valley Forge, PA 19481
(215) 768-2204

The American Lutheran Church

ALC Hunger Program
American Lutheran Church
422 South Fifth Street
Minneapolis, MN 55415
(612) 330-3221

Lutheran World Relief
360 Park Avenue South
New York, NY 10010
(212) 532-6350

Assemblies of God

Division of Foreign Missions
Assemblies of God International Headquarters
1445 Boonville Avenue
Springfield, MO 65802
(417) 862-2781

Association of Evangelical Lutheran Churches

AELC World Hunger Appeal
12015 Manchester, Suite 80LL
St. Louis, MO 63131
(314) 821-3889

Lutheran World Relief
(same address as above)

Christian Church (Disciples of Christ)

Division of Homeland Ministries
222 S. Downey Avenue
P.O. Box 1986
Indianapolis, IN 46206
(317) 353-1491

Christian Methodist Episcopal Church

General Board of Social Concerns
P.O. Box 92284
Atlanta, GA 30314
(404) 525-8827

Christian Reformed Church in North America

Christian Reformed World Relief Committee
2850 Kalamazoo Avenue, SE
Grand Rapids, MI 49560
(616) 245-8557

Church of God (Anderson, IN)

Board of Church Extension and Home Missions
Box 2069
Anderson, IN 46018
(317) 644-2555

Church of God (Cleveland, TN)

World Missions
Keith Street at 25th NW
Cleveland, TN 37311
(615) 472-3361

Church of the Brethren

Global Justice
Church of the Brethren
110 Maryland Avenue, N.E.
Box 50
Washington, D.C. 20002
(202) 546-3202

World Ministries Commission
1451 Dundee Avenue
Elgin, IL 60120
(312) 742-5100

Church of the Nazarene

Division of World Mission
6401 The Paseo
Kansas City, MO 64131
(816) 333-7000

The Episcopal Church

Episcopal Hunger Office
815 Second Avenue
New York, NY 10017
(212) 867-8400

Presiding Bishop's Fund for World Relief
(same address as above)

The Evangelical Covenant Church

Covenant World Relief
5105 N. Francisco Avenue
Chicago, IL 60625
(312) 784-3000

Lutheran Church in America

Division for Mission in North America
231 Madison Avenue
New York, NY 10016
(212) 696-6785

LCA World Hunger Appeal
(same address as above)

The Lutheran Church-Missouri Synod

Board for Social Ministry Services
1333 South Kirkwood Road
St. Louis, MO 63122
(314) 965-9000

The World Relief Committee
(same address as above)

Mennonite Church

Mennonite Central Committee
21 South 12th Street
Akron, PA 17501
(717) 859-1151

Moravian Church in America

Moravian Church in America
Board of Christian Education
Drawer Y, Salem Station
Winston-Salem, NC 27108
(919) 725-5811

Department of Education
Ministries and Board
of World Mission
P.O. Box 1245
1021 Center Street
Bethlehem, PA 18016
(215) 867-7566

National Baptist Convention,
U.S.A., Inc. 1059

Foreign Mission Board
701 S. 19th Street
Philadelphia, PA 19146
(215) 735-7868

Presbyterian Church (U.S.A.)

Presbyterian Hunger Program
475 Riverside Drive
New York, NY 10115
(212) 870-3108 and
341 Ponce de Leon Avenue, NE
Atlanta, GA 30365
(404) 873-1531

Progressive National Baptist
Convention, Inc.

Home Mission Board
601 50th Street, NE
Washington, D.C. 20019
(202) 396-0558

Reformed Church in America

Program and World Mission
Reformed Church in America
475 Riverside Drive, 18th floor
New York, NY 10115
(212) 870-3071

Religious Society of Friends
(Quakers)

American Friends
Service Committee
1501 Cherry Street
Philadelphia, PA 19102
(215) 241-7000

Friends Committee on
National Legislation
245 Second Street, NE
Washington, D.C. 20002
(202) 547-6000

World Hunger/Global
Development Project
15 Rutherford Place
New York, NY 10003
(212) 777-4600

Reorganized Church
of Jesus Christ
of Latter Day Saints

Outreach Ministries
Commission
P.O. Box 1059
Independence, MO 64051
(816) 833-1001

The Hunger Committee
(same address as above)

The Roman Catholic Church

Campaign for Human
Development
U.S. Catholic Conference
1312 Massachusetts Avenue, NW
Washington, D.C. 20005
(202) 659-6650

Catholic Charities, U.S.A.
1319 F Street, N.W., 4th floor
Washington, D.C. 20004
(202) 639-8400

Catholic Relief Services
1011 First Avenue
New York, NY 10022
(212) 838-4700

Conference of Major Superiors
of Men
8808 Cameron Street
Silver Spring, MD 20910
(301) 588-4030

Leadership Conference of
Women Religious
8808 Cameron Street
Silver Spring, MD 20910
(301) 588-4955

Office of International Justice
and Peace
U.S. Catholic Conference
(address above)
(202) 659-6812

Southern Baptist Convention

Christian Life Commission
901 Commerce, #550
Nashville, TN 37203-3620
(615) 244-2495

Human Needs Department,
Foreign Mission Board
P.O. Box 6597
Richmond, VA 23230
(804) 353-1051

Home Mission Board
1350 Spring Street, NW
Atlanta, GA 30367
(404) 873-4041

Woman's Missionary Union
P.O. Box C-10
600 North 20th Street
Birmingham, AL 35283-0010
(205) 991-8100

*Unitarian Universalist
Association*

Unitarian Universalist Service
Committee, Inc.
78 Beacon Street
Boston, MA 02108
(617) 742-2120

United Church of Christ

Hunger Action Office
United Church of Christ
475 Riverside Drive, 16th floor
New York, NY 10115
(212) 870-2951

The United Methodist Church

Board of Church and Society
100 Maryland Avenue, NE
Washington, D.C. 20002
(202) 488-5600

Board of Discipleship
P.O. Box 840
Nashville, TN 37202
(615) 327-2700

Board of Global Ministries
475 Riverside Drive
New York, NY 10115
(212) 870-3600

APPENDIX D - KEY NATIONAL HUNGER ORGANIZATIONS

For a more extensive listing of hunger organizations, please see the following two resources:

Fenton, Thomas P., and Mary J. Heffron, eds. *Third World Resource Directory.* Maryknoll, NY: Orbis Books, 1984. Available for $17.95 (plus $1.50 shipping and handling) from Third World Resources, 464 19th Street, Oakland, CA 94612.

Kutzner, Patricia L., and Nickola Lagoudakis. *Who's Involved With Hunger: An Organization Guide.* Washington, D.C.: World Hunger Education Service, 1985. Available for $8.00 (plus $2.00 shipping and handling) from Bread for the World, 802 Rhode Island Avenue, N.E., Washington, D.C. 20018.

The organizations listed below are by no means the only ones working on hunger issues. Those organizations which are primarily affiliated with one particular denomination are listed in Appendix C. Many other organizations which do excellent relief and development work are not listed here. The list is predominantly hunger organizations which can assist you in hunger organizing work or provide special organizing resources.

Africare
1601 Connecticut Avenue, N.W.
Washington, D.C. 20009
Primarily a development organization working in Africa, but they develop some good resource materials on Africa.

Alternatives
Box 429
Ellenwood, GA 30049
(404) 961-4622
Focuses on life-style change, including the need to simplify lifestyles in a hungry world. Excellent
resource materials for alternative ways to celebrate holidays such as Christmas.

Bread for the World
802 Rhode Island Avenue, N.E.
Washington, D.C. 20018
(202) 269-0200
A Christian citizens' movement which works on public policies on hunger. Members of Bread for the World contact elected leaders about upcoming legislation. Membership is $25 a year (or contribute what you can if the fee is a hardship). Monthly newsletter targets upcoming legislation. Many worship aids and organizing resources produced.

Brethren House Ministries
6301 56th Avenue, N.
St. Petersburg, FL 33709
Develops hunger resource materials for children and youth.

Care
660 First Avenue
New York, NY 10016
Primarily a relief and development organization, however their *CARE Briefs* are excellent study materials.

Children's Defense Fund (CDF)
122 C Street, N.W.
Washington, D.C. 20001
(202) 628-8787
Advocates on issues related to U.S. children. Provides good resource materials on poverty and children.

Church World Service Office on Global Education
2115 N. Charles Street
Baltimore, MD 21218
(301) 727-6106
Develops hunger education resources for church groups. (See further description below.)

Clergy and Laity Concerned
198 Broadway
New York, NY 10038
(212) 964-6730
An interfaith peace and justice group which organizes on justice issues, including hunger.

Community Nutrition Institute (CNI)
2001 S. Street, N.W.
Washington, D.C. 20009
(202) 462-4700
Provides detailed information on U.S. federal food programs.

Impact on Hunger
145 E. 49th Street, Suite 3D
New York, NY 10017
(212) 750-9893
Works to influence education programs. Has designed hunger curriculum for high schools.

CROP (Community Hunger Appeal of Church World Service)
P.O. Box 968
Elkhart, IN 46515
(219) 264-3102
Organizes and provides resources for organizing CROP Walks. Church World Service is the relief and development arm of the Division of Overseas Ministries of the National Council of Churches of Christ in the U.S.A. Thirty-one Protestant and Orthodox denominations cooperate in supporting Church World Service.

Food Research and Action Center (FRAC)
1319 F Street, N.W.
Washington, D.C. 20005
(202) 393-5060
A public interest law firm that analyzes regulations and legislation and advocates improvements for the U.S. federal food programs. Excellent guides to the programs.

Heifer Project International
P.O. Box 808
825 West Third Street
Little Rock, AR 72203
(501) 376-6836
Primarily a development organization, but they provide excellent educational resources for youth and children.

The Hunger Project
2015 Steiner Street
San Francisco, CA 94115
(415) 346-6100
Provides educational and media resources on hunger. Organizes hunger briefings.

Institute for Food and Development Policy
1885 Mission Street
San Francisco, CA 94103
(415) 864-8555
Researches and writes on hunger issues. Very readable education materials.

Interfaith Action for
Economic Justice
110 Maryland Avenue, N.E.
Washington, D.C. 20002
(202) 543-2800
A coalition of national Protestant, Roman Catholic, Jewish and other religious agencies that work together to achieve just and effective policies on a range of social issues. Solid background materials on legislative issues.

National Committee for
World Food Day
1001 22nd Street, N.W.
Washington, D.C. 20437
(202) 653-2404
Serves as a clearinghouse for activities focused around World Food Day. They send out a collection of material prepared by other organizations. Useful mailing list to get on.

National IMPACT Network
100 Maryland Avenue, N.E.
Washington, D.C. 20002
(202) 544-8636
An interfaith lobbying network on social justice issues, including hunger. State affiliates, which work on state hunger legislation, operate in nineteen states.

Network
806 Rhode Island Avenue, N.E.
Washington, D.C. 20018
(202) 526-4070
A Catholic lobby on social justice issues, including hunger.

Oxfam America
115 Broadway
Boston, MA 02116
(617) 482-1211
Primarily a development organization, but provides good organizing materials for the Oxfam Fast.

Results
245 Second Street, N.E.
Washington, D.C. 20002
(202) 543-9340
A hunger lobbying organization

that organizes local chapters.The chapters do excellent work with the media.

Save the Children Federation
54 Wilton Rd.
Westport, CT 06880
(203) 226-7271
Primarily a development organization, but several good resource materials on children in poverty, both here and overseas.

SEEDS
222 East Lake Drive
Decatur, GA 30030
(404) 378-3566
Originally formed to help Southern Baptists get more involved in hunger concerns. Works now to provide educational resources on hunger, including *SEEDS* magazine ($12/year). All the material is very usable within churches.

World Hunger
Education Service
1317 G Street, N.W.
Washington, D.C. 20005
(202) 347-4441
A clearinghouse on hunger and development issues. Maintains an excellent resource collection of hunger materials.

World Hunger Year
350 Broadway
New York, NY 10013
(212) 226-2714
Provides a useful hunger education magazine.

U.S. Committee for UNICEF
331 E. 38th Street
New York, NY 10061
(212) 686-5522
Educational materials on UNICEF and efforts to save children's lives. Their new Campaign for Child Survival is a collaborative effort seeking greater public awareness of child survival techniques. Some good materials for children.

Home delivery
from
Sheed & Ward

Here's your opportunity to have bestsellers delivered right to you. Our free catalog is filled with the newest titles on spirituality, church in the modern world, women in religion, ministry, small group resources, adult education/scripture, medical ethics videos and Sheed & Ward classics.

Please send me a free Sheed & Ward catalog for home delivery.

NAME _____

ADDRESS _____

CITY _____ STATE/ZIP _____

If you have friends who would like to order books at home, we'll send them a catalog to —

NAME _____

ADDRESS _____

CITY _____ STATE/ZIP _____

NAME _____

ADDRESS_____

CITY _____ STATE/ZIP _____